D1161858

TWO WORLDS FOR MEMORY

Alfred Noyes.

TWO WORLDS for MEMORY

Alfred Noyes

J. B. LIPPINCOTT COMPANY
PHILADELPHIA AND NEW YORK

PRINTED IN THE
UNITED STATES OF AMERICA

FIRST EDITION

The quotation from "Miss T" is from *Peacock Pie* by Walter de la Mare and is used with the permission of the publishers, Henry Holt and Company, Inc.

"Roger Casement" by W. B. Yeats is from *The Collected Poems of William Butler Yeats*. Copyrighted 1940 by Georgie Yeats and used with the permission of The Macmillan Company, publishers; of The Macmillan Company of Canada, and of Mrs. W. B. Yeats.

The quotation from "Compline" is from *Poems of Duncan Campbell Scott,* published by The Ryerson Press, Toronto, Canada, and is used with the permission of the publishers.

Library of Congress Catalog Card Number 53-5420

Contents

CONTENTS

Illustrations

TWO WORLDS FOR MEMORY

I

Boyhood

Once, on the far blue hills,
Alone with the pine and the cloud, in those high still places;
Alone with a whisper of ferns and a chuckle of rills,
And the peat-brown pools that mirrored the angels' faces,
Pools that mirrored the wood-pigeon's grey-blue feather,
And all my thistledown dreams as they drifted along;
Once, oh, once, on the hills, thro' the red-bloomed heather,
I followed an elfin song.

IN WRITING AN autobiography there is always the danger of dwelling upon details recorded in a diary as if they were the things that mattered most. Looking back at my own childhood, there is a small sunlit spot which nobody knew but myself, and my memory returns to it again and again.

It was half-way up a steep and almost untrodden mountainside, a tiny sunny nook fringed about with bracken. Below it there was a wood of young fir trees impenetrable to grown-ups, but a boy of nine in quest of wood-pigeons' eggs (to be hatched under his pigeons at home) could twist and turn or creep through it over the fragrant fir needles until all sense of direction was lost. It was in just this way that I came upon the little eyrie on the mountainside, with something of that wonder of discovery which children feel perhaps even more keenly than any grown-up can. Above it there were great boulders of rock encrusted with golden lichen, and over the tops of the young fir trees that guarded its other three sides it commanded a wide prospect: a valley with a river winding down to a long and lonely coast line, and west of this coast line "the immeasurable tremor of all the sea."

It was a place of discovery in more senses than one; for when I first came out of the wood into that sunlit space (it was only about twelve feet in diameter) the first thing I saw was not the wide prospect but something quite small that almost took my breath away with what I believe was my first conscious recognition of the spirit of beauty. On a smooth stone right in front of me there blazed in the sun something more beautiful than any crown jewel; the colours on its wings were not those of wild nature, for they were exquisitely organized in a complicated pattern. The natural history books at home might tell me its name—Tiger Moth or Fritillary—but they could never explain what I first saw there, and half a century later tried to say in a chapter of *The Unknown God.*

It must have been about this time that one morning very early I got up and, without any conscious purpose of my own, wrote what I believed to be a poem. It had an effect upon me which I recorded many years later in some lines entitled "The Song-Tree." What I have said there is in every detail true, but I have never been able to understand it:

> It was at break of day,
> Well I remember it,—
> The first note that I heard,
> A magical undertone . . .

My mountain nook was for me the place where the springs of poetry rose. The tree in "Buccaneer Days," with "a magpie's big mud-plastered nest in its old crooked heart" originally grew in that wood where no companions came. In a passage describing the boyhood of Drake the tree with the raven's nest had its roots in the same place.

There was something else which I discovered in this mountain nook. It was there that I brought my first copy of Spenser's *Faery Queen,* in the old Chandos Classics. Among the bracken and the fir trees, and with nothing around me but the things that had not changed their ways through the intervening centuries, the bewitching woods of the poem merged into the woods around me, and at any moment the sun might glint upon a shield

> Wherein old dints of deep wounds did remain.

I never unravelled the intricacies of the story, which is nothing more or less than a ramble through a wild country of enchantment, but there were certain passages in it that have always lingered in my mind. Beyond and above all its sensuous beauty, there were lines that made a deeper and more lasting impression:

> And is there care in heaven? And is there love
> In heavenly spirits to these creatures base?

Lines like these unlocked for me a whole treasure-house of wonder.

Keats and Wordsworth, and much of Walter Scott, I read in the same place. The leaf-shadows dancing on the pages, and the sparkle of the sea beyond the fir trees, are as vivid in my mind to-day as they were then. The poem "Sparkle of the Sea" in *Orchard's Bay* recalls them. Books were not lifeless things on shelves, but something speaking from the very heart of nature.

And it was not only the famous poets who accompanied me there. A little pocket edition of Sydney Dobell was one of my favourites. He fascinated me by his way of suddenly touching a few notes, a "string of soft recall" which seemed to breathe the innermost spirit of poetry, and then just missing the perfection which they promised. Some of these lines remain in the mind like a fragrance from unforgotten fields—opening lines that had an original movement of their own, like

> In the Spring twilight, in the coloured twilight,
> Whereto the latter primroses are stars,

and occasionally a deeper passage:

> Before every man, the world of beauty
> Like a great artist, standeth day and night,
> With patient hand retouching in the heart
> God's defaced image.

This passage I marked, when I was about fourteen years old, with three vertical lines in the margin, and I think it must have been my first apprehension of the idea that in the beauty of nature we recognize the expression of a spirit akin to our own.

I read a great deal at home, too. Boswell's *Johnson* I must have read through three or four times on winter evenings by the fire, and the whole Johnsonian circle, Reynolds, Goldsmith, Burke, were very real personages to me. As a result, I was led on to other eighteenth-century books. Addison's essays on Milton and Pope in the *Spectator* interested me enormously by their comments on the technique of verse; and this again led me to the poems themselves. But the reading diary which I kept at the time discloses an omnivorous appetite for books. It included Ballantyne's *Coral Island,* Fenimore Cooper, G. A. Henty, Harrison Ainsworth, Mark Twain, Stevenson, and almost the whole of Dickens. There was also a series of twopenny-coloured penny-dreadfuls, in which Deadwood Dick had blood-curdling adventures among cowboys and Indians. These delicacies were not recorded in the diary, and were subject to confiscation. Perhaps, in conjunction with Ainsworth's *Rookwood,* they were the germ of my "Highwayman."

All this jostled elbows with Pope's *Essay on Criticism,* the *Idylls of the King,* Scott's *Rokeby* which I specially loved for the grim character of Bertram of Risingham, and *Paradise Lost* which I loved, perhaps for a similar reason—the character of Satan, though its most lasting impression was the beauty of the invocation to Light which opens the third Book. I pored over it incessantly in the large edition, illustrated by Doré.

Despite this heterogeneous collection, however, it was only the poets that I took to my mountain eyrie. I had more time for reading than most boys, for I was never sent to a boarding-school. There happened to be a small private school near my home, of which the head was Mr. R. A. Pope, a Cambridge man (of Sidney Sussex College) and a former Master of Shrewsbury School. He was not strong physically, and at Jasper House School, as it was called, he had only about a dozen boarders and twenty-five day-boys, of whom I was one. But there were enough of us to play football and cricket in matches at home and away, and I missed none of those normal activities of boyhood. We had swimming contests and "athletic sports" in which I won the 100-yards in not very good time (just under eleven seconds). A small sailing-boat and sea-fishing occupied much of my time in the holidays, but when I went fishing I usually had a book in my pocket.

I fear that I must be unfashionable enough to say that my school-days were exceedingly happy, and in ways quite different from the usual picture. Once, for instance, when I was supposed to be studying

Euclid I had hidden my Spenser behind an exercise-book and was surreptitiously reading him (I had not yet been informed by Miss Edna St. Vincent Millay that Euclid alone knew beauty bare). Suddenly I felt the rap of some hard knuckles on my head, and heard a stern voice asking coldly what I was reading. I handed over the book and was expecting trouble, when to my bewilderment Mr. Pope gave a little exclamation of pleasure, and actually held up the book to the rest of the class as if it were a kind of miracle. From my own point of view the miracle was that I escaped chastisement.

My ideas on the relationship between punishment and crime were further confused during a visit about this time to an austerely kind uncle. He was an extremely Low Church Anglican clergyman, who used to preach in a black gown and who was described in an obituary notice as "a Puritan of the Puritans, holding the doctrines of John Calvin as embodied in the XVII Article of the Church of England. He was of the most gentle disposition and never dogmatic; but on matters of doctrine he would not be moved one hairsbreadth." The only austerity I suffered personally was one which at this distance of time has a touch of Gilbertian humour about it.

My young cousin Herbert, while we were playing at Red Indians in the garden, hit me a violent blow on the head with his tomahawk. My gory head created a sensation when I ran into the house. My Calvinistic uncle, who had hitherto appeared to be detached from the things of this world, passed sentence upon Herbert: for an entire week he was to have no pudding at his mid-day meal. The following day was Sunday, when the Redskins were privileged to take that meal with their elders. Bandaged and complacent, I was looking forward to the moment when I was to assuage my appetite and perhaps gloat a little over the spectacle of a hungry Herbert across the table. My aunt gave me a generous helping and I was about to begin when my uncle surprised me by saying: "Now, wouldn't you like to give an example of self-sacrifice?" Reluctantly putting my spoon down, I said yes; whereupon my uncle handed my plate over to my still more surprised cousin. My aunt, all too kindly attributing to me angelic virtues, at once offered me another helping as a reward, but my uncle said firmly: "No. There would be no self-sacrifice in that."

I am afraid I did not appreciate his good intention at the time; for the little devil opposite (when his parents were not looking) waved his spoon about, licked his lips and patted his tummy, to indicate that he was enjoying himself immensely. And the sacrifice continued for the entire week. It was all a little confusing for me. My uncle was perfectly sincere and impartial; but I realized that if I had tomahawked my cousin I would have had the pudding.

Though I was born in England and my forbears on both sides were English, much of my boyhood was spent on the sea-coast and among the hills of Wales. This always seemed a foreign country to me, but its spontaneous musical genius spoke a universal language. Songs that I heard echoing through its valleys have haunted me like the sound of a mountain stream or a wind-swept pine wood.

I went for long walks with a young Scot, the son of an Art Master. He introduced me to Fitzgerald's *Omar,* and struck a chill to my fifteen-year-old heart by saying, with a certain pride in his own reading, that all the evidence pointed to the inevitable foundering of the Christian creed. Under this influence, and I think sharing his immature pride, I am ashamed to say I wrote a long letter to a kindly schoolmaster, using my newly acquired agnostics to pick holes in his belief. The schoolmaster answered, with a wise and gentle letter which even to-day makes me feel ashamed of myself, that I had attacked his deepest faith and he could not answer me now, but he believed the day would come when I would find there was no conflict between science and religion.

He was a good and a broad-minded man, and he offset my agnostics to a certain extent by lending me Carlyle's *Sartor Resartus.* This was the period which I have tried to describe in the early chapters of *The Unknown God.* I need say no more about it here but that the reading of Locke helped to extricate me from the materialistic tangle, and all the more effectively when I discovered that T. H. Huxley himself found unsuspected depths in Berkeley.

Behind all this, moreover, there was something which I find it difficult to put into words, but which I believe now to have been by far the strongest element in my life—the sense of a hidden meaning in the universe. We were not "the guests of chance." At certain conjunctures, as I have described in *The Unknown God,* there were fragmentary glimpses of a scheme in human life, like broken bits of a great symphony which could only be fully understood when heard in its completeness *post hoc exilium.*

II

First Beginnings

I SUPPOSE that for a proper autobiography I should find something caustic and subtly dissective or condemnatory to say of those to whom in childhood I owed everything, including my own existence. But I have been writing now for fifty years, and during that time I have seen many fashions come and go. I have therefore some ground for optimism about this fashion. It will go, and indeed it is already going as the others have gone.

I have nothing sadistic to report of my elders, nor can I utter a single agonized cry of self-pity, even though they gave me on my seventh birthday what I now regard as a very wicked book, *The History of the Fairchild Family.* In fact I thoroughly enjoyed the passage in which Mr. Fairchild seats his infantile offspring under the gallows, and proceeds to tell them the history of the unfortunate man who was swinging in chains above their heads. It is not recorded whether any bones dropped. I particularly enjoyed the chapter in which those three little horrors of piety unexpectedly got drunk on the cider with which a farmer's wife had carelessly regaled them.

It is all very well to despise the narrowness of the Victorians, but what modern child's book could be so broad-minded as to let the little angels get drunk?

I have to record here a fact which, if the fashionable autobiographies are reliable, must seem so strange as to be almost incredible: When I was about fourteen I had written what I believed to be a poem, in a metre of my own invention, on Echo and Narcissus. I think I had found the story in Lemprière's *Classical Dictionary.* I had written most of it in my mountain eyrie. It opened:

I, the child of the mountain caverns, faintly, faintly, out of the distance,
Murmur, hovering over the pine-woods, over the purple far-away . . .

I don't remember any more of it in its original juvenile form, and I wouldn't if I could, though a very much revised version appeared in my first book. I showed the manuscript to my father, and he read it carefully through. By all the rules, he should have regarded me with horror. Instead of this, he looked at me very kindly; then, turning to my mother with obvious pleasure at what I gather is to most people an appalling thought, he said: "I believe he will be a poet."

It was my first favourable review, and though in later life I have been fortunate far beyond my deserts, it is still the one that gives me the warmest glow of happiness.

Looking back on my childhood, I could only wish that the barrier of shyness between father and son had been broken down more completely, so that I could feel sure he knew of the love and gratitude which I was unable to express to one whose own affections were as reticent as they were deep.

In his early days he had greatly wished to be ordained in the Anglican Church like his three brothers, but it was not possible for all four to go to the University, and when he made way for a younger brother it was only the beginning of an entire life of unselfishness. At school he had shown unusual promise in scholarship. He had been sent to one of those ancient grammar schools in which the classical education was of a far higher standard than is common to-day. One of them bears the onus of having taught Shakespeare "small Latin and less Greek," but in one of the prizes which my father won for Greek and Latin there is preserved a Greek examination paper with which only the very exceptional school-boy of the present day would be able to cope at all. It was his quotation of passages from Virgil that first opened my eyes to the beauty of Latin poetry. The lines were not those which are usually picked out by the critics. Two of them have haunted my imagination ever since I first heard them in his voice:

> *"Olli dura quies oculos et ferreus urguet*
> *Somnus. In aeternam clauduntur lumina noctem."*

He made me see, as clearly as if I were looking at a piece of sculpture, how the heavy word *"somnus,"* carried over and placed at the beginning of the next line, gave the effect of the warrior's head bowing forward into the night of death. He used to quote his favourite passages from Cowper, George Herbert and Tennyson, and in these the religious note was predominant—though he never spoke of it but conveyed it simply by his own sincerity.

He had a dry humour, too, which was quite his own. Tennyson's "Vision of Sin" can hardly be regarded as a humorous poem, but there were certain passages in it with which, assuming a ghoulish air, my father could always amuse his children:

> Wrinkled ostler, grim and thin,
> Here is custom come your way.
> Take my horse and lead him in;
> Stuff his ribs with mouldy hay.

He gave me his Greek Testament, and taught me at a very early age enough Greek to follow the Gospels in it at Church.

After his early disappointment his first thought was that he might turn to authorship, and he began to write a historical novel. It is with something like heartache that I look back now on my discovery of his unfinished manuscript, hidden away on an upper bookshelf behind Boswell's *Johnson,* the *Poems* of Walter Scott and *St. Ronan's Well*—curiously enough his favourite among Scott's novels. The description in this manuscript of an old castle holding out against the Cromwellian forces made a vivid impression on me at the time. It seemed to me that the characters moved like life itself, and their talk had a naturalness which in recollection sometimes made me feel that I had met them in some previous existence. Possibly the story was suggested to him by a picture of Ludlow Castle by my great-grandfather Robert Noyes. My father had a number of his paintings (there is a collection of Robert Noyes' water-colour drawings in the Salt Library at Stafford. His son, H. J. Noyes, occasionally exhibited in the Academy; he painted a portrait of my great-grandmother which I value exceedingly because the kind grey eyes in it are so like those of my father).

His life was in religion, and no man that ever lived had a truer religious vocation. If he had been ordained as he once hoped, he would have been found in some quiet country vicarage, where he might have lived the life of a George Herbert.

With that unworldliness which, as a newspaper said of my Calvinistic uncle, may be detached from common sense, but may be attached to something better, my father married early, and, in the deepest and truest sense of the word, for love; but after the birth of my younger brother my mother's health broke down, and she became a life-long invalid. It was one of those distressing nervous illnesses which preclude all the normal relationships of life, and for the rest of his own life my father devoted himself to caring for her with a deep and tender devotion, utterly regardless of self. He had one great strength—his religion; and his care for my mother became what the Catholic Church would have called his vocation. In some extraordinary way he succeeded in sheltering his children from any sense of unhappiness in their home life, and he took their mother's place in all those tender graces of heart and mind which otherwise they might have missed. It was at his knees that their first prayers were said. Outwardly, to the unseeing eye, his life during those patient years might have seemed commonplace to the point of dullness. He could follow no professional calling that would keep him away from home, but his life was a perfect exemplification of his creed and the sacredness of the greatest contract that can be made between two human beings on this earth. If I ever had any doubts about the fundamental realities of religion they could always be dispelled by one memory, the light upon my father's face as he came back from early Communion.

III

Oxford

IN 1898, when I went up to Exeter College, Oxford, I was a year younger than the average undergraduate of that time. The many changes that in the twentieth century have come upon that "dreaming city" had not yet begun to operate. It was still the Oxford that Matthew Arnold had described as "whispering from her towers the last enchantments of the Middle Ages," by which I suppose he meant that the great cultural traditions of Christendom still influenced its life. The undergraduates may not have been aware of it, but it was in the air they breathed; it sounded in its bells and haunted its cloisters. Its living presence was all the more potent because the past was alive in it.

The undergraduates who climbed the Martyrs' Memorial and called it "Magger's Memugger" were brothers in blood to those of many centuries, and exulted in the fact that if the police became too officious there were appeals to Caesar and the law of an ancient State within the State.

Once, I remember, a festive troupe of students made an enormous bonfire in the middle of the Broad, in which they tried to burn, not only a piano belonging to an unpopular man, but a bus belonging to the municipality. The police arrested the ring-leaders, but were discomfited by the dramatic arrival of the Proctor and his bulldogs, who claimed the prisoners as subjects of the University. This aroused the anger of a crowd of townsmen who thought (quite mistakenly) that the offenders were going to escape punishment. They began to boo and hiss the Proctor and jostle him so roughly that the offending undergraduates had to protect him. One of these protecting offenders happened to be the captain of the Exeter eight, and also one of the best heavyweight boxers in the University. They escorted the Proctor, in his billowy gown, to the gates of his own College, where he removed his cap with a stately bow and said:

"For this courtesy much thanks, gentlemen, but I must ask you to come and see me at nine o'clock to-morrow morning."

There was really no nonsense about University discipline in those days.

Among my undergraduate friends there was one remarkably fluent and witty speaker, Herbert du Parcq, who as President of the Union seemed to be marked out for a great political career. He once said to me that he would like to marry a thoroughly wicked woman, because it would be so interesting to watch her and see what she would do next. Fortunately he did not achieve this ambition. He married very happily and became a distinguished Judge, so that he was able to survey the wickedness of the world with more comfort, and perhaps with even greater scope when he became a member of the Committee on Persistent Offenders. He was a little too sensitive to cope with the worst phases of crime. At his first murder case he fainted in Court, and to his relief soon afterwards became a Lord Justice of Appeal. He was one of those judges who, like Lord Darling, were seldom at a loss for a witty comment or retort if the need arose. But there was one occasion when du Parcq was left speechless: A man in the witness box said of another witness that he was "drunk as a Judge." The Judge suavely interposed, "I presume you mean 'drunk as a Lord.' " "Yes, my Lord," said the witness cheerfully.

I was very fortunate in having R. R. Marett as my tutor at Exeter. H. J. Massingham's description of him, many years later, in *The Times Literary Supplement,* could hardly be bettered:

> As an oblique light upon the indominitableness and gracious scholarship of the late Dr. Marett, I hope you can find space for a brief extract from the letter he wrote me with his own hand on the day of his death:
>
> > "I have nothing wrong with me except what may be called annodominitis. Meanwhile, a week or two in bed has given me a taste of what Plato calls 'drone's honey.'
> >
> > *Otio qui nescit uti*
> > *Habet ille plus negoti*
> >
> > (which is Ennius turned into rhyme)."

In those few words I find a synthesis between the great scholar, the humanist, and the island seigneur [like du Parcq, he was a Jersey man]. He wore the Norman heritage of the last to such perfection that it became the quality of a great countryman and not the least endearing of his many fine gifts.

My first acquaintance with Marett was at a debate in the junior Common Room on some philosophical subject, when he gave my youthful mind rather a jolt by a retort to a speaker with whose views on the universe he did not agree. "If that is God's universe," he said, "then God is no sportsman." He was of course only maintaining the justice of God, but I had not yet become hardened to what may be called the irreverent phraseology with which the scholar hid something deeper, and for some time I looked upon Marett as a kind of Oxonian Voltaire. When I mentioned this to him on a visit to Oxford in later life, he exclaimed: "Good heavens! Didn't you realize that I was one of the pillars of the Church?"

One of the things Marett said to me was that of course all my real work would have to be done during vacations; this was partly because in my first year I got into the College "torpids" and the following summer into the College eight. For a time rowing became the most important thing in life, and as we went up a good many places on the river, our eight rowed at Henley. But our luck was broken when we were drawn against the winning crew for the Ladies' Cup.

I had, however, one of those disappointments which to an undergraduate loom very large. I had done no rowing before I went to Oxford, so I was greatly excited when a note informed me that I was wanted to row at number six in one of the trial crews from which the blues are chosen to row against Cambridge. The procedure was rather harrowing to tense nerves, as it was only from day to day that you were told, by a note left at the porter's lodge, whether you would be wanted. For about a week the notes continued to arrive, then they stopped, and my heart sank. I had hardly expected to get my blue, since for that only eight men can be picked from the twenty-odd Colleges, but it would have been something to be chosen as one of the sixteen who row in the preliminary trials. I made all sorts of calculations, hoping to convince myself that there was some slight chance since our own College crew had been going up steadily on the river. Suddenly another note arrived at the porter's lodge, asking me to come once more to the University barge. I thought this must mean that somebody else had been tried and found wanting. The notes continued for two or three days more, and then, alas, stopped altogether. But for some brief moments of glory I had at least the good luck to row behind those two very fine American oars, the brothers Milburn (famous also in the polo field) who both eventually got their blue.

Despite these distractions, from the lectures of Marett and Cyril Bailey I at least learned to appreciate much of "the best that is known and thought in the world."

There was a little group of undergraduates at Exeter who were keenly interested in literature, and especially in poetry. We formed ourselves into what we called The Essay Club, and met weekly to read papers on various authors, from the Elizabethans to Browning and Stevenson. There were many discussions lasting into the small hours,

> Where once we held debate, a band
> Of youthful friends, on mind and art
> And labour, and the changing mart,
> And all the framework of the land.

One thing that struck me very forcibly in later years was the marked enthusiasm of that earlier generation for the work in art and literature of its immediate predecessors. I do not remember a single paper read before that Club in which the subject had not been chosen because the speaker was enthusiastic about it. If a man liked Thackeray better than Dickens, he would give us a paper on Thackeray and would waste no time in condemning roast beef and home-brewed for not being champagne and oysters.

Marett's prophecy about my being unable to do any work except in vacation may have been true so far as lectures and examinations were concerned, but I did an immense amount of reading, and in my fourth year completed my first volume of poems. The publisher to whom I sent it wrote a very cordial letter in reply, asking me to come to see him in London. The letter arrived just before my final examinations were to begin. His words were so alluring, and questions about Gothic so unalluring, that I went up to London in a state of glorious excitement, cut the examinations altogether, and produced a volume of poems instead of getting a degree.

Somewhat to my surprise, I incurred no blame from the University authorities. In my final year I had been taking the newly formed English Literature school, in which my tutor had been Ernest de Selincourt (the editor of Keats and Wordsworth). When I showed him my poems (one of which, entitled "The Symbolist," had been published in *Literature,* as *The Times Literary Supplement* was then called) and told him what I had done, there was a long silence, while I nervously awaited his comments. Then, to my utter amazement, he remarked, looking at a letter I had shown him from the Editor of *Literature,* inviting further contributions: "This is much more important." Few young writers have been more fortunate than that.

A good many years later Marett, who had then become Rector of Exeter, and incidentally one of the most eminent of anthropologists, sent me his volume of Gifford Lectures, with an inscription in Latin verse which, I felt, completely absolved me from my academic transgressions:

Non anthropologis divinitus atque poetis
Pellendi tenebras unquam fuit aequa potestas.

At a dinner given for my seventieth birthday the Chairman, Sir Shane Leslie, jestingly observed that if I had committed such transgressions at Cambridge I should have been given an honorory degree; but at Oxford something happened to me which I valued far more.

It was in the last year of the Rectorship of Dr. W. W. Jackson (editor of Dante's *Convivio*), when I was revisiting the College. He asked me to lunch, and afterwards, with the amiable twinkle of one who is hiding a pleasant surprise, he said: "Have you been to see the windows in the College Hall yet?"

I went to the Dining Hall as he suggested. The tall windows commemorate members of the College who are alleged to have acquired merit in various ways, from Elizabethan times downwards. A pane carries the initials of each, with the date of birth. One of these windows is devoted to literature and the arts, beginning with John Ford and coming down to William Morris and Burne-Jones. The last pane in this window I discovered had been given to me, and I felt that my Alma Mater had laid a very gentle and generous hand upon my unworthy head. The memory of it has remained for sustainment and benediction all through my life.

IV

The Loom of Years

THIS CHAPTER must be regarded as an expression of gratitude.

My first book of poems, *The Loom of Years,* came out in 1902, while I was still at Oxford. The title was suggested by the lines about the Loom of Time which Carlyle translated from Goethe's *Faust.* I was more than fortunate in the reception of my book.

A youngster of twenty-one could hardly be blamed for being elated when George Meredith wrote that one of the poems was "worthy of praise, not only as a performance, but as an intimation of strength coming," and suggesting, in a delightfully Meredithian phrase, that when my wings became more flexible, they might "mount and fly." But an undergraduate takes prophecies of that kind almost for granted, and I believe I innocently wondered why he did not think them flexible enough already.

A letter from W. B. Yeats told me that he was arranging for one of my poems to be chanted to the accompaniment of what he called a "psaltery" (I believe at the Abbey Theatre). This apparently was an instrument peculiarly appropriate to the Celtic twilight. So, for what might be called one brief moth-hour, I floated in that dim green air, catching distant glimpses of curd-pale moons.

But the greatest encouragement of all came from a member of the

Punch Round Table. R. C. Lehmann was one of those writers who kept the Horatian tradition of verse alive in *Punch,* and through that periodical, by their kindly satire and sense of style, had a salutary critical influence on the literature of their generation. He was then Editor of the *Daily News* and Acting Editor of the *Speaker* (afterwards the *Nation*), the leading Liberal weekly, and he wrote inviting me to become a contributor to that periodical. His letter was followed by a most generous article in the *Speaker,* one sentence of which I quote here because it embodies a theory of poetry that for me has always been the ideal which I have tried to follow: "Fine thought is wedded to a haunting rhythm, and the music vibrates and vibrates away, and is caught and repeated, and fades and swells as the hand of a poet touches the strings."

I have some pride in the recollection that in the *Speaker* I was one of the first to proclaim the genius of G. K. Chesterton, who, although somewhat older than I, began to write at about the same time. Of course at that early age I had to show off a little. Reviewing his book on Browning, I believe I said he was a genius with some straws in his hair. His book *The Wild Knight and Other Poems* may have suggested this, but it is a curious fact that in much of Chesterton's later work there is occasionally a delightfully lunatic quality which, developing from the mad tea-party in Lewis Carroll, has a serious philosophical undertone, and might have been used to illustrate a textbook of logic.

My contributions to the *Speaker* involved me in one fantastically comic episode: A Spaniard with literary ambitions, who had been at Oxford and was now resident in London, noticed some of my reviews, and calling one afternoon at my digs, left a huge manuscript novel, about twice the length of *Don Quixote,* with an entreaty that I should read it and help him to find a publisher. There was something about his wild eyes which made me think that he, too, might be a genius. I began to read it as soon as he had gone, but quickly discovered that in his anxiety to attract readers he had resorted to a trick which in recent years has become only too familiar, baiting his hook on almost every page with dirty little worms for the unwary fish.

It was the first time when, as a critic, I had to discriminate between work which seriously and honestly faces reality, and that other work which in the name of "realism" attempts to exalt into an artistic method the scribbling of filth on lavatory walls. There is always something a little ludicrous about these pretensions, and my Spaniard was no exception.

I had his book wrapped up again, in thick brown paper through which nothing could crawl, and gave instructions that when the author called again it was to be handed back to him without comment.

This was done quite early one morning, and resulted in an operatic scene at the front door, in which my landlady and her daughter participated. There were interminable recitatives on the theme of "What! No message!" and "No message," of which the climax was the statement in a resounding tenor: "Then I shall come in on my own responsibility." A moment later there was a flaming eruption of the Spaniard into my sitting-room, where he demanded an explanation.

The explanation was brief and easy, and concluded by a chorus from my landlady and her two daughters: "He said he'd go in on 'is own responsibility, and now he's come out on 'is own responsibility."

On the afternoon of the same day I received my first and only challenge to a duel, a missive so precious that I have often thought of having it framed:

> Mr. —— presents his compliments to Mr. Noyes and begs to apologise for his intrusion in his room this morning. He is likewise ready to give him satisfaction and will meet him in France or in any country where duelling is allowed. He waves aside his right of choosing weapons, but will fight him with either sword or pistols, as Mr. Noyes prefers. He awaits Mr. Noyes' answer before communicating with his own second in France, who will be glad to hear from the intermediary that Mr. Noyes will choose to act for him.

At the age of twenty-three one does not neglect opportunities of this kind, and I thought it would be rather fun to ask a certain retired Major, a melancholy man with a long drooping moustache and no sense of humour, to act as my second. After expressing his great willingness to act for me, in spite of the irregularities of the challenge, he asked if I had any particular choice in weapons. I told him I had heard that the Spaniard was a dead shot and an expert fencer, which of course meant certain death for me, and that I would therefore like to choose battle-axes, with which I thought the Spaniard would not stand a dog's chance as I was a larger man than he. The Major thought this an excellent idea, and, tugging at his moustache, remarked, "I will call upon him immediately."

With this friendly suggestion he called upon my opponent, but, as they say at the Peace Conferences, no progress was made. In fact the Spaniard intimated that honour was satisfied. I never saw him again; and, so far as I know, his book was never published.

Quite apart from anything else, the English in which it was written was rather like that of a novel an American publisher told me was once offered to him, containing the following striking paragraph:

> Suddenly he blew his nose off. Stooping almost to the floor, she picked it up and returned it to him with a charming smile in her pocket handkerchief.

My week-end visits to the Lehmanns' house at Bourne End were among the happiest events in my life of those days. R. C. L. was very much in the centre of things, political and literary, and he had an extraordinarily wide range of interests. Among the writers whom I remember meeting there, were C. L. Graves, Asistant Editor of the *Spectator,* A. A. Milne, E. V. Lucas and G. K. Chesterton. I have a vivid recollection of Chesterton standing in the library, which had two large windows at opposite ends; the sun was shining in at one side and there was a slight April shower on the other, which induced Chesterton to quote the lines from William Morris:

> Folk say a wizard to a Northern King
> At Christmastide such wondrous things did show
> That through one window men beheld the Spring
> And through another saw the summer glow,
> And through a third the fruited vines a-row,
> While still unheard, but in its wonted way
> Piped the drear wind of that December day.

At lunch that day Chesterton suddenly produced from his pocket and arranged on the table before him a number of little brass figures,

Mr. Pickwick, Mr. Micawber, Sam Weller and other characters from Dickens, giving one an almost uncanny sense that Gulliver held them alive in his hands.

It was through R. C. L.'s friendship that I came into contact with H. W. Massingham, who later edited the *Nation,* and J. A. Spender, Editor of the *Westminster Gazette,* both of whom published many of my poems.

I have never been able to give myself any political label; but at this time I was already imbued with a sense of approaching catastrophe, and was writing whenever I could in the cause of peace. I had, however, two sides to my head, and believed that the strength of England might be one of the greatest factors in that cause; her fleet was a defensive, not an offensive, weapon, and the weakening of it might be an invitation to aggression all over the world. It was with this conviction that I wrote "The Phantom Fleet," in which the great sailors of the past were depicted as coming to England's aid. I showed it to Lehmann, who I knew shared my views on both sides of the question. The poem, even if it had been shorter, would hardly have suited the *Speaker,* but R. C. L. at once opened for me the door of a famous old periodical on the other side. "The Phantom Fleet" eventually occupied several pages in *Blackwood's Magazine,* and was quoted very widely in the newspapers. The Navy League made use of it on Trafalgar Day in several subsequent years, and presented me with a walking-stick made of the oak and bronze of Nelson's *Victory.*

At a distance of fifty years I look back with a kind of amazed gratitude at the generosity with which a very young writer was aided in his first efforts, and I am still puzzled that such consistently good fortune should have accompanied me. I had come to London with no resources but my pen and a small cheque which the *Spectator* had paid me for a poem. I had no introductions to the literary world, and I was naïve enough to think that all I had to do was to rent a couple of rooms and begin life as a poet. Then, as if at the waving of a magic wand, these unbelievable kindnesses began to happen. It is true that Grant Richards, who had published my first two books in a series uniform with Chesterton's *Wild Knight,* very soon went bankrupt, but I don't think the publication of my books had anything to do with it, for of these he had sold the entire stock.

Subsequent letters from R. C. L. encouraged me greatly about the project upon which I embarked in 1903, of writing an epic on the subject of Drake. I was full of this when I wrote to R. C. L. in 1905 a letter which Mrs. Lehmann has kindly allowed me to print in 1953:

I enclose the first three books of "Drake" which you kindly said you would like to see. I should have written before to thank you for your letter which set me to work like a steam-engine again, but I began to make a copy of what I had done to send you, and began altering and re-writing and re-arranging as I wrote, so that it has taken all this time. I began, for instance, with Drake's boyhood in the first book, but came to the conclusion that it was better, after all, to plunge right into the middle of things and work in the earlier part incidentally as I went along. You may, perhaps, see rough edges and traces of this re-arrangement; but I think when I finally go over it, I can make that all right. I shall be very anxious to hear your opinion as to whether I am on the right tack. Personally, I can't help thinking "Drake" far and away the best thing I have done, but perhaps I am cheating myself with the imagined glories of the next nine books. There ought to be some opportunities when they get into the Pacific, and I wanted to make them (in capturing the great galleon that came once a year from those parts to Spain) get hold of a survivor of the Cortes and Pizarro expeditions, or at least someone who was able to tell them of those wonderful conquests of Peru and Mexico, in the same way as the Angel told Adam of the war in heaven. There are some wonderful stories I could weave in (though this part couldn't occupy more than two books) and the Aztec poetry and mythology were absolutely wonderful. Think of the mere names of their temples—the Temple of the Moon (all of silver); the Temple of the Sun (all of gold); the Temple of the Rainbow (all of precious stones); the Temple of the Thunder and the Temple of the Unknown God, all culminating in that. I could use all this to heighten the grandeur of the Spanish conquests and so eventually to heighten the effect of the downfall of the Armada.

The lyrics are an experiment, I suppose, but I think they help. I shall be on tenterhooks until I hear from you. One thing I feel "Drake" possesses, and that is a much more uniform or sustained control over the harmonies of the vowel-sounds on which blank verse, I suppose, depends. . . . By the bye, do you think it would be possible to publish it in parts, or should I finish the whole thing straight away? . . .

I am, in fear and trembling for your judgment,

Ever gratefully yours.

"Maga" did something almost unique in the history of publishing: Mr. William Blackwood decided to use *Drake* as a serial, dividing some of the twelve books into two parts, so that it ran continuously for more than a year; and it may be noted that this most unconventional behaviour took place, not in a new and experimental periodical, but in a magazine that had been established for almost a hundred years. When one remembers that each section of the poem ran to a good many pages, it may be doubted whether anything of the kind had happened before. The following letter from R.C.L. refers to the first installment of *Drake* in *Blackwood's Magazine:*

"March 6:06. . . . I was delighted to see Book I of *Drake* in Blackwood. It gives a proud exultant Tudor air to Maga. I haven't seen Lang's article. Could you send it to me?"

Andrew Lang had written a column about *Drake* in the *Morning Post,* in the course of which he said that I had touched the centre of the shield with my lance, though he pointed out an anachronism which—let me confess it—I owed not to the history books but to Sir Walter Scott. The generosity of R. C. L. thought that Lang should have ignored this fault. For my own part, I was naturally only too delighted that Lang should have written as he did, and indeed he exonerated me in the following letter:

8 Gibson Place,
St. Andrews, Scotland.
March 7.

. . . I do not know in exactly what year you pitch Lady Robert Dudley's view of the moon, but it must in any case be long after her demise. As the public knows nothing about any of these things I hope you agree with me that you have as free a hand as Homer. Elizabeth, in fact, was a destestable person, but as long as the public does not know, she is as fair a heroine of epic as Helen of Troy. It really took a "oner" to behave worse than Mary Stuart did, but Elizabeth did so without an effort. . . . Lady Robert had about as much right to be alive after Leicester's second marriage (as she perhaps is) as Lady Boyne to be at Fotheringhay in one of Swinburne's plays. All is fair in love and poetry.

But the article did not please R. C. L. He wrote:

March 8:06. . . . I return Andrew Lang's article from the M. Post. It is one of his infernally niggling productions. It idly compliments the poet, but says precious little about the poem—precious little that has any discrimination (I don't speak of generosity) or bearing on the work. This is our brindle-haired Andrew in his mood of historical and garrulous sub-acidity. . . . I wish you would come and see me some day at 59 Ashley Gardens, when you've got nothing better to do. If you turned up about 12:30 we could go and lunch in the House of Commons.

The next letter from R. C. L. refers to a poem entitled "A Prayer for Peace" in which the approaching catastrophe of 1914 is foreshadowed:

Oct. 6:06. That is a very fine poem both in its stately workmanship and in the ringing force of its appeal. I think the extract at the head of it is unnecessary and somewhat confusing. I advise its excision. The title also might be improved. . . . I want something that will warrant the appearance of the poem almost immediately. I believe the Speaker would pay a special rate for it, so I am sending it to Hirst *on that condition*. If he cannot, the *Westminster* shall have it.

The next refers to my book on William Morris, in the *English Men of Letters* series, edited at that time by John Morley who corrected the proofs and incidentally one of my quotations:

Oct. 14:06. . . . I am really delighted to hear you are to do the William Morris book for Macmillan's. . . . Helen has just cut and to some extent eaten her birthday cake—with its decoration of seven candles. She is standing at my side (and jogging my elbow) and begs me to thank you for your message—which made her smile. But at that age one doesn't doubt at all that the going on *will* be for ever. Anyhow, I hope her ever will do its proper duty by outlasting mine.

"Betsy," one of his most delightful poems about children, had just appeared in *Punch*. I wrote to congratulate him upon it, and he replied:

Nov. 29:06. . . . Last Thursday, when I got home from the House of Commons at 11:30, I remembered that unless I wrote something at once I should miss the next *Punch*. In a flash I saw "Betsy" in her metrical dress before me. I took a pencil, wrote with enthusiasm, posted without re-writing and went to bed. Then I began to doubt, but next day I got the proof and began to fall in love with it—mainly, I daresay, for its subject's sake—but I did fancy I had somehow hit it off by one of those rare inexplicable chances that sometimes come to a man. Your letter has bucked me up immensely. Hearty congratulations on your conquests of Exeter and "The Pines." You must tell me all your news.

"Betsy" was inspired by his youngest daughter, Beatrix, who already, at the age of three, had an elvish, almost an impish, gift of impersonation. Later this gift, in more serious roles, brought her distinction on the stage. In the child depicted by R. C. L. one could hardly foresee the vividness and power of the part she played in *Mourning Becomes Electra:*

She's a dancing,
Glancing,
A most entrancing
Bundle of life,
At strife
With reason,
And quick to seize on
Your slightest word
In a manner absurd
To help herself,
The Elf.

. . . . . .

Oh, she's the one
In the midst of her fun
To make or pick names
The queerest nicknames,
For you and the rest;
To give herself airs
With the very best
As she walks downstairs
With an invalid doll wrapped up in a shawl
And a dandy bandy peppery dog
With his tail stuck out and his ears agog,
Who never never obeys her call.
Who was it said
That word of dread?
In spite of her pleading, wheedling wiles,
In spite of her tricks and songs and smiles,
Shaking her touzled golden head,
She is seized, God Bless her, and marched to bed.

About this time Beerbohm Tree wrote suggesting that he would like to make a Christmas play out of my poem *The Forest of Wild Thyme* "for children under ninety." R. C. L. wrote.

May 5:07. Helen has taken to writing stories.

I was very glad to hear from you. I saw your beautiful "Niobe" in the *Nation,* and judged you must have seen Massingham. I think you could make a delightful children's play out of the "Forest of Wild Thyme" but—there's a but—the grace of the original, depending, as it does, on poetry, would be gone, and you would have to seek a new grace, or rather you would have to develop in action the other grace that underlay the poetical grace. . . .

I'm your man for tea at the House on Tuesday next. We look for the new member of the Fieldhead Boat Club towards the end of this month.

This was an intimation of the birth of John Lehmann who, a quarter of a century later, was to be the editor of *New Writing.*

R. C. L. sent me one of the little stories that Helen had been writing (I think it was only about ten lines long), and I showed it to the editor of the *Bookman,* who promptly said he wanted to publish it. The "blue" in the following letter was of course the newly arrived John Lehmann, and the opening sentence refers to my approaching marriage:

June 21:07. . . . Bravo! I'm delighted to hear you are going to take that jolly plunge so soon. It's good to hear that your work flourishes. My warm regards to Miss Garnett.

The "Blue" flourishes. He's a huge boy. His mother is doing splendidly.

I wish you had seen Helen's pink delight at beholding her masterpiece in print. Please tell Lobban that, if he doesn't mind, I shall not pay in the 2/6 cheque. She endorsed it quite properly, and I mean to keep it.

R. C. L. had a great many interests and was leading a very active life, but he could always find time for the little things that give pleasure to others, as when, for instance, during a busy political session he took the trouble to send the following message: "Oct. 23:10. . . . It may interest and amuse you to know that you have been quoted in the Cambridge University pulpit—and with only one word wrong! I enclose report of the sermon."

V

The Meynells

IT WAS indirectly through Charles Dickens that I was introduced to another section of the literary world in 1903. In the village at the edge of Bagshot Heath where I wrote "The Highwayman" and part of *Drake* there lived a Catholic priest with whom I occasionally played chess. He told me that he would like me to meet one of my neighbours, Mrs. Thompson, who had some extremely interesting Dickens letters and was the mother of Alice Meynell and Lady Butler, the painter of "The Roll Call." Accordingly one afternoon he piloted me to a little cottage which reminded me of Tennyson's description:

> Almost to the martin-haunted eaves,
> A summer burial deep in hollyhocks.

It has always remained in my memory as a little nook in Paradise; and its occupant, who lived there alone with her books, her music and her painting, was one of the most fascinating characters I have ever known.

Her letters from Dickens were of considerable length, and have been quoted in several biographies, including that of Alice Meynell by her daughter Viola. Half-way through the twentieth century, in the year which has just celebrated the hundredth anniversary of Alice Meynell's birth, it pleases me to remember that I was able to hear her mother talk of Dickens and of those early days in Italy where the Thompsons brought up their children.

Mrs. Thompson's little house was full of flowers, books and pictures, these last her own work. Ruskin said of her painting that nobody could get certain effects of sunlight in a garden as she could; and though he may have spoken with the affection of a friend, he was too good a critic not to mean what he said. The possessors of these pictures, whoever they may be, are fortunate.

She was also an accomplished musician, and at the age of eighty could play two or three sonatas of Beethoven at a sitting. If you passed her house in the evening you would sometimes hear her playing to herself, though, according to her own story, not without an audience invisible to others, for she was something of a visionary and once told me quite simply that after playing one of the sonatas she had looked up and seen Beethoven standing in the sunlit doorway that opened into the garden.

She talked of the flowers and the birds very much as St. Francis of Assisi must have spoken, and although she did not actually use the words she gave the impression that she looked on them all as her little brothers and sisters. She was clearly the fountainhead from which the genius of her two famous daughters was born, and I have known nobody in whom the feeling for beauty in nature, art and literature was more sensitive. She had composed a lengthy musical work, illustrative of the *Midsummer Night's Dream,* and I can never hear some of the lines of that play without recalling the air to which she set them:

O happy fair,
Your eyes are lode-stars and your tongue's sweet air
More tunable than lark to shepherd's ear
When wheat is green, when hawthorne buds appear.

It was through her that after I went to London I found myself a frequent visitor on the Sunday evenings when Wilfrid and Alice Meynell were at home in their Kensington house at Palace Gate.

Some privately printed lines by Coventry Patmore exquisitely suggest in one and the same picture the impression made by the poetry and the personality of Alice Meynell:

Sharp honey assuaged with milk
Straight as a stalk of lavender,
Soft as a rope of silk.

On my first visit there I arrived early, and at once felt the atmosphere of poetry in an environment where it was the stuff not of dreams but of life itself.

The poetry of Burns was not what I expected to find there, yet my first recollection is of entering a long and beautifully proportioned room, and seeing at the far end, across a shining floor, one of the Meynell daughters seated at a piano, and a dark, rather romantic-looking young man leaning over it and very softly, almost inaudibly, singing to her quiet accompaniment:

Oh my luve's like the melodie
That's sweetly played in tune.

Those evenings at the Meynells' were a delight to me. Through all the conversation there was the sense of something deeper, of the underlying perennial philosophy which gave strength, vitality and permanence to everything that Alice Meynell wrote and said. Wilfrid Meynell's wit had an extraordinary quality which was, I think, due to this underlying philosophy. He could say something that appeared to be mere persiflage and yet carried a quite profound meaning, as for instance an epigram in verse:

Great saints and monarchs all are dead,
And still their symbols stand.
There is a crown on every head,
A palm in every hand.

Tom Hood could not have bettered it in levity, and Blake could hardly have bettered it in its deeper sense.

He anticipated De la Mare's delightful lines,

It's a very odd thing—
As odd as can be—
That whatever Miss T. eats
Turns into Miss T.

and could bewilder the agnostic by explaining to him that in his digestive process at supper he was co-operating in a kind of transubstantiation, and would follow the somewhat startling jest with a more serious remark which really comprehended the heights and depths of the sacramental principle in art, nature and religion.

Physically, Wilfrid Meynell looked very like the author of *The Ring and the Book,* and one afternoon at our house in Hanover Terrace, when he suddenly entered the room, another guest, Dum-Dum

(Captain Kendall) of *Punch,* exclaimed in my ear: "Good God! Here comes Robert Browning!"

Once or twice he lunched with us at Hanover Terrace when Chesterton was among the guests, and he drew some remarkable extemporaneous fireworks from Chesterton, whose conversation was as gloriously vital as his writing. Wilfrid Meynell told us that in a recent conversation with Edith Wharton he had mentioned a certain American as an admirable subject for one of her novels. Edith Wharton had rejected the idea on the ground that the American in question had once been a dentist in Philadelphia. This greatly amused Wilfrid Meynell, and Chesterton, rolling his Johnsonian body from side to side, gave a deep grunt, and ejaculated: "But surely dentistry is a great art, chryselephantine art in its most universal form."

Once at lunch a quiet little mouse of a man, not one of the literary world, informed us that he was a constant reader of the *New Witness,* which had recently taken its place among the English weeklies. Meynell surveyed him with the closest attention, as if taking note of every detail.

"That is *very* interesting," he murmured. "I have often met contributors to the *New Witness,* but I have never before seen one of its readers."

Shortly after Francis Thompson's death, Wilfrid Meynell gave me the manuscript of an unfinished article which Thompson had been writing for the *Academy* on my early poem, *Drake.* In the earlier editions of that poem there were certain lines which so closely followed the Protestant historical tradition that I was a little surprised at his cordiality.

Thompson's unfinished article was afterwards published in Walter Jerrold's book on my work in the *Modern Writers* series.

VI

The Highwayman, and Drake

IN THE little cottage on the edge of Bagshot Heath where I had taken rooms shortly after I left Oxford I wrote "The Highwayman" and hoped to complete my poem on *Drake*. Bagshot Heath in those days was a wild bit of country, all heather and pinewoods. The Highwayman suggested itself to me one blustery night when the sound of the wind in the pines gave me the first line

The wind was a torrent of darkness among the gusty trees.

It took me about two days to complete the poem. Shortly afterwards it appeared in *Blackwood's Magazine*. It illustrates the unpredictable chances of authorship, that this poem, written in so short a time, when I was twenty-four, should have been read so widely. During the last half century it has been reprinted in scores of anthologies and several hundred schoolbooks in England and America. Two cantatas have been based upon it, and one of these, by the American composer Deems Taylor, has been performed all over the United States. It has been broadcast repeatedly during the last ten years in both England and America, and now, nearly half a century after its appearance in the sober Scots magazine, it has been elaborated for production in Technicolour by the Allied Artists, and distributed by Messrs. Pathé to hundreds of cinema theatres. Still more surprising, perhaps, is the fact that in this picture, produced in Hollywood, the poem itself is used and followed with the most artistic care.

I think the success of the poem in all these ways was due to the fact that it was not an artificial composition, but was written at an age when I was genuinely excited by that kind of romantic story.

Shortly before the Technicolour film was released, another Hollywood production, based on my poem "Dick Turpin's Ride," was being shown, and one of the newspapers confused the two in a way that inspired a Scots parodist, Ian Crawford, with a delectable rhapsody on what he supposed was happening in the Hollywood studios:

IS THERE NOTHING SACRED?

An American film company has announced that they are "shortly to film *Dick Turpin's Ride,* which is based on the poem The Highwayman, by Alfred Noyes." Such is Hollywood! Some scenario writer, no doubt, has mistaken "Bess, the landlord's black-eyed daughter" for Dick Turpin's Black Bess!

We have had, of course, *Gunga Din* "based" on Rudyard Kipling's poem—and it wasn't at all a bad film. Good luck, then, to *Dick Turpin.*

The poem naturally will have to be adapted to fit the screen. So, with profuse apologies to Alfred Noyes (who was responsible for "Come down to Kew in lilac-time") we have re-written the poem and offer it to the company concerned with the thought of no reward except a small place among the credit titles:

HOLLYWOOD HIGHWAYMAN

The wind was a twenty-foot fan, sirs, blowing a gusty breeze,
The moon was a baby floodlight greening the Hollywood trees,
The road was a painted backdrop, so was the purple moor,
And the highwayman came riding—
Riding—riding—
The highwayman came riding, up to the sound-set door.

Over the cobbles he clattered (noise off by cocoanut shells)
His Wonder Horse was stamping, in the background were the belles,
He crooned a blues to the window, and who should be waiting there?
Black Bess, the landlord's daughter
(Renamed Nell, a colonel's daughter)
Plaiting a Technicolour love-knot into her bottle-blonde hair.

"One kiss, my bonny sweetheart. Gee! That's the way I feel,
But I shall be back with the crown jewels before the end of the reel
And if they fade me early or dissolve me through the day,
Then look for me by limelight,
(5,000 watts of limelight)
I'll come to thee by limelight, though Karloff bars the way."

He did not come in the Third Reel; he did not come in Four,
They switched on reds for sunset, with Nell posed at the door.
Then, with the theme-song blaring, the camera tracking before

A Red-Coat troop came marching—
        Marching—marching—
The extras all came marching with a chorus (and encore).

There's comedy with the landlord (with gags about being a "red")
They also "gagged" his daughter—and tied her to the bed.
Two of them knelt at the casement, with six-guns at their side,
There was a fade-in to a window,
        The gunman at that window
And Nell could see, on the backcloth, the road that *he* would ride.

Tlot-tlot, in the frosty silence—a clever long-range shot.
Nearer he came and nearer, her face picked out by a spot.
Her eyes grew wide in a close-up, the mike picked up a breath,
Then her finger moved in the darkness,
        A gun-flash shattered the darkness,
Shattered her breast (and a call-boy) but warned him with her death.

Back he rode like Fairbanks, his grease-paint just renewed,
The tarmac unreeling behind him and telephoto viewed.
Blood-red were the kliegs on the scaffold, the music rose to a peak,
Then they ambushed him on the highway,
        (*Pianissimo* for the highway)
He lay in tomato-juice on the highway as the screen flashed "All Next Week."

And still of a winter's night, they say, when the wind is in the trees,
When the moon is a ghostly galleon tossed upon cloudy seas,
When the road is a ribbon of moonlight—and sighs breathe o'er the air
Comes Hollywood's "Turpin" riding
        Riding—riding—
Comes Louis Hayward riding, on his Metro-Goldwyn-Mayer.

But even at the time of writing "The Highwayman," very different thoughts and events were occupying another part of my mind. Some of these are reflected in incidental passages of *Drake,* which, although it was a tale of piracy and warfare, had actually set sail for a wider horizon. In the dedicatory verses to the American edition of *Drake* there was a foreshadowing of that

        federation of the strong and weak
    Whereby the weak are strengthened and the strong
    Made stronger in the increasing good of all,

and there was a direct plea for that co-operation of the English-speaking world which to-day is the chief hope of civilization. As poetry the dedicatory verses were not good, and later I omitted them; but they did embody a hope which at that time (half a century ago) seemed remote.

Verses of mine expressing this hope have been used on two War Memorials in the United States, one in 1915 and another in 1951. I wish I could think that they might one day be remembered when the hope is accomplished.

VII

Maga

IN 1906 shortly after the publication of *Drake,* I went to stay with the Blackwoods at Gogar Mount, near Edinburgh.

Mr. William Blackwood, head of that famous publishing firm and editor of the magazine, was even then a venerable figure, tall, lean, shrewd, generous, with a character as strongly marked in its own way as that of John Knox, profoundly religious, and on occasion exceedingly plain-spoken.

The letter in which he invited me to come to Gogar Mount must, I think, be almost unique as an example of a publisher's care for the well-being of a youthful poet. As will be observed, he had as strong an objection to tobacco as James VI of Scotland:

MY DEAR NOYES:

We shall be delighted to welcome you at Gogar Mount on 16th and bring your tennis racket and flannels with you as Jimmie [his nephew, afterwards head of the firm] expects to have some good games with you. Come by ten A. M. express from Kings Cross to Edinburgh from where you will get a train at 6.55 to Gogar Station. You are due to arrive at Waverley Station Edinburgh at 6.15 and you start from same station for Gogar. You come by Great Northern, Northeastern and North British Railway Cos. and take a tourist return ticket third class which is most comfortable, and write beforehand to Station Master Kings X to reserve a corner seat for you in non-smoking compartment, facing engine or not as you prefer.

You get an excellent lunch and tea in train and be sure you go to first luncheon (this to avoid tobacco smoke there). If you can extend your trip to see more of Scotland than Edin. get one of Cook's books of tours in Scotland. What I would recommend your doing is to see Glasgow and a trip down the Clyde and back and you can do that in one day from us. Another one is to the Trossachs, Loch Catharine and Loch Lomond, also a one day one from us. Only a case of early rising and late getting back, both of which we are accustomed to in our house. Jim and his bride may possibly go on one of the trips with you. How long can you spare time to be with us? Fix your own and don't hurry away.

I was glad to hear that Andrew Lang had been so appreciative.

Yours truly,

WILLIAM BLACKWOOD

Merely to arrive at a station called Waverley, to meet Sir Walter Scott in marble on Princes Street, to walk up the Canongate with Robert Louis Stevenson's poems in my pocket and the rhythm of "Bonnie Dundee" in my head, almost expecting to meet their authors at any moment, excited me with the feeling that I was being introduced into the great literary tradition of Scotland. The "Old Saloon," the famous room in the publishing offices of the magazine at 45 George Street, was still haunted by the ghosts of its old contributors, Christopher North and the Ettrick Shepherd. Mr. Blackwood himself had a lively memory; as a boy he had seen de Quincey rushing into the room and begging to be concealed from the creditors who were hunting him and would have had him in a debtors' prison. William Blackwood had vivid memories of George Eliot, who spoke to him of her books as "her children."

It was during this visit that I wrote my poem on Edinburgh:

> City of mist and rain and blown grey spaces,
> Dashed with wild wet colour and gleam of tears. . .

My stay at Gogar was one of unmixed pleasure. Jim and George Blackwood, the two nephews, had arranged a compromise over their uncle's grim objection to smoking, by fitting up a small outbuilding as a smoking-room, and in this we had many pleasant pipes together.

But Gogar Mount was the most hospitable house, and gave me my first introduction to those wonderful Scottish breakfasts, which to-day seem so incredibly remote.

In old Mr. Blackwood the combination of scrupulous thrift and lavish generosity was amazing. His comfortable country house "snowed of meat and drink," but he so hated waste that he had little receptacles here and there for used match-sticks, which were to serve again as spills for lighting candles. In the third of a century during which he published my books, I never had a contract with him. He would merely write a friendly letter telling me that my book was going to the printers and informing me of the royalty he proposed to pay—but he was invariably better than his word.

Every morning the whole household, guests and servants, were assembled for family prayers, and when dear old William Blackwood announced that he was going to read this or that chapter from Matthew or John (he never used the prefix saint), it always sounded to me as if they too were members of the firm.

A departing guest would sometimes be slightly embarrassed by an extempore prayer on his behalf. I think I was suspected of having liberal views, and was somewhat taken aback on the morning of my own departure to hear William Blackwood addressing the Almighty with a request that "our young friend, who is now leaving us for London, may be saved from the wiles of that wicked man Lloyd George!"

VIII

Swinburne at The Pines

A RED-LETTER day of my early life in London was that on which an invitation reached me to dine at The Pines with Swinburne and Watts-Dunton. When I was still an undergraduate I had walked past that house with an Irish fellow-student who had an ecstatic admiration for *Songs Before Sunrise,* and always took off his hat as he passed the gate. Outwardly it was an unprepossessing house, and Swinburne himself was almost inaccessible in those days to the younger generation. I arrived therefore with a sense of awe.

There were only the three of us at dinner, and as both Swinburne and Watts-Dunton were extremely deaf I soon became aware that there was no need for me to be anything but a good listener. I think I made a few quite sensible remarks but I was rather glad that they escaped notice. I was just becoming comfortably accustomed to the idea that it didn't matter much what I said, when to my horror, after I had made a casual remark about the weather, Swinburne became alive to the fact that my lips had moved, and, looking extraordinarily interested, asked me what I had said. I told him I believed we were going to have rain; whereupon he turned to Watts-Dunton, asking eagerly, "What did he say?" Watts-Dunton did not hear him, and Swinburne repeated, almost shouting, "What did he say?" Watts-Dunton turned to me, and apparently assuming that I also was deaf, shouted, "Swinburne wants to know what you said to him." After all this excitement it was impossible for me to repeat my casual remark about the weather, so I hastily improvised another in the form of a question asking whether Matthew Arnold, in "Thyrsis" and "The Scholar Gypsy," hadn't owed a great deal to the Odes of Keats, of which the long stanza, with a short line towards the end, has very much the same metrical effect. It was a relief to find that Swinburne agreed with this. Matthew Arnold, he thought, was one of the most derivative of our poets, though this did not lessen the great beauty of his work.

From this point onwards Swinburne happily did all the talking, and he talked brilliantly, almost consistently in praise of his favourite poets, especially Landor and Hugo. He said nothing about contemporary writers, with one exception: he dismissed Bridges as "a pedant, and a dull pedant." Rather to my surprise, for it seemed to belong to a different world, he became eloquent over Dickens, and especially over *Great Expectations.* On this subject he revealed what was perhaps his most human side. For him the remark of Sainte Beuve that great literature is contemporary with all the ages was an obvious truth; Dickens was one of the great company which included John Ford and Dekker, Ben Jonson and Shakespeare himself. Swinburne's kindness to me as a young writer made me feel that I was being inducted into the fellowship of the Mermaid Tavern. I did not send him some verses which I published in the *Fortnightly Review* on his seventieth birthday, but I believe the editor, W. L. Courtney, did, for Swinburne wrote to me: "I wish I could hope that my appreciation of your praise could give you half the pleasure that Hugo's too generous appreciation of my tributes repeatedly gave me."

During my first visit he launched into a long description of a solitary walk he had taken years earlier on the East Coast, which he describes in his poem "By the North Sea." It was an extraordinarily vivid recollection, and he went into the most minute details about certain "lozenges of colour" that he had seen in some of the rock-pools. For some reason or other he turned once or twice to Watts-Dunton, remarking, "You were not with me on that occasion."

One very definite fact I did observe, and I feel it should be recorded here. Max Beerbohm's description of his own visit to The Pines was an exceedingly clever caricature deliberately designed to be amusing, and very artistically shaped to that end and to that end alone. But in the interest of literary history it should be said that it omits everything of real value and goes woefully astray on many points of demonstrable fact. There was, for instance, far more of Rossetti and William Morris than of the suburban early Victorianism upon which Max Beerbohm insists in a description of the interior of the house. Incidentally, a house crammed to overflowing with books of the Elizabethan period as well as from the Kelmscott Press, falls completely out of the category in which Max Beerbohm tried to place it.

In spite of his small stature, Swinburne had just that personal dignity of which the caricaturists robbed him. He was a contemporary in many ways of those who frequented the Mermaid Tavern, but there was another side of his character in which he was akin to Sir Walter Scott. He loved riding in the North Country; and his interest in the old Scottish ballads and the Scottish Queen, for whose house his fathers fought, made a striking contrast with the picture of him as a mere aesthete of the 'nineties. One of his favourite lines was "We are what suns and winds and waters make us," and those are influences of which the Lytton Strachey school knows very little.

Swinburne was sometimes said to be very reticent about the work of the younger generation at that time, but when *Drake* appeared he wrote a cordial letter (this was published in the book on my work by Walter Jerrold in the *Modern Writers* series). It was followed by a gift from The Pines of the fine edition, published by the Florence Press, of *Songs Before Sunrise,* inscribed by Watts-Dunton with a very generous expression of Swinburne's own friendship to my work.

The complexity of Swinburne's character should not be over-simplified. I think it may be said (he himself said) that many of his superficially anti-Christian diatribes were directed, not against the Eleven, but against Judas. In the first quarter of an hour of my first visit to The Pines he tried to shock me by saying, of some brutal incident that was filling the newspapers, "Christianity itself has conceived nothing more ghastly." Finding that this did not disturb me, he changed his tone completely.

It has been said that the "Triumph of Time" records an early love affair in which the cloister prevailed over poetry:

> You have chosen and clung to the chance they sent you,
> Life sweet as perfume and pure as prayer,
> But will it not one day in Heaven repent you?
>
> . . . .
>
> The gate is straight; I shall not be there.

In one of Swinburne's letters to his mother on the death of the blind poet Philip Bourke Marston (whom Swinburne had helped to save from want) he wrote:

> . . . His poor father sent me a note announcing it on the very day that he—as I do hope and trust and believe—passed from a life of such suffering and sorrow as very few can have known to a happy one.

In a later letter, about Mazzini, he says of this faith:

> . . . The most wonderfully and divinely unselfish man I ever knew, Mazzini, whose whole life was self-sacrifice, was so intensely possessed by this faith that if he could have been uncharitable it would have been towards the disbelievers and preachers of disbelief in it.

The true Swinburne, untrammelled by art or artifice, is expressed in the lines on the death of his father, Admiral Swinburne:

> Whose sail went seaward yesterday from shore
> To cross the last of many an unknown sea.
>
> The life, the spirit, and the work were one
> That here—ah, who shall say, that here are done?
> Not I, that know not; father, not thy son,
> For all the darkness of the night and sea.

This was the real Swinburne, the Swinburne who, as I saw him at The Pines, impressed me with the essential nobility of his mind and spirit.

IX

First Marriage

THE FOLLOWING year, 1907, I was married to Garnett, the daughter of Colonel and Mrs. Daniels, of Washington, D. C., an event which brought me into my first close association with America, although we did not actually visit the United States until a few years later.

For the first years of our married life we rented a tiny house at Rottingdean. We had my pen and about £50 between us when we were married, but we were so inexperienced that we felt no anxiety about the future, and, strangely enough, our lack of anxiety was justified. Garnett's father, Colonel Daniels, who had died about a year before our marriage, was one of those optimists who make no provision for the future, and he had left her mother and sister with a very small income.

Those years at Rottingdean, when every cheque from a publisher was an event, were without a cloud. In the twenty years of our married life, Garnett and I were never parted for more than a few days. Her father, whose commission in the American Army, as a very young man, was signed by Abraham Lincoln, had come to England in the Consular Service after his retirement from the Army. My wife's mother had been a Miss Upham and was born in Cambridge, New England, at the flowering time of many of its famous names, including that of her own kinsman Charles Wentworth Upham, and she was a connection by marriage of Oliver Wendell Holmes (the Autocrat of the Breakfast Table).

Two of my own kinsmen had gone to New England in the seventeenth century, and George Noyes, one of their descendants, on the faculty of Harvard, is mentioned in a class-day poem by Oliver Wendell Holmes, who proposed his health in the following cheerful lines:

> Then here's to the classen vocatam (the boys),
> Et eorum tutorem cui nomen est Noyes.

My wife's mother, as a child, had known Emerson and Longfellow, and when my wife and I visited New England there was almost a sense of homecoming, for Longfellow's daughters entertained us at their father's house in Cambridge, and Emerson's son at the house which still contained his father's library in Concord. In the dedication of the American edition of *Drake* I tried to give expression to this feeling of homecoming.

My kinsmen Nicholas and James Noyes, who were the progenitors of a numerous clan in the United States, had sailed to America in 1633, in the good ship "Mary & John of London. Robert Sayers, Master," to escape the ecclesiastical tyranny of Laud. They were both ministers of the Anglican Church, but were of a strongly Puritan disposition. This had a somewhat grim result in the son of Nicholas, who, it is recorded in the *Annals of Salem,* "officiated as clergyman at the hanging of the witches on September 22, 1692, and after they were dead, said, 'What a sad sight it is to see those eight firebrands of hell hanging there!' " I did not know this when, answering an Englishman's statement that "there are no ghosts in America," I wrote my "Ghosts of the New World," which included this stanza:

> No ghosts in Salem town
> With silver-buckled shoon?

> No lovely witch to drown
> Or burn beneath the moon?
> Not even a whiff of tea,
> On Boston's glimmering quay?

However, later, the son of Nicholas repented of his part in the witchcraft persecutions, and "did what he could to assist the dependent families." Brattle says of him: "His talents were good, his literature general, his acquaintance with theology extensive, his attachment to the ministry strong, and his life both useful and desired. A learned, a charitable and a good man, described as being extremely fat.

"The Rev. Nicholas Noyes wrote several poems, one on the death of his colleague Mr. Higginson in 1708, which was bound with the sermon preached by Cotton Mather on the same occasion, and another on the death of Mr. Green:

> Under this Sorry Heap of Stones
> Rich treasure Lyes, dear Joseph's Bones. . . ."

This seems to me an anticipation of the Laureate rather than of myself.

A more cheerful relationship is that of James Noyes, who became a founder and co-trustee of Yale College, of which some two centuries later I was privileged to become an honorary graduate.

My sense of homecoming was increased by my wife's connection with the New England group in which my own kinsman had been so pleasantly toasted by the Autocrat of the Breakfast Table.

X

Music in Scotland

TO EACH of the two volumes of *Drake* shortly after publication *The Times Literary Supplement* devoted its main article, one of them extending to more than a page, and I was told afterwards that these articles were written by Quiller-Couch. In the second article the writer spoke of the unusual fact that a poem of this kind should be read aloud in country houses. I don't know who told him of the country-house reading, but it probably referred to an occasion when my wife and I were staying with the Bruces at Seaton House, near Arbroath.

We visited the Blackwoods shortly after our marriage, and from there went on to the Bruces, with whom, between 1907 and 1912, we passed many delightful weeks.

It was a remarkable household. Frederick Bruce, a brother of Lord Elgin (Viceroy of India), was a great lover of music, and his large family of sons and daughters had inherited that love. They had studied music in Berlin under Joachim, and every evening after dinner their own family quartette would give us an hour or more of Mozart.

I have heard many famous players, but nothing has brought me nearer to the soul of music than those long evenings among the Scottish hills, when there was no audience but ourselves, and the players were so filled with the love of what they were doing that everything else was forgotten. Occasionally the programme was varied by readings of poetry. Frederick Bruce often read aloud and held his listeners enthralled with pages from his favourite books—and very few indeed of them were written within the last hundred years. He was a student of philosophy as well as of music, and although some of us knew them by heart, passages from the *Symposium* or the *Apology* of Socrates (Jowett's translation) seemed to acquire a new significance from the music that introduced and followed them.

A matter that sometimes came up for discussion was the British treatment of "subject races." What interests me to-day in looking back on these discussions is their honest idealism. Public debate on such matters is often marked by hypocrisy or by cynical scepticism. It is all very well for cynics to say that the British only talk of self-government when they are forced to it; but the hypocritical use of liberal ideas by disingenuous men does not detract from the good faith of those who honestly hold them. There are parts of the world to-day (in West Africa for instance) where, according to the "democratic" propagandists of the extreme Left, the tyrannical British are carrying out a very wicked programme, eliminating the completely democratic habit of cannibalism, and are building schools and teaching those methods of self-government by which eventually the wicked British controls will inevitably be supplanted. To say that we have no interest in the matter would of course be hypocritical. Even a missionary with a cannibal's cooking-pot in sight might be moved by self-interest to introduce the works of Mrs. Beaton, or that American classic *The Joy of Cooking.*

To deny that there is an idealistic motive sometimes amounting to a religious passion in the men who are doing the work is about as reasonable as to deny the existence of goodness because you have read the story of Judas Iscariot. Fifty years ago, at any rate, when we thought a great deal of our "Indian Empire," the family of one of its Viceroys was discussing in private whether the British had any right to be there at all, except as servants of the very process which would hasten their departure.

Mrs. Bruce, like Thomas Hardy, thought it uncivilized to kill animals for food, but she was more consistent than Hardy. Her household was run on strictly vegetarian lines, the only concession to her large and healthy family being that she had a superb cook whose mysterious "cutlets" were so much better than the real thing that they might have converted one of Kipling's "five-meal meat-fed men." Theoretically I believe she was right. As Chesterton once remarked, the inhabitants of another planet might find something grimly Dantesque and horrible in the fact that the inhabitants of ours kept themselves alive by thrusting pieces of other animals into holes in their heads.

Mrs. Bruce could not convert everyone in the world by the delicious achievements of her cook, but occasionally she would surprise the family by bringing back a flock of sheep which she had met on their way to the slaughter-house and had ransomed at considerable cost. Fortunately there was ample grazing for them, and the practical difficulties that often confront the tender-hearted did not stand in her way. The rest of the family sometimes suspected that some farmer who had wanted to make a quick profit had deliberately crossed her path with a pathetic herd of cattle. But her influence was wise and beneficent and she did a great deal of good in the more general field of human kindness.

During one of our visits the pianist Donald Tovey (afterwards Reid Professor of Music) was staying in the house, and with Charles Bruce and his violin we had a feast indeed. The Bruces' former musical tutor, Mr. W——, himself a fine musician, was often added to the orchestra.

In the summer of 1914 W—— was visiting some musical friends in Berlin, and when the war came he was imprisoned in one of the worst concentration camps. Frederick Bruce wrote to me (I was then lecturing at Princeton) asking if I could do anything through my American friends to get him out. I wrote at once to my friend Carl Stoeckel, an American of Austrian descent, who from time to time had arranged for the performance of works by European composers at an auditorium in his country house in Connecticut. These works were always conducted by the composer in person, and admission was only by invitation. (Coleridge-Taylor had gone there to conduct the first performance of his cantata based on my *Tale of Old Japan.*) Sibelius had conducted a work there, and Carl Stoeckel's name was well known to many leading figures in the European musical world, including of course leading figures in Germany. My own acquaintance with him dated from the performance of *A Tale of Old Japan.*

In my letter to Carl Stoeckel I dwelt on the fact that music spoke an international language. Stoeckel at once wrote to me saying that he would do everything in his power. A few weeks later I received a telegram from him saying tersely: "W—— is to be exchanged. Carl Stoeckel Norfolk Conn."

A few months later I was in England and the Bruces asked me to lunch to meet W——. They told me that he did not like talking about his imprisonment; but after lunch he broached the subject himself and spoke of one horrible incident. In a hut next to his own he heard the cries of a prisoner who was being brutally maltreated by some of the guards. When he next met this prisoner he was horrified to see that one of man's eyes had been gouged out!

W—— said that he was puzzled about the way in which he had

been released. "They told me I'd never get out," he said, "as there were too many people trying to arrange it; then in a few days I was taken away and given a very good dinner and sent home. I understand that I was being exchanged for some prisoner called Carl Stoeckel in Norfolk."

"Yes," I said, "but not a prisoner and not the English Norfolk." I had the telegram in my pocketbook, and showed him the signature: "Carl Stoeckel Norfolk Conn."

The curious way in which the incidents of one's life weave themselves into a pattern—the Bruces, their music, the *Tale of Old Japan,* Carl Stoeckel and his musical friends, all contributing to a little personal drama, is further illustrated by a sequel:

At a much later date I was dining one night with the Jellicoes on the Isle of Wight. After dinner one of the guests, a naval officer, told me of his own imprisonment in Germany, and I recounted the adventure of W—— and Carl Stoeckel. He gave a gasp of surprise.

"Why, that explains it," he said. "W—— and I were in the same concentration camp. He was trying to organize some music for us, and we wondered why he had been released. It put an end to our music. Of course we were glad he got out, but we were sorry to lose him."

Oddly enough, the last words W—— had said to me were, "You know, although it was so horrible, I felt almost sorry to go, leaving those fellows behind."

My poem "Mountain Laurel" arose out of those musical gatherings at Carl Stoeckel's home in Connecticut, when the hills and valleys were bright with blossoms of the "rose-dappled snow-drifts, warm with the honey of May."

> If I never should find you again, O lost companions,
>   When the rose-red month begins,
> With the wood-smoke curling blue by the Indian river,
>   And the sound of the violins,
> In dreams the breath of your green glens would still haunt me,
>   Where night and her stars, drawing down on blossom and tree,
> Turn earth to heaven and whisper their love till daybreak.
>   Wild laurel for me!

XI

Asquith and Swinburne

EVERY YEAR Edmund Gosse gave a birthday dinner at the National Club, at which Mr. Asquith was a guest. It was at one of these that I first met the leader of the Liberal party, who had recently become Prime Minister. He talked with me about poetry and, possibly because the sweeping Liberal victories of that decade had made him a little optimistic about the future, he quoted with real feeling some very fine lines from the *Songs Before Sunrise:*

"All these things in your day
  Ye shall see, O our sons, and shall hold
Surely; but we, in the grey
Twilight, for one thing we pray,
  In that day though our memories be cold;

To feel on our brows as we wait,
  An air of the morning, a breath
From the springs of the east . . ."

The way in which he breathed those last two lines made a curious impression upon me. There was no doubt about the political idealism, the desire for that undiscoverable country where liberty shall be the only light; but there was something else which has long haunted and puzzled me. There was no immediate prospect of war at that time (Dec. 8, 1908), but there was something in the aspect of this man, the coldly legal face with the strange streak of coldly rational enthusiasm, which made me think of Byron's prophecy, "blood will be shed like water." It was an unreasonable feeling on my part, and I have never been able to analyze it, but it has remained with me for more than forty years.

He went on to quote some of those anti-Christian lines in which

Swinburne, despite the amazing verbal music, was at his worst intellectually. To me it has always seemed that the great lyrical genius of Swinburne was summed up with complete justice, to both his strength and his weakness, by Tennyson, who said that he was a *reed* through which everything blew into music. Asquith had not noticed that the reed swaying in the wind of the anti-Christian poems was blown in the opposite direction in the very poem which he had first quoted, where Swinburne quite inconsequently couples "the blood-bright splendour of Brutus" with the "snow-bright splendour of Christ." The truth of the matter is, of course, that confronted by certain aspects of the universe, Swinburne, unlike Job, was ready to curse God and die. Confronted by other aspects he was swept into ecstasy, equally ready to praise God and live. It seemed ironical that the Prime Minister, fresh from appointing Bishops in the Church of England, so particularly admired the passage about the "pale Galilean," and the comparison between the Mother of Christ and Aphrodite:

"For thine came pale and a maiden, a sister to sorrow; but ours,
Her deep hair heavily laden with odour and colour of flowers,

. . . . . .

For thine came weeping, a slave among slaves, and rejected, but she
Came flushed from the full-flushed wave, and imperial, her foot on the sea."

I remember he said, "That's how I should like to write, if I were a poet."

Asquith had known Swinburne in earlier days, when the poet had a mane of flaming red hair. As I had recently dined with Swinburne he asked me many questions about him, his conversation, his appearance, and the colour of his hair. With the memory of Swinburne's bald dome shining above his venerable fringe of grey locks, I assured the Prime Minister that the general effect was now pink.

"Pink?" he exclaimed.

"Yes," I said firmly, "pink."

John Morley I met only once, and again it was Gosse who introduced me to him. His resignation from the Asquith Cabinet over the declaration of war in 1914 has apparently puzzled people for many decades. The reason he gave to Asquith was not disclosed at the time; but most people to-day would regard it as remarkably prophetic. His view was that to bind ourselves to Russia was to be confronted eventually with demands that we could not meet.

It was some years after this that I was introduced to Lord Morley. He was ill at the time, but I felt that he was a far greater man than his books had led me to suppose. There was something of Roman grandeur in his personality and even in his physical appearance as he lay on his couch with a great rug loosely wrapped about him, like a senatorial toga.

Strongly as I have criticized some of his views in my *Voltaire,* I felt that in actual life he was a man of absolute integrity, and of incomparably greater stature than the political colleagues with whom he had disagreed about the war.

Whatever else may be said about it (and there were of course fearful wrongs on both sides), it is a fact that within a few hours of that disagreement one of the greatest tragedies in the history of the world was precipitated by the flat refusal of Russia to consider the frantic midnight appeal of the British Cabinet and King to defer her general mobilization; and that we were accordingly swept into acquiescence in something which we believed to be so wrong that the Prime Minister had called upon the King in the middle of the night to concert measures for stopping it. What does puzzle me very much indeed is the public statement recently made by a member of Asquith's former Cabinet (who, incidentally had been involved in the Marconi affair) that he had not the slightest idea why Lord Morley resigned. Of his wisdom in the political field perhaps only the history of the far future will be able to judge.

It was at Gosse's house at dinner one evening that Lord Haldane startled me by suddenly asking me across the table what I thought was the best proof in literature of the existence of God. It was an appalling incident in the life of a shy young man, for the philosopher was profoundly serious. Everyone was listening and there was an awful hush for a moment. I murmured faintly that certain passages in Dante's *Paradiso* gave all that human language could convey on that subject. His reply was devastating:

"Oh, but that's poetry!"

In essence, the best of these passages happen also to be Aquinas, but Haldane could suggest nothing better. Moreover he had committed himself to a whole-hearted acceptance of poetry in his Gifford Lectures, *The Pathway to Reality,* where he uses, as the connecting thread of the whole series, the last lines of Emily Brönte on that ultimate self-existent Being which, having no cause beyond Itself, is supra-rational and supernatural:

> Though earth and man were gone,
> And suns and universes ceased to be,
> And Thou wert left alone,
> Every existence would exist in Thee.
>
> There is not room for Death,
> Nor atom that his might could render void:
> Thou—Thou art Being and Breath,
> And what Thou art may never be destroyed.

In essence these lines constituted his religion, though apart from Hegel he seemed to find its most philosophical satisfaction in Buddhism.

XII

The Velvet Paw

EDMUND GOSSE once remarked that he modelled himself on the cat. Stevenson in fact affectionately addressed him as "wicked old cat-like poet." The offering of the velvet paw, followed by the unexpected scratch, certainly amused both Gosse and his friends. Few of his victims were without affection for the author of their suffering. He had a keen sense of the ridiculous, but was nevertheless extremely touchy on little occurrences which would have amused him intensely if they had happened to others. (He was not alone, perhaps, in that.) On several of these occasions I was an enthralled observer.

At one of his dinner parties at 17 Hanover Terrace, one of the guests, Sir Edward Marsh ("Eddie" of the Georgian Poets) had omitted the slight formality of talking to the lady on his left because of his interest in the lady on his right. Gosse was annoyed by this, and when the men had been left to their port he suddenly hissed at the offending but astounded Eddie the single word, "Beast!" The vehemence of the hiss caused Eddie's monocle to fall with a rattle on his stiff shirt-front. Gosse then gave him the other barrel, "Beast!" with even greater vehemence, which to my astonished eyes had the curious effect of jerking the monocle back again. There were a few hurried words in a corner, and Eddie left the house in what I believe is known as high dudgeon.

Gosse and Marsh were both members of the Savile Club, and for twelve months after this contretemps, whenever Gosse and Marsh passed one another in the Club, Gosse elevated his nose and gave Eddie the cut deliberate. At the end of the year the eminent Librarian of the House of Lords felt that it was time for the happy bells to ring out across the snow. But how to break the ice? A charming thought occurred to him. Both were friends of Arthur Christopher Benson, who had been seriously ill but was now convalescing. What could be more pleasant and appropriate than that they should shake hands over an old friend's recovery? Accordingly, with a smile of rosy benevolence, Gosse suddenly accosted the unprepared Eddie, extended the velvet paw and said sweetly: "Isn't it good to hear that Arthur Benson is almost well again?" Taken aback by this change of weather, Eddie fixed his monocle more firmly in his eye, and squeaked in his curiously high soprano voice, "I didn't know he had been ill." It was merely the reply of embarrassment, but the fixing of the monocle gave it the chilliness of a rebuff to the fiddle-string nerves of Gosse, who promptly turned on his heel, walked away, and refused to speak to the forlorn Marsh for another year. The quarrel was eventually made up, I believe, with the presentation of a rare first edition from the penitent "Eddie" of the "Georgians" to the Sainte Beuve of the *Sunday Times*.

Gosse had a gift for saying the amusing thing at the psychological moment. At a luncheon in the House of Lords, when one of the Georgian Poets (T. Sturge Moore) appeared in exceedingly shaggy attire, Gosse murmured, "A sheep in sheep's clothing!" It is alleged that Mr. Churchill used the same description of Mr. Atlee, but Ferris Greenslet, Advisory Editor of the *Atlantic Monthly,* who accompanied me to Gosse's luncheon party, confirms its earlier date in his book *Under the Bridge*.

J. M. Barrie was one of the guests on that occasion, and told me an extraordinary story about his crippled friend W. E. Henley: Barrie had once seen Henley and Oscar Wilde coming out of a London theatre. They had apparently been engaged in some dispute. After they had parted on the brightly lighted pavement Wilde called something out to him, whereupon Henley turned, drew back a little, and, with all the force of Long John Silver, hurled his crutch at Wilde's head. Henley was said to be the original of Stevenson's Silver, but the crutch of the critic appears to have been less effective than that of the pirate.

Not long after the death of Swinburne Gosse was engaged on the Bonchurch Edition of the poet's works, in collaboration with that extraordinary character T. J. Wise (whose achievements as a "bibliophile" deceived many book collectors, apparently including Gosse. These achievements are impressively recorded in that rather startling volume *Forging Ahead,* by Wilfrid Partington, published by G. P. Putnam's Sons, New York). On one of the crowded Sunday afternoons at 17 Hanover Terrace, a telephone message was misunderstood by the parlourmaid who took it. Knowing nothing of the death of the great poet, she stood in the doorway, and to my amazement announced, "Mr. Swinburne to speak to you on the telephone, sir!" Greatly as he appreciated Swinburne, it was an opportunity not to be missed by Gosse. In the breathless hush which had naturally followed the rather appalling announcement, all eyes were fixed on his glittering spectacles as he exclaimed, "Mr. Swinburne to speak to me on the telephone? I shall certainly not speak to Mr. Swinburne. I don't know *where* he may be speaking from."

Possibly the message came from T. J. Wise. If so, it was among the more successful demonstrations of his virtuosity.

As literature, Gosse's biography of Swinburne is well written and amusing, but it belongs to the genre in which Lytton Strachey excelled. It is a piquant cartoon rather than a veracious history. The Swinburne with whom I dined at The Pines was certainly not the Swinburne of Max Beerbohm or Gosse. Gosse, of course, did recognize that Swinburne was one of the great lyric poets of the world, and said that for anything to compare with "Hertha" we must go back to the masterpieces of ancient Greece. But this was only incidental to the caricature, whereas the caricature should surely have been incidental to the appreciation.

Curiously enough, it was Barry Pain, one of the most humorous writers of the day, who in his own turn criticized this aspect of the matter, in some unpublished verses he sent to me:

DEAR NOYES,

After reading Gosse's article last night, the devil entered into me, and I hitched the principal points of it into rhyme—"lest we forget, lest we forget."

SWINBURNE BY GOSSE

i. *His Concealment of His Age*

Poems and Ballads was his first success;
He then was twenty-four, so said the press,
And so said Algernon. The trick is dirty
To say you're twenty-four when you are thirty.

ii. *A Coincidence*

"Algernon took to you at once." Thus stated
A letter at the close of '70 dated.
To prove its truth I need but add that we
Were not on friendly terms till '73.

iii. *Another Coincidence*

When I've been talking, and then said Goodnight,
He'd fall asleep e'er I put out the light,
Sleep where he sat as if exhaustion forced him,
And yet what could have happened to exhaust him?

viii. *His Vanity*

He'd often bring his poems round to read,
And yet, when asked, appear surprised indeed,
Profess reluctance to comply, and then
Spout out the lot. The vanity of men!

ix. *His Tendency to Low Company*

At Lamb's Centenary he gave a show,
Five of us had dinner in Soho,
Four men and I. And one was T. Purnell,
No friend of mine, who rudely shouted "Hell!"

Swinburne rebuked him, pointing out that "Hades"
Was what a man should say before the ladies.

x. *His Sad End*

When I had talked to him for several years
The wretched man grew deaf in both his ears.
At forty all his mind grew ossified;
He failed to love French realists; and died.

Postscript by the Versifier

Whatever ill our thorny path attends,
May God Almighty save us from our friends,
Or—if His wisdom still ordains that cross—
Spare us at least a eulogy from Gosse.

In several of his works Gosse was an exponent of a form of literary biography which, however delightful to read, lays innumerable pitfalls for the future historian. Lytton Strachey and others carried it on with even more surprising effects, and the same preference for what they would call the "creative imagination." It was perhaps only a fortunate coincidence that, on a visit to the British Museum as a young man, the future biographer of Swinburne should have met two strong men carrying a chair in which was an extraordinary object with a mane of red-gold hair dabbled in blood, and that this object—Swinburne of course—should have so conveniently succumbed at exactly the right moment for the future biographer to settle the otherwise undeterminable question whether Swinburne ever had an epileptic fit, but, as Gosse himself remarks, with characteristic "sensibility," this, his very first glimpse of the poet, was "terrifying in the extreme."

It was Gosse's habit to make his articles interesting by very amusing additions to literary history. Probably he hardly expected either his hearers or his readers to mistake his playfulness for actual fact, but the process was occasionally carried too far. He would begin an essay somewhat after this fashion (the "creative imagination" in this case is my own): "Many years ago I remember walking through St. James's Park and seeing the eminent philosopher Herbert Spencer seated on a park bench with George Eliot. They were engaged in an animated conversation of a kind which did not appear to be wholly acceptable to the author of the *First Principles.* I took the opportunity of passing the bench two or three times, both in front of and behind the interesting couple, but was able to catch only a few fragments of their talk, which apparently turned upon the theories of G. H. Lewes on marriage. I was fortunate enough to see Mr. Spencer bring the discussion to a close by snapping on the famous ear-clips, which precluded him from hearing any opinions but his own. He then rose to his feet with an angry snort and walked rapidly away in the direction of Buckingham Palace."

This method of course had its charm for the innocent. Lady Gosse said to me, quite simply, "Don't you think that Edmund's style grows more and more flexible as time goes on?"

There were two distinct men in Gosse: The first, the real Gosse, was the author of that fine and true biography, the life of his father, the naturalist Philip Gosse. The second and more sophisticated Gosse was the author of *Father and Son.* This had something of the detached wit of Anatole France, and was far more widely read than the former biography because, in accordance with contemporary fashion, the son in the later book made fun of the father. But the picture, necessarily one-sided since the father could not reply, had also the defect of Anatole France in that it subordinated more important considerations to epigrammatic effect. In fairness to Gosse it should be remembered that he lived in an age of cynical scepticism, in which the rapier of wit is sometimes the only effective weapon, and the heart worn upon the sleeve would certainly be pecked by innumerable daws.

In my personal relationship and correspondence with Gosse it should be said here that I met only the first of these two, the real

Gosse. His letters to me were consistently generous, and I think sincere, but I sometimes found myself in a dilemma when the velvet paw unexpectedly scratched others who were also my friends. I could not agree with what he said in the following letter about Watts-Dunton:

> In a few days I am going to send you my "Recollections" of S in the *Fortnightly*. Watts-Dunton is a she-bear for raging, but we really must not allow him to monopolize and reconstruct a Swinburne of his own. You must support me in rejecting a Swinburne whose hair was black and whose voice was bass and who was in complete and humble unison with the tenets of the Church of England. Sooner or later we shall have to march over the body of Watts-Dunton to the grotto of the Veritable Algernon.

(All very amusing, of course, but quite untrue to the characters and relationship of the two friends.)

Like many of his contemporaries, and a little jealously, Gosse underrated the value of Watts-Dunton's friendship to Swinburne, and also his very fine qualities both as a critic and as a poet. Swinburne's own estimate of him as "the largest-minded and surest-sighted critic of this or perhaps any age," is of course far too sweeping, but Swinburne was not a fool in such matters, and the long essay on poetry by Watts-Dunton in the 1911 edition of the *Encyclopaedia Britannica* covers the whole field in a way that it would be difficult to match elsewhere. On the death of the poet, as I know from letters I received from them, Gosse was joking while Watts-Dunton was grieving. As for his friendship for Swinburne, whatever Watts-Dunton's faults may have been he unquestionably saved Swinburne from disaster and enabled him to write many more books which, if not all equal to his former best, are in some cases certainly not inferior to it, and in others distinctly better. I have never been able to understand the passionate lamentations of outsiders that Swinburne was not allowed to die young and preferably in a state of debauchery. These queer Jeremiahs have never once considered or quoted a single word of what Swinburne wrote about the man who devoted his life to him:

> There is a friend who, as the wise man saith,
> Cleaves closer than a brother. Nor to me

Hath Time not shown through days like waves at strife
This pearl most precious found in all the sea
That washes towards your feet these waifs of life.

In these dedicatory lines there is a touching recognition of the fact that without his friend he was without a helm.

The co-operation of Gosse and Wise, in the Bonchurch Edition of the poet's work, was unfortunate. This edition, in twenty handsome volumes, professed to be complete, but it would have aroused the indignation of Swinburne to find that the dedication of his own first collected edition, which he made to his "best and dearest friend" in a long prefatory letter of twenty-five pages, had been entirely omitted; while a preface by Gosse, in which there is a sentence depreciating that friendship, had taken its place. Furthermore, the dedication to Theodore Watts which Swinburne printed on the fly-leaf at the beginning of *Tristram of Lyonesse,* is also omitted, although the dedicatory poem to the unnamed friend is retained. The name of Theodore Watts is also omitted from the dedication of the volume entitled *A Midsummer Holiday,* a holiday which Swinburne spent with that friend. Among all the various dedications of Swinburne's volumes, these are the only omissions which are made. It is all the more marked, because the dedication to Theodore Watts, of a few unimportant rondels about Guernsey, is retained, while the important dedications to him are omitted. Whether Watts-Dunton deserved it or not, this was simply playing tricks with literary history.

The dangers of the "creative imagination" in literary history are aptly illustrated by the gay little stories which the inventiveness of Gosse placed at the disposal of Wise. The most absurd of these is the story about the verses which appeared in *Fraser's Magazine* between 1849 and 1851 over the initials A. C. S. Swinburne was twelve years old in 1849, and Wise was eager to bring out a privately printed "first edition" of these "juvenilia." Gosse was apparently doubtful at first, but after discussing the matter with Wise he calmly stated in the article on Swinburne which he was writing for the *Dictionary of National Biography* that Swinburne's mother (Lady Jane Swinburne) had sent these verses to *Fraser's Magazine.* Watts-Dunton, with genuine critical perception, described the attribution as "monstrous," and through his efforts it was discovered that these "juvenilia" were the work of the elderly Sir Anthony Coningham Sterling, K. C. B. Gosse, in a panic, wrote to Wise, "Keep the Old Man of Putney Hill quiet."

If the "creative imagination" was not at work in the remarkable parody of himself, attributed to Swinburne by Gosse and Wise, it is certainly one of the most incredible pieces of self-condemnation ever made by a poet. He is said to have suppressed it in favour of the much less devastating "Nephelidia." I don't know where the manuscript may be, but in this poem he describes his work as a mad mixture of Frenchified offal, prurient, while his free-thought is nothing but wind, and the mere sight of a church, he says, sets him "yelping." If Swinburne wrote this there is no need for any other critic to dwell on his weaknesses, and, as I have done in other cases, I prefer to dwell upon his real values.

Swinburne's best work has the perfection of Catullus. Sometimes his music, to a degree almost unnoticed by conventional criticism, carries him up to a height where he becomes a worshipper of the unknown God. A striking feature of these passages is that they are immeasurably superior in technique to some of the work which is regarded as most characteristic of him. Compare, for instance, the doggerel

> Those lie where thy foot on the floor is,
> These crown and caress thee and chain,
> O splendid and sterile Dolores,

with certain stanzas in the *Songs Before Sunrise,* which remind one of the masterpieces of Italian religious painting. His picture of St. Catherine of Siena, for instance, is among these:

> And the house midway hanging see
> That saw Saint Catherine bodily,
> Felt on its floors her sweet feet move,
> And the live light of fiery love
> Burn from her beautiful strange face,
> As in the sanguine sacred place

Where in pure hands she took the head
Severed, and with pure lips still red
Kissed the lips dead.

. . . .

Then in her sacred saving hands
She took the sorrows of the lands,
With maiden palms she lifted up
The sick time's blood-embittered cup,
And in her virgin garment furled
The faint limbs of a wounded world.

. . . .

There on the dim side-chapel wall
Thy mighty touch memorial,
Razzi, raised up, for ages dead,
And fixed for us her heavenly head:
And, rent with plaited thorn and rod,
Bared the live likeness of her God
To men's eyes turning from strange lands,
Where, pale from thine immortal hands,
Christ wounded stands;

And the blood blots his holy hair
  And white brows over hungering eyes
That plead against us. . . .

Again in the stanza which uses, with so exquisite an art, the Italian words borrowed from Dante, his transfigured Italy becomes a type of something infinitely higher:

With other face, with speech the same,
A mightier maiden's likeness came
Late among mourning men that slept,
A sacred ghost that went and wept,
White as the passion-wounded Lamb,
Saying, "Ah, remember me, that am
Italia." (From deep sea to sea
Earth heard, earth knew her, that this was she.)
"Ricorditi."

Even technically, there is no comparison between these and the superficially blasphemous verses in which he apparently prefers to curse God and die. I say "apparently" because the God whom he attacks is not God at all. Intellectually, Swinburne lived at the very centre of an agnostic generation; but, like those other agnostics of whom I wrote in *The Unknown God,* he continually reaffirmed one or another article of the faith. Tennyson once asked him if it was fair to abuse the Deity in language borrowed from the Hebrew prophets; but the borrowing went deeper than that, and was often an instinctive acceptance of a reality that transcended language.

In his extraordinarily terse and powerful little play *The Duke of Gandia* he wrote part of the drama he had planned about the Borgias. Whether his portraits are true or false, the spirit of evil broods over the play like a thundercloud. In one scene Pope Alexander talks with Caesar Borgia who had murdered his brother on the preceding night. The Pope, unaware of this, vies with the murderer in irony at the expense of a God whom they apparently believe to be non-existent. Gradually it is borne in upon Alexander that some terrible revelation is about to be made. A messenger arrives to tell him the appalling truth. The thundercloud of evil is discharged in a single concluding line, like a lightning-flash of judgment, as the Pope cries,

"O God, Thou livest, and my son is dead!"

XIII

A Dublin Comedy

IN 1909 Sir Herbert Beerbohm Tree purchased a dramatization of *The Forest of Wild Thyme,* which he was good enough to tell me he liked better than the *Blue Bird*. This remark was not so encouraging as it sounded, for he also told me that he had lost two fortunes by underestimating the taste of the public! He had in fact rejected the *Blue Bird* itself, and also, more surprisingly, Barrie's *Peter Pan.* His mournful reminiscence was not a direct reflection upon *The Forest of Wild Thyme* but it led to many reflections on my own part.

I did a considerable amount of work with him on the script of this play, for which he was preparing, in imagination at least, a very elaborate production at His Majesty's Theatre. He was interested in the scenic possibilities of a dream world in which the children, who had been magically dwarfed to the size of ladybirds, wandered through an enchanted forest in which stalks of thyme towered like eucalyptus trees over daisies ten feet high. He liked the melodramatic possibilities of the Spider, who was of course the villain of the piece and had long wished that he might meet children of an eatable size in his native jungle.

There was one blood-curdling scene in which the Spider, or Hideous Hermit as we called him, was discovered preparing his web for the little visitors, who were being lured by Glow-worm (an old man with a green lantern) into the depths of the forest. Hideous (for Tree insisted on calling him by his Christian name) was to be a kind of Arthur Rackham creature, half spider and half human, and he was to bear a resemblance to Mr. Spinner, the children's tutor in the work-a-day world. Tree himself, fresh from a triumph as Caliban in *The Tempest,* was to play the part of Hideous whenever the spider spoke, and when gymnastics were necessary (as in the making of the web) he was to be doubled by an expert acrobat. Tree, with his huge and strangely luminous eyes, long thin legs and well-nourished middle, was perfectly designed for the part, and his peculiar humour delighted in it. He had elaborate music composed for the play by Coleridge-Taylor.

And then there began the long series of delays and difficulties which make writing for the theatre so hazardous an enterprise for the young author. There was what Tree called the "obstinate success" of his production of *Henry VIII,* which ran for over two years at His Majesty's Theatre; and then came the War.

In the meantime, however, there was a good deal of interest and a certain consolation in finding myself behind the scenes of that curious world in which art and box-office receipts, vanity, jealousy and genius, play an unending comedy of their own. Tree was very urgent that I should write for the stage, and I became a frequent visitor at the theatre. He lived in a large flat in the dome of His

Majesty's, where he gave supper parties after the play, and of course never ceased to act. The walls were hung with the tapestries which he used in producing Shakespeare. They lent a certain grandiosity to what might be called his banqueting hall, in which he doubled the parts of potentate and court jester.

I sometimes suspected that there were pre-arranged cues for some of the epigrams apparently born at these supper parties. Once, for instance, Tree fixed his almost phosphorent eyes on his daughter Viola at the other end of the table, and with an air of unutterable melancholy remarked:

"Viola, when I die I shall have my ashes put in a beautiful urn and sent to you."

Whereupon Viola, fixing her equally luminous eyes on his lugubrious countenance, breathed softly: "That would be a very nasty jar for me, Papa."

Prepared or not, these exchanges were always effective, and the company could enjoy them without restraint but there were some embarrassing moments to the inexperienced visitor. A novelist was the protagonist in one of these incidents. He wrote books of considerable beauty, but he was reputed to be the ugliest man in London. During a supper party one of Tree's pompous footmen in silk stockings, knee-breeches and powdered hair, suddenly announced the unexpected arrival of the novelist. Tree rose hastily from his seat, and said in a loud whisper: "Mr. —— is coming; put out the nuts." The remark was apparently harmless enough, but when the eminent novelist a few moments later shambled into the room, looking decidedly arboreal, he must have been puzzled by the fact that several of those to whom he was introduced appeared to be afflicted with strange tremors and asthmatic gasps.

It can hardly be supposed that Tree arranged for an explosion to take place in a neighbouring garage as a cue for an even more formidable blast at the expense of Arthur Boucher, but I really suspected it at one of the rehearsals of *Henry VIII* at which I happened to be present. Tree took the part of Wolsey in this play and gave a very fine performance; but Boucher, who took the part of Henry VIII, looked so much like the Holbein portrait of the royal bluebeard that he stole too many of the scenes to please the actor-manager. It seemed almost too fortunate a cue for Sir Herbert that just after Boucher had made one of his exits we should have heard a terrific explosion somewhere outside, which shook His Majesty's from foundation to dome. There were about sixty players on the stage at the moment and they seemed to be paralyzed by the concussion, but Tree was master of the situation. Rolling his great eyes around at the petrified faces of his cast he said, with a kind of tragic satisfaction: "Boucher's head has burst."

For some years he stuck to the idea of producing *The Forest of Wild Thyme* and we did quite a lot of work on it together, but I was always kept in uncertainty about it. After one period of several months, during which it was completely shelved, I suddenly had a telegram from him asking if I would come to Dublin, where he was then playing for a fortnight, and work on the play with him. Accordingly, with visions of a dazzling première for the following Christmas intoxicating my youthful ambition, I hurried off to Dublin, although my instincts warned me that I was probably wasting time. The idea was that we were to breakfast together every morning and work upon the play between breakfast and lunch. Breakfasts and suppers took place, but we got little work done, although Tree made some very useful and imaginative suggestions.

There were some interesting guests at these supper parties after the theatre. Among them I remember most vividly J. P. Mahaffy, erudite Provost of Trinity College, Dublin. His stories had an inimitable Irish touch. He told us of an Irish country-woman who wanted to obtain a divorce and had consulted one of his lawyer friends about it. The lawyer had great difficulty in extracting from her the least hint of any ground for the action.

"Has he been unfaithful to you?"

"Niver in the world."

"Has he been cruel to you?"

"Niver was any man more kind and considerate."

"But you must give some grounds for wanting to be divorced from him."

Very reluctantly at last the fateful grounds were given in a husky whisper:

"Well, y'r Honour, I have reason to believe he's not the father of me fourth child."

There were two outstanding incidents which illuminated the queer world of the theatre for me. One of these also illustrated the volatility of the Irish.

The play which Tree was producing in Dublin was by Justin Huntly McCarthy, and at the first performance which I attended there were some unexpected reactions. Possibly if it had been performed by an all-Irish cast there would have been no trouble, but Tree had a way of interposing a slight facetiousness even in the most serious moments of Shakespeare. There were one or two lines in the McCarthy play about the descendants of Irish Kings which Tree induced the players to render in a manner not wholly serious. When the curtain fell at the end of the first scene a fiery individual, with burning blue eyes and shaggy red hair, rose in the pit, and in a burst of oratory that might have roused a nation to war, declared that the play was an insult to Ireland. When the curtain went up on the second scene the astonished players were greeted with a storm of hissing and booing that drowned all their attempts to make themselves heard and left them helplessly staring at one another and more than a little panic-stricken. Tree was on the stage at the time, and he saved the whole situation by a comic stroke of that psychological intuition which is probably the secret of every successful actor. The scene was to end with an Irish reel, and although not a word had yet been spoken and the scene had only just begun, Tree made a signal to the orchestra, which at once broke into the completely irrelevant dance music. The players were too stupefied to realize what Tree was doing, and he had to hiss at them, "Dance! For God's sake dance!" and like the Light Brigade at Balaclava they obeyed him. The hissing and booing stopped like the bawling of a child when it is offered a sugar-plum. The tune was as Irish as it could be, and every face in the theatre became attentive, lips parted and eyes glistened, and when the reel came to an end there was a burst of applause from at least a third of the audience. But Tree was not satisfied with that. He made another and more vigorous signal to the orchestra, and before the audience had time to change its mind the Balaclava brigade was at it again, dancing as if for very life. At the end of the encore the applause was still more enthusiastic, and came from at least half the audience. But Tree was still unsatisfied. He made yet another gesture to the orchestra like one who felt that he was now conducting the entire house, and again the players (some of them, like Hamlet, rather fat and scant of breath) were swept into a third demonstration. When the curtain fell on this, the triumph was complete—the entire audience was applauding vociferously.

I went round to the back of the stage to congratulate the victors, and there I saw a sight as remarkable, I should think, as any in the history of the drama: The entire company lay flat on their backs, panting, with the impressive bulk of Beerbohm Tree in the midst looking very like a whale. Some joy to the world was lost in that the curtain did not rise then and there. The liveliness of the reel, which had been intended to last only a minute or two, had replaced a whole scene. They had come near to consummating victory in death.

The applause beyond the curtain grew louder and louder, and there were appalling cries of "encore." The distressed players looked at their great leader imploringly. He rose nobly to the occasion. Fine actor as he was, he was in no fit condition for athletics, but he would take the call himself. As he came before the curtain his whole body seemed to heave with the effort to regain his wind. The applauding spectators began to shout "Speech! Speech!" and at last words came, tactful and engaging as the circumstances demanded:

"Fellow Hibernians," he began, "I am not so frightened now as I was half an hour ago, but I think I should explain that I lost my brogue at the Battle of the Boyne." The rest was drowned in a roar of laughter that continued until the curtain went up on the next scene. Curiously enough, there was no further question about the success of the play. It ran to full and appreciative houses until a more important event closed the doors of the theatre.

The newspaper reports of the illness of King Edward VII had

become increasingly serious at this time, and one night as we were at supper in Tree's suite at the hotel, his telephone rang. Tree took the call and dramatized it. Lifting up a solemn hand and rolling his eyes round in search of his audience, he exclaimed: "He is dead!" exactly as if he had been Macbeth announcing the death of Duncan.

The next morning I found Tree in great excitement dispatching letters and telegrams to key personages. One of the telegrams was to the Lord Chamberlain, announcing majestically: "I am closing my theatre in London and my theatre in Dublin." At the moment, in my innocence, I could not imagine why he was giving this important information to the Lord Chamberlain at a time when that personage must have had many matters more immediately pressing. My education, however, was enriched a few mornings later when at breakfast an important letter was brought by a boy in buttons, who regularly announced his own entrance at the door by making a low bow and crying in a high soprano voice: "Sir Boomtree, the page." The letter was from the Lord Chamberlain's office and Sir Boomtree seized it with an eagerness which seemed slightly out of keeping with its black edges. "It's come!" he cried, and actually capered round the room in his excitement. It was a personal invitation to the funeral. Perhaps noticing my astonishment at this extraordinary reception of so melancholy a missive, he added, not very convincingly: "I don't care a rap about the invitation, but I should have been damned angry if they hadn't sent it."

It was not long before it became clear to me that one might waste many years in the attempt to write poetic drama. The greater part of *The Forest of Wild Thyme* had been in prose, and I had thought it possible that in a play of this kind the verse might still be used in the occasional songs. The dramatic use of the lyric was a subject that had always interested me. In several famous plays, even in modern times, a song has been used not merely as a decoration but as bringing the whole drama up to a climax. Something of this is suggested in Browning's "Pippa Passes," where each scene is consummated in a song of the little silk-weaver. But for some strange reason it is generally assumed in the theatrical world that the medium in which the majority of the world's dramatists have succeeded, the medium of verse, can bring nothing but failure in the future. I still believe that if verse is handled in the right way and spoken by those who understand it, audiences will respond as readily as they do to music; but you cannot have orchestras if your players have not mastered the elementary technique of the violin. I think Charles Lamb was right in his criticism of the way in which poetic drama was beginning to be murdered on the stage. It is said that when one of his own plays was hissed, the hissing and booing was led by Lamb himself from the front row of the stalls, and there is a possibility that it was not his play but the insincerity of the players that gave vigour to his booing.

When Miss Lena Ashwell produced my *Sherwood* at a small theatre in London the verse was beautifully spoken and I do not think the audiences had any feeling that an artificial medium was being used. Later, when it was played by the same company, not in regular theatres but in provincial town-halls, the verse was accepted quite naturally, and it seemed to me that it certainly held their attention throughout.

However, I felt that I would rather make sure of writing a few books, into which I could put my best work, than lose time in trying to convert the box-office into a temple of the muses. My final disillusionment about the commercial theatre came when I had the privilege of reading *The Forest of Wild Thyme* to one of the Broadway potentates in New York. There was one scene in the play which closed on a religious note. Incidentally, it was the scene for which Coleridge-Taylor had composed some particularly beautiful music. The potentate, who had been slowly absorbing a large cigar, removed it from his mouth at this point and remarked, "Yeah! I'd cut that out. I'd put in a leg-show there." It happened to be the scene which Tree liked best, so that if there was a question of theatrical experience the doctors were at variance. I decided, therefore, that it was best to write for the theatre inside my own head, and I began the *Tales of the Mermaid Tavern*.

One curious adventure, however, befell me before I said good-bye to any project of writing for the theatre. Tree wanted to produce an opera bouffe version of Orpheus and Eurydice, and invited me to do the script and lyrics in collaboration with Frederic Norton, who was to adapt the music of Gluck via Offenbach. It was entitled *Orpheus in the Underground* and was produced at His Majesty's during the Christmas holidays, with great *éclat* as far as I could judge from the illustrated papers. I never saw it because I was ill in a nursing home at the time.

In subsequent years, despite my disappointment about *The Forest of Wild Thyme,* there were other and more satisfactory contacts with the theatre, on which I shall touch in a later chapter.

XIV

The Arrest of the Playboy

DURING MY visit to Dublin, I went to see Francis Meynell, who was then an undergraduate at Trinity College, and I made the acquaintance of his fellow-undergraduate Maurice Healy. Poetry at that time interested the future K. C. more than the law, in which he afterwards became so distinguished a figure. He called at my hotel with real treasure-trove from young Ireland, and wrote afterwards:

"I was very sorry to miss you this afternoon as I have very slight prospect of running up against you for a little time to come. I brought with me a small consignment of what I consider to be representative Irish talent, and trust that you found it awaiting your arrival. The book of Colum's poems is really Francis' gift, and if you will accept the rest from me as a little token of my pleasure at thus meeting you I shall feel very much honoured.

"I think that the extraordinary Gaelic revival in Ireland, which had its origin about 1893 and has been forging ahead ever since, has reacted most favourably upon Anglo-Irish literature. Of course there is a vast and magnificent literature of Ireland which remains a sealed book or almost so to most of us; and it too is making great progress, while excellent translations are day by day adding to the heritage of us poor ignorants. But apart altogether from this, the group of young men, who are conveniently termed 'the Abbey Theatre school,' are doing work which ought to win modern Ireland some place in current literature.

"Of these the most remarkable is Colum—I except Yeats for he has evidently abandoned his pen altogether. Colum is a quite young man, country-bred and with all the woodland sweetness about him. Mayne has done some very good work, but he has spoiled his best play *The Drone* by the addition of a third act. I tried to get Synge's poems, but all I could find was the much discussed *Playboy of the Western World;* and while as one familiar with country nature in the west and south of Ireland I must protest against the picture of our country, I cannot deny him the merit of very fine character-drawing, and a delicate touch of phrase that raises the play from its surroundings of vulgarity. I am sorry I could not get his masterpiece, *Riders to the Sea,* but I hope to send it to you one of these days.

"Lady Gregory is a very remarkable old lady with a wonderful knack of catching the phraseology of the country people. I might have sent you any of her Abbey plays—but I think the *Kiltartan History* is about the most typical piece of her work one could find. Read the notes at the end before you tackle the history proper.

"Finally there is James Stephens, a queer little shrimp of a fellow who writes some strangely fine verse, and at times, if I may say so, reminds me of your own work. But if you read the *Nation* every week you will be very familiar with his poetry, for Massingham has taken a great fancy to it."

I crossed the trail of *The Playboy of the Western World,* when I was a fellow-guest with Lady Gregory, the godmother of the Irish Players, at the house of LaBarre Jayne in Philadelphia. When the play was performed there in 1912 it gave rise to one of the most delicious comedies ever enacted in a Police Court.

Its picture of Irish life, which Maurice Healy had deprecated, so roused the wrath of a citizen of Irish descent in that city that at his instance the police raided the theatre and arrested the players.

When the players were brought into Court the Magistrate asked what charge was preferred against them, and a witness, pointing to the chief character, who in the play had laid his father out with an axe, charged him with attempted murder!

There was more fun in the Police Court that day than had been seen in the theatre for a very long time. The Philadelphia newspapers had interviews with prominent men on the legal aspects of the case. One of them cabled for the opinion of Mr. Bernard Shaw, and got a typical and I am sure undeserved cable in reply: "All decent people are always arrested in the United States."

The little volume of Padraic Colum's early verse, entitled *Wild Earth,* which Maurice Healy gave me, is still treasured in my library. Colum went to the United States and became an American citizen, and it was thirty years later when I met him in New York where he came to one of my readings. He allowed me to use some of his poems in my anthology, *The Golden Book of Catholic Poetry.* There is nothing lovelier in modern Irish poetry than the lyric beginning: "O men from the fields, come gently within." But, like many authors, Colum felt that his earlier work should not overshadow the more mature. He wrote: "It was a pleasure to hear from you and I should be happy to have your selection of my poems in your anthology. . . . I like the poems you mention but they belong to a distant period. Could you find anything of my later work to your liking? As it is a Catholic anthology, perhaps my 'Fuchsias in Connacht' would fit." I compromised by including both, and also his remarkable lines on the Stations of the Cross in the Chicago Cathedral.

XV

Acceptances

IN 1911 I wrote for the *Fortnightly Review* an article entitled "Acceptances," which, though I did not realize it at the time, was my first definite step on the road to the perennial philosophy of Catholicism. The main thesis of that article was that we were in a world of scientific specialists, each pursuing his own line of thought along a diminishing road, always explaining the greater by the less, until the road ran into the void.

We had to choose, in short, between a universe which had nothing behind it and was therefore meaningless, and a universe which had something infinitely greater than itself behind it, so that you might

> . . . see a world in a grain of sand,
> A heaven in a wild flower,
> Hold infinity in the palm of your hand
> And eternity in an hour.

What seemed quite impossible to me was that the universe should be a meaningless and purposeless chimera, originating and ending in nothing.

This thesis was suggested in a comparison which I then used for the first time, and afterwards incorporated in *The Torch-Bearers,* saying that a modern materialist is like a man who should explain a Beethoven symphony (quite accurately as far as he went) by tracing to their sources the wood and catgut of the instruments, and forget both the significance of the music and the mind of the Composer, who, although He does not appear on the scene, speaks through physical instrumentalities to the minds of His listeners. Analysis had gone so far that we were in peril of robbing the universe of meaning. An illustration of this I drew later in *The Torch-Bearers* and in *The Unknown God* from the new theories of the nature of matter. Undoubtedly these have led to great practical results (including the atomic bomb), but, in the discovery that all matter consists of revolving systems of electrons and protons, materialists were in danger of losing sight of something far more important. Flowers and human faces, if they could be magnified to a certain extent, would show us nothing but these revolving systems. The thing which we call a flower, the expression which a child sees in its mother's face, would vanish utterly. There is no possible place in the scientific analysis for the very thing that gives them meaning and value. For Virgil's exquisite line: "*Incipe, parve puer, risu cognoscere matrem,*" we should have to substitute

Begin, little neutron, to roll
With that bunch of revolving electrons.
Don't call it mother, poor brat.
It is just an electrical whirlpool."

On the other hand, the analyses of science had revealed an unsuspected order in the minutiae of the physical universe. A grain of dust was no longer an insignificant particle blown about by the winds of chance, but a microcosm in which "the armies of unconquerable law" marched with no less precision than they did across the skies of the astronomer. To make a synthesis, which we call beauty and poetry, of what science has analysed, so that these myriads of little constellations might be seen once more miraculously grouping themselves into flowers and faces, was one of the aims of *The Torch-Bearers:*

Up-whispered by what Power,
Deeper than moon or sun,
Must each of the myriad atoms of this flower
To its own point of the coloured pattern run;

Each atom, from earth's gloom,
A clean sun-cluster driven
To make, at its bright goal, one grain of bloom,
Or fleck with rose one petal's edge in heaven?

What blind roots lifted up
This sacramental sign
Transmitting their dark food in this wild cup
Of glory, to what heavenly bread and wine?

What Music was concealed,
What Logos in this loam,
That the celestial Beauty here revealed
Should thus be struggling back to its lost home?

Whence was the radiant storm,
The still up-rushing song,
That built of formless earth this heavenly form,
Redeeming, with wild art, the world's blind wrong;

Unlocking everywhere
The Spirit's wintry prison,
And whispering from the grave, "Not here! Not here!
He is not dead. The Light you seek is risen!"

Everything in nature became a parable. In a somewhat analogous way in my poems on pagan or classical subjects, I had found ancient images illuminating modern scientific and philosophical ideas—the Sphinx, for instance, the body of a beast culminating in a human face, becoming a symbol of the unsolved mystery of "evolution." In "Mount Ida" a Greek legend led up to what Alice Meynell called "the heights with summits" of the perennial philosophy. In my poem on Pythagoras in *The Book of Earth,* I found the old doctrine of reincarnation, adumbrating what Hegel called "the eternal history of spirit," its fall and its redemption—a fall from the eternal world of the Platonists rather than from the Eden of Genesis, but nevertheless a fall; and a struggling back by the road of evolution rather than by the road of redemption, but nevertheless a struggling back—all of which received its full significance only in the perennial philosophy towards which it was groping.

Guard the immortal fire.
Honour the glorious line of the great dead.
To the new height let all thy soul aspire;
But let those memories be thy wine and bread.

Quench not in any shrine
The smoldering storax. In no human heart
Quench what love kindled. Faintly though it shine,
Not till it wholly dies the gods depart.

Close not thine eyes in sleep
Till thou hast searched thy memories of the day,
Graved in thy heart the vow thou didst not keep,
And called each wandering thought back to the way.

Pray to the gods! Their aid,
Their aid alone can crown thy work aright;
Teach thee that song whereof all worlds were made;
Rend the last veil, and feed thine eyes with light.

Naught shall deceive thee, then.
All creatures of the sea and earth and air,
The circling stars, the warring tribes of men,
Shall make one harmony, and thy soul shall hear.

Write not thy thoughts on snow.
Cut them in rock to front the thundering sky.
From Earth and Time, when it is time to go,
Take the dark road; bid one more world good-bye.

Out of this earth, this dust,
Out of this flesh, this blood, this living tomb,
Out of these cosmic throes of wrath and lust,
Breaks the lost splendour from the world's blind womb.

Thou that wast brought so low;
And through those lower lives hast risen again,
Kin to the beasts, with power at last to know
Thine own proud banishment and diviner pain;

Out of this prison of clay
With lifted face, a mask of struggling fire,
With arms of flesh and bone stretched up to pray,
Dumb, thou shalt hear that Voice of thy desire:

Courage, O conquering soul!
For all the boundless night that whelms thee now,
Though worlds on worlds into that darkness roll,
The gods abide; and of their race art thou!

The long process of evolution had culminated on a height where it seemed that man had been met half-way by the creative power in which all those meanings and values originated, a power so infinitely above man's comprehension that those meanings and values could only come to him in hints and momentary glimpses, until they were focussed into definition at that meeting place where the Word was made Flesh (*Et Homo Factus Est*).

XVI

First American Tour

IT WAS in 1911 that the first suggestion of a lecture tour in America was made to me by my American publishers. I had never done any lecturing, and in fact had always been afflicted with stage fright at the mere prospect of having to make a speech of any kind. But when Clayton Hamilton, the dramatic critic, came over to England that summer, and visited us at Rottingdean, where Garnett and I had a small house full of books, he was so keen about the scheme that my hesitations were temporarily overborne. Clayton Hamilton at this time was prominent in the literary world of New York; he had come to England primarily to collect material for his book *On the Trail of Stevenson,* from friends like Sidney Colvin and Barrie. He had many conversations with Gosse, but found him "too frivolous" to be really helpful. We had some very pleasant days in Sussex together.

At this time, though I knew little of politics and could only feel instinctively that a tempest was approaching, I wrote several poems on the subject of international peace. "A Prayer for Peace," mentioned in an earlier chapter, and "The Wine-Press" were among them. The former was set to music by Coleridge-Taylor. One of these peace poems had a wide circulation in America; it was quoted in Congress and afterwards printed in full in the *Congressional Record* (the American *Hansard*), on the initiative of Robert Underwood Johnson. He had given up his editorship of the *Century Magazine* to serve the cause of peace in Washington, and subsequently represented the United States as Observer at the League of Nations, and as Ambassador to Rome (where, incidentally, he founded the Keats-Shelley Memorial).

Nearly all my writing on the subject of world peace turned upon one fact of which I was convinced then, and in the ensuing half century have become more and more certain, that the whole future of our civilization depends upon the co-operation of the United States and the British Commonwealth of Nations. Without that co-operation the world would tear itself to pieces. This is a commonplace to-day, but at that time there was little belief in it.

Clayton Hamilton thought this should be the subject of my proposed lectures, and after his return to the United States he wrote to me:

"I began early in May to organize a conspiracy to import you to the United States. Don't look worried until I tell you what I mean. The business of the peace poem impressed upon me that what you have to say in behalf of international peace needs to be said in America as well as in England. There is an enthusiastic young chap in Bill Morrow's (Stokes's) office named Sinclair Lewis; and him I sent to see Hamilton Mabie" (one of the leading critics of that day) "to ask him what he thought of this idea. Mabie wrote a letter in support of the project. I then wrote a statement of my own, and collected some of your peace poems. This gave me a little bundle of material,—viz. (1) my statement, (2) Mabie's letter, and (3) your poems; and I had several copies made of the collection. These copies I turned over to Dean Keppel of Columbia College. . . . Keppel brought them to the notice of President Butler" (Nicholas Murray Butler) "of Columbia University, who is one of the Trustees of the Carnegie Peace Foundation. Keppel subsequently mailed copies of my material, accompanied by letters of his own, to other people influential in the Peace Societies. All of this, let me assure you, I did in the most dignified manner. The people who are helping me in the project are all men of high position. . . .

"My idea was, further, that you should also lecture on poetry, and on two or three specific poets,—say Tennyson, Swinburne and Morris (because of your books). . . .

"In a word, sir, come on over and dine with me: The Players is a good place.

. . . . . .

"Yet, personally, I should rather have you come now to New London 'on the wings of a dove,' and swim with me by the light of the full golden moon which is rolling up this evening from the sea. I have a little bungalow here which overlooks a sand-dune, with the sea beyond it widening to a far horizon. I haven't any white walls or rolling downs, but there are woods of deep trees and a cove for canoeing, and a wonder of a harbour to sail around."

However, my hesitations returned, and though I agreed to go I was almost appalled when in the autumn a cable informed me that a large auditorium was engaged for my first appearance in New York, and that there would be present eight hundred ministers of many religious denominations.

The lecture was to be entitled "The Great Green Table," and the subject was the sinister gamble for power that was then drawing the nations more and more inexorably towards a world war. But the prospect of speaking for the first time in my life to a large audience, so many of whom would be much better practiced than I in the art of speaking, unnerved me. It was only three weeks or so before I had to sail; all the arrangements had been made for a prolonged tour—but I had not anticipated those eight hundred ministers, who were more alarming to me then than they would be now. With my heart in my mouth and an uneasy sense of guilt I hastily sent off a cable to say that unexpected obstacles would make it quite impossible for me to come to America (I did not explain that the obstacles wore clerical collars).

Garnett and I then went up to London, hoping to forget all about it in a few days of music and the theatre. When we returned to Rottingdean at the end of the week, I found a pile of cables from America, declaring that, if I failed to come, my friends there would find it difficult to save me from the consequences of about fifty broken contracts, while my agent would lose very heavily as a result of his expenditures on preliminary announcements. The most staggering of these messages came from my friend Clayton Hamilton, who cabled:

> Cancellation causes friends great financial loss and personal embarrassment Our honour is involved please come.

Accordingly, again with my heart in my mouth, I sent another cable saying that I would come as arranged. One or two kind friends in England had told me that it was not in the least likely that I should be able to make myself heard in a large auditorium, and I therefore tried over the telephone to make an appointment with a coach who had been recommended to me. Rather to my astonishment he replied that he would be very glad to see me if I wished, but that I need not have the slightest fear of not being able to make myself heard, as from the timbre of my voice on the telephone he could assure me that I would have no difficulty. It puzzled me somewhat, as my voice was naturally low-toned, but his prophecy turned out to be true.

I had many misgivings, however, on the way to America, and I practiced my first lecture with an open porthole during a mid-Atlantic storm, trying to imagine that the winds and waves were a hostile audience.

By a very fortunate circumstance, on the afternoon of that first lecture in New York, something happened which made me forget my stage fright: A musically-minded member of the Committee wanted to arrange for musical interludes, during which one of his friends would sing songs from Schumann. I was to speak for ten minutes, then we were to have Schumann, after which I was to speak for another ten minutes, again sit down for more Schumann, and so on for nearly an hour and a half, completely destroying the continuity of my address. I could have sympathized if they had put it on the ground that they couldn't stand more than ten minutes of me at a time, but when I realized that it was to promote a forthcoming concert I fought against the arrangement as if I had never heard of peace! Eventually it was agreed that the music should take place after the lecture, but the discussion was heated. The singer was evidently afraid that the audience would leave prematurely—and so was I—but the effect upon myself was quite salutary, as I was very angry when I went on the platform and all nervousness was banished. One of the ministers said afterwards that the speaker appeared to be inspired. Perhaps he was, but I am afraid to some degree from below rather than from above. In any case, it broke the ice for me as a speaker, and from that time onward I have had nothing but good fortune with my audiences in the United States.

I felt more at home in my next lecture in New York, for this was on the subject of poetry, and was given to the MacDowell Club, an institution founded in memory of the distinguished American composer.

My lectures were largely on the music of poetry, and the element of "song" which had been an essential characteristic of poetry for over two thousand years. From the days of Homer, century after century, the poets had spoken of their work as a kind of "song" The rugged Browning (no less than Homer, Virgil, Dante, Milton, Keats and Shelley) had the same aim:

> Never may I commence my song, my due
> To God who best taught song by gift of thee,
> Except with bent head and beseeching hand.

This thesis enabled me to draw upon innumerable illustrations from the poets, in which the music of poetry is itself a symbol of a greater music:

L'amor che move il sole e l 'altre stelle.

I was particularly fortunate in the next lecture, at Boston, also on poetry, with some readings from my own work. The chair was taken by W. D. Howells, the Dean of American letters at that time. It could hardly have taken place under happier auspices. Afterwards my wife and I drove out to Cambridge and had lunch with him and his daughter, who acted as hostess.

I went on to Wellesley, which, with its beautiful campus of lake and woodland, was the queen of American women's colleges. There was a large gathering of its students, and I felt as if I had been suddenly introduced into the enchanted halls of Tennyson's Princess.

After this I lectured on English and American poetry, and was asked to give readings from my own work, at many American educational institutions, where I met with kindnesses which I should be ungrateful indeed ever to forget.

The success of the tour led to a repetition on a larger scale, and in 1913, on our arrival in New York, my wife and I were asked by Mrs. Douglas Robinson to meet her brother, Theodore Roosevelt, who had not long retired from the Presidency of the United States. There were no other guests, and Roosevelt talked very freely on a great variety of subjects, from the philosophy of Bergson, whom he had met a few days earlier, to Wordsworth. He quoted from many of the poets, with only one mis-quotation when he transposed "land" and "sea" in the line "the light that never was, on sea or land."

He asked me what I thought of contemporary American poets, and whether I did not think George Sylvester Viereck was perhaps among the best of the younger generation. As Viereck seemed to me very far from that, I said quite frankly what I thought of him. This opinion was adequately borne out by subsequent events, though some of these events had nothing to do with poetry.

I told Roosevelt how much I liked the poetry of Brian Hooker and Edwin Arlington Robinson. I am glad to think that my appreciation of the latter was almost the first in the field. Robinson wrote to me later:

"I faced the denizens of the Colony Club, being told that you were to read there, and was glad to see you again and to hear you. The better acquainted I become with your work the more I wonder at your lyrical way of doing things. I can't do it myself and accordingly I wonder at it all the more. No doubt I'm a little jealous underneath.

"I still see occasional references to your remarks about my work—I regret on your account that they were so magnified—and I wish to thank you again for your friendliness in making them. I hope that I may see you and Mrs. Noyes again sometime before you leave this unfocussed but promising republic."

Brian Hooker in his early days wrote some very beautiful lyrics, but he was lazy and did not make the most of his great gift. His poem on that mother of men, old Yale, is perhaps the best college song ever written. His poem about college men who died in the first world war was set to music, and is one of those things which once heard are never forgotten. His version of *Cyrano de Bergerac* and his *Vagabond King* (based on the life of Villon) were successful in the theatre, and perhaps made work unnecessary, but in the intervals between the arrival of royalties he was often in difficulties, out of which he was sometimes helped by Clayton Hamilton. Clayton, one of the most popular members of the Players Club, was not wealthy and liked to live within his means, for he had a wife and children of his own. Leonard Bacon told me that one day Clayton was seen pacing up and down outside the Players Club, with an expression of profound gloom on his usually cheerful face, and on being asked what troubled him, he replied quite simply: "Brian Hooker is going to have another baby, and I'm not sure whether I can afford it."

Two young Harvard poets of that day, Witter Bynner and Hermann Hagedorn, are happily still with us. Once Witter Bynner was responsible for a literary hoax of which the reverberations continue forty years later. "Atticus" told part of the story recently in *The Sunday Times,* much to the amusement of Witter Bynner, who was spending a week-end with us in the Isle of Wight.

Nearly forty years ago Witter Bynner and Arthur Davison Ficke prophetically parodied some of today's serious "poetry." The book, entitled *Spectra,* was published under the pseudonyms of Emanuel Morgan and Anne Knish, and dedicated to Remy de Gourmont in lines which gave fair warning, but the advanced critics took it all quite seriously.

To Remy de Gourmont

Poet, a wreath!—
No matter how we had combined our flowers,
You would have worn them—being ours,
On you, on them, the showers—
O roots beneath!

Their prophecy in the dedication has been amply fulfilled.

The critics were lured down the garden path of "Spectrism" by an engaging preface, which declared that we had seen things too long under the white light of day, and they should now be touched with the colours of the spectrum:

"It is the aim of the Spectric group to push the possibilities of poetic expression into a new region. . . . Spectric speaks, to the mind, of that process of diffraction by which are disarticulated the several coloured and other rays of which light is composed. It indicates our feeling that the theme of a poem is to be regarded as a prism.

A growing acquaintance with Chinese painting is surely liberating in our poets and painters a happy sense of the disproportion of man to his assumed place in the universe. By this weapon, man defends his intuition of the Absolute."

There was a chorus of praise from the unwary. Opus 15 was described by a leading English journal as a "brilliant example of that sharp-edged imagery with which some of the more adventurous of our younger poets are experimenting today."

> Asparagus is feathery and tall,
> And the hose lies rotting by the garden wall.

The futuristic beauty of Opus 9 was of course clear to everyone:

> When frogs' legs on a plate are brought to me
> As though I were divinity in France,
> I feel as God would feel were he to see
> Imperial Russians dance.
>
> These people's thoughts and gestures and concerns
> Move like a Russian ballet made of eggs;
> A bright-smirched canvas heaven heaves and burns
> Above their arms and legs.
>
> Society hops this way and that, well-taught;
> But while I watch, in cloudy state,
> I feel as God would feel if he were brought
> Frogs' legs on a plate.

And what could be more Freudian than Opus 104:

> How terrible to entertain a lunatic!
> To keep his earnestness from coming close!
> A Madagascar land-crab once
> Lifted blue claws at me
> And rattled long black eyes.
> That would have got me
> Had I not been gay.

The climax of the little hoax was reached during the first world war. Ficke was now a Colonel in the American Army. He was approached one day by a young soldier, who asserted that a certain pseudonymous work entitled *Spectra* was written by himself. He entrusted Colonel Ficke with a sealed envelope by which his claim was to be substantiated in the event of his death. Colonel Ficke accepted the sacred trust gravely and without comment.

XVII

Lowell Lectures, the Aldriches and Others

LORD BRYCE in 1913 was still British Ambassador in Washington. I had read his famous book on the Holy Roman Empire when I was at Oxford. He very kindly asked me to lunch when I was in Washington, but much as I enjoyed meeting him, I felt that his interest in the subject of my lectures might be embarrassing. A little later that year I received a letter from him which, though it contained only a hint, made me feel that behind the diplomatic scenes events were being shaped on which no rough-hewing could have any effect. It startled me to find him saying that war might be inevitable; and, with an Olympian detachment from the appalling tragedy that he envisaged, bidding me remember that if there had been no Trojan War there would have been no *Iliad*.

Shortly afterwards I was invited by President Lowell of Harvard to give the Lowell Lectures. The subject I chose was "The Sea in English Poetry." The auditorium in Boston (at the Massachusetts Institute of Technology) was filled to overflowing, and I was asked to repeat the entire series there a little later in the same season.

The lecture field is one in which human nature does not always show at its best, and the European lecturer visiting America has all too often mistaken kindness and hospitality for acknowledgement of a somewhat exaggerated estimate of his personal importance, with effects which might be more annoying if they were not so amusing. When Count Keyserling (at one time taken quite seriously in England as a philosopher) visited America, the manifesto which he caused to be issued to his prospective hosts was an almost perfect example of how things should not be done. A copy of the manifesto is before me as I write:

MEMORANDA re COUNT KEYSERLING

The following will help you to understand Count Keyserling's preferences better than anything else.

He is a charming and fascinating guest as long as his wishes are considered, but when they are disregarded he becomes upset and this reacts on his speaking ability. Any further information which you would like to have will be given with a great deal of pleasure.

The Count dislikes sight-seeing.

He dreads his room over-heated.

He never attends theatres, concerts, or the like.

He would like to walk from two to four hours a day away from the heart of the city.

He never sees anything [*sic*] later than six hours before a lecture.

He *must have* a lectern or pulpit on the platform to keep his material on.

He does not dine before a lecture. However, half an hour before he is to go on the platform he would like to have served a strong cup of coffee and a sandwich of roast beef or chicken (white meat).

He does not care to meet anyone after closing a lecture. He wishes to leave the platform and the auditorium immediately for the home of his host, or for the place where a sitting-down supper will be served, if he is to meet anyone later in the evening.

He is nervously and physically exhausted after finishing a lecture. If he is to meet anyone after his lecture, he would enjoy doing so at somebody's home under the following conditions: He prefers to have an opportunity to change his clothes. Secondly, he is famished and must eat immediately after a lecture. Therefore he does not want to meet anyone unless he can have a sitting-down supper at which he will be served French wines or champagne. The champagne or French wine may be served to him in his room with a supper if it can't be served in public.

If he does not have to talk with anyone after his lecture he does not need the wine or champagne, but he must have the supper. The following is a quotation from one of Count Keyserling's letters to us: "Champagne is what helps me best to get over the nervous strain produced by a lecture. But if this can't be had then good claret (French red wine) will do. I can't stand German white wines and strong spirits like whiskey and short drinks." Later he said he did not care for cordials.

He is delighted to attend dinner parties and luncheons to meet interesting people. The Count refuses to attend dinners with men only.

He cannot eat raw fruit, salad, vegetables, etc.

He eats no vegetables except potatoes (boiled or mashed).

He cannot eat ice-cream or sweets, and nothing heavy or spicy.

He lives chiefly on fresh fish and fresh oysters, dozens of them on the half-shell, and beef, lamb and white meat of fowl.

He enjoys the society of attractive young women.

In the next few years, during which Garnett and I frequently visited America, Boston became a second home to us. Some of our happiest days were spent at No. 59 Mount Vernon Street, with the family of Thomas Bailey Aldrich. It was a house of many memories. Dickens had visited the Aldriches in their younger days, and Edwin Booth, the famous American actor, a friend of Thomas Bailey Aldrich, had been playing in Boston on the night when his brother murdered Abraham Lincoln at a theatre in Washington. When the tragic news reached Edwin Booth he was crushed by it, and shut himself up in his house, feeling that his name would be an object of execration. Aldrich was one of the two friends whose companionship, by day and by night, pulled him through those terrible months. When Booth recovered something of his composure they smoked pipe after pipe together, Aldrich trying to persuade him that his great career might yet be saved from the wreck. The pipe which Edwin Booth had been smoking was a peculiar one. The meerschaum bowl was in the shape of a large human thumb, crooked upwards, with a broad thumb-nail of amber. Booth gave it to Aldrich when he left, and it was given to me by the Aldrich family, with an inscription on the stem relating the circumstances. The crooked meerschaum thumb discoloured by nicotine, with the large amber thumb-nail, still somewhat gruesomely suggests the hand of the assassin who put so bitter a cup to the lips of his brother and his country.

Mrs. Aldrich must have been the only person in existence who had seen Harriet Beecher Stowe drunk, and in fact she was unintentionally responsible for that equally unintentional lapse. Mrs. Aldrich's account of this historical event, as I heard it from her own lips, was inimitable.

It happened in the first days of her married life, when the Aldriches were living in a much smaller house called Rose Cottage. Here one afternoon the young bride was tremulously expecting a visit from the author of that world-famous book *Uncle Tom's Cabin;* tremulously, for Mr. Aldrich had told her that the conversation would probably be lofty, since Harriet Beecher Stowe at the age of ten had written a thesis entitled "Can the Immortality of the Soul be Proved by the Light of Nature?" He also suggested that as the weather was very hot a claret-cup should be prepared. He was called away for the afternoon and would not return until dinner-time. To the recipe which he had given her for the claret-cup, the young hostess, wishing to do all possible honour to so distinguished a guest, added something from a curiously shaped bottle which she understood came from a Carthusian Monastery. What could be more appropriate? Had not Mr. Matthew Arnold (also a recent visitor to Boston) written a poem on the Grande Chartreuse?

Mrs. Stowe arrived, looking wispy, frail, and (as Swinburne might say) "pale with bitter summer." Almost her first remark was "I'm *so* thirsty!" Instantly free from all fear of conversation about the immortality of the soul, the proud young hostess produced her beverage and poured out a full tumbler. It vanished rapidly. A second tumbler followed, and, to Mrs. Aldrich's amazement, Harriet Beecher Stowe's conversation assumed a nautical turn. She asked why the sofa was going up and down, and said she would like to get into her berth and take a nap, "if only it would keep still." The hoop-skirt that she wore added to the nonchalant effect of her recumbent position on the sofa; and Mrs. Aldrich, who was expecting other guests, began to wonder what she could do about those white cotton stockings and flowery garter ribbons. There were attempts to cover the inebriated Mrs. Stowe, only to be met with indignant little kicks, and the remark: "I won't be any properer than I've a mind to be. Let me sleep."

Sleep, in fact, lasting until dinner-time, saved the situation, though alarm again assailed the young hostess when she heard her guest describe to Mr. Aldrich the strange dizziness which she thought "had been caused by the train journey."

Thomas Bailey Aldrich had died in 1908, but his book-lined studies at 59 Mount Vernon Street and at Tenants Harbor, their summer home on the coast of Maine, were exactly as he had left them, and the hospitality of his family opened both to me as havens to which Garnett and I could return in the intervals of lecturing from end to end of the continent. There followed several summers at The Crags (Tenants Harbor) on that beautiful coast of Maine where almost untrodden pine forests go down to a sea of Mediterranean blue; and scores of little islands, crowned with dark pines, tempt you to endless explorations.

The village of Tenants Harbor was an isolated cluster of small wooden houses. Some of its inhabitants belonged to a religious sect at whose meetings, rather like those of the Quakers, complete silence was maintained until someone in the congregation was moved by the spirit. On one of these occasions the silence was prolonged until (to the general alarm, for he had never done it before) the village lunatic rose and, concentrating the venom of a lifetime into a single sentence, exclaimed: "My brother Bill says there ain't no Hell," then joyously, "but HE'll see!"

It was the prelude to grimmer, as well as more ludicrous incidents.

A young Norwegian painter who lived in the village often came to The Crags in the evening. For some unexplained reason the lunatic had taken a dislike to him and began to lie in wait for him at dark corners of the road, from which he would emerge with a sinister expression when the young painter passed. "Nordy," as we called him, always looked as if his hair were standing on end, with his eyes popping. The effect was impressive when one evening he told us that the lunatic had now begun to sharpen a knife on his doorstep at five o'clock in the morning. We thought he must have imagined it, but a little later, when some cattle were mysteriously mutilated in a neighbour's field, things began to look more serious. One of the lunatic's hallucinations was that he was in communication with historic personages of the remote past and could write letters to them. The climax was reached when he rowed across the harbour to the little post-office which stood on the other side, and frightened the postmistress out of her wits by his appearance with a blood-stained knife in one hand and a telegram in the other, which he insisted she should send to King Charles I. Her screams for help resulted in the lunatic's arrest and conveyance to safe quarters elsewhere.

News of these happenings did not reach The Crags until the next afternoon, and in the meantime comedy entered.

Talbot Aldrich (the poet's son) and I had gone out in his motor launch for some sea-fishing. We had a very pleasant morning and caught a great many rock-cod. On our return to The Crags I found a letter from Frederick Stokes, the publisher, saying he had received a request from the Duchess of Buckingham and Chandos for the use of my poem "The Highwayman" in a book which was being prepared for some good cause in England; he thought that as the letter had been delayed I might like to send her a cable.

Accordingly I got into a rowing-boat at once without changing my blood-stained jeans, and made for the little post-office on the other side of the harbour, where I wrote out my telegram:

DUCHESS OF BUCKINGHAM AND CHANDOS, DUNCRAIG CASTLE, SCOTLAND
My highwayman entirely at your service.

I handed it to the postmistress. Then I suddenly became aware that there were white rings around her eyes, and that she was staring with horror at my blue-jeans smeared with the blood of cod-fish. Before anything could be done about it she was out through the back door, with a scream for help that might be heard a mile off. Knowing nothing of what had happened the day before, I stood there mystified but patiently awaiting developments.

Presently I heard sounds of many shuffling feet outside the post-office door, where some kind of consultation appeared to be going on; then the door was opened very cautiously, just wide enough for a head, remarkably like Uncle Sam's, to take a quick glance at me. The sight of my blood-stained jeans appeared to confirm some awful suspicion, for the head was quickly withdrawn and there was a further consultation, into which a high-pitched voice apparently brought fresh evidence. The door was cautiously opened again, and after another glance Uncle Sam took a chance on it, and came into the room.

"Ain't you the feller that's staying up to Aldrich's?" he asked.

I made the mistake of trying to be funny, and said, "I hope so," at which there seemed to be renewed consternation among the villagers at the door. But Uncle Sam reassured them, and turning to me made a graceful little apology:

"My wife had a feller in here yesterday trying to send a cable to King Charles I, and she thought you was another of 'em."

The Aldrich house, The Crags, stood in its own pine woods about a quarter of a mile from the village and so near the sea that you could throw a fishing line from the verandah into the clear green water. Three-masted ships of the old days occasionally passed close inshore on the way to Rockland. The place was haunted by memories of the French and Indian Wars, and the combination of these with the recollections of London, Paris and Rome, which met you in the house and in Talbot's studio, gave it a charm and an atmosphere which I have found nowhere else. Something of this I tried to recapture in some verses which I wrote there:

THE CRAGS

(*In Memory of Thomas Bailey Aldrich*)

Falernian, first! What other wine
Should brim the cup or tint the line
That would recall my days
Among your creeks and bays;

Where, founded on a rock, your house
Between the pines' unfading boughs,
Watches through sun and rain
That lonelier coast of Maine;

And the Atlantic's mounded blue
Breaks on your crags the summer through
A long pine's length below,
In rainbow-tossing snow,

While on your railed verandah there
As on a deck you sail through air,
And sea and cloud and sky
Go softly streaming by.

Like delicate oils at set of sun
Smoothing the waves the colours run—
  Around the enchanted hull,
  Anchored and beautiful.

. . . .

But best of all, I think, at night,
The moon that makes a road of light
  Across the whispering sea,
  A road—for memory.

When the blue dusk has filled the pane,
And the great pine-logs burn again,
  And books are good to read—
  For his were books indeed—

Their silken shadows, rustling, dim,
May sing no more of Spain for him;
  No shadows of old France
  Renew their courtly dance.

He walks no more where shadows are,
But left their ivory gates ajar,
  That shadows might prolong
  The dance, the tale, the song.

His was no narrow test or rule,
He chose the best of every school—
  Stendhal and Keats and Donne,
  Balzac and Stevenson;

Wordsworth and Flaubert filled their place.
Dumas met Hawthorne face to face.
  There were both new and old
  In his good realm of gold.

The title-pages bore his name;
And, nightly, by the dancing flame,
  Following him, I found
  That all was haunted ground;

Until a friendlier shadow fell
Upon the leaves he loved so well,
  And I no longer read,
  But talked with him instead.

Aldrich himself was the poet of memory. There are few lyrics that give more perfect expression to one of its strangest characteristics than those exquisite lines:

MEMORY

My mind lets go a thousand things,
Like dates of wars and deaths of kings,
And yet recalls the very hour—
'Twas noon by yonder village tower,
And on the last blue noon in May—
The wind came briskly up this way,
Crisping the brook beside the road;
Then pausing here, set down its load
Of pine-scents, and shook listlessly
Two petals from that wild-rose tree.

Years afterwards, in *The Secret of Pooduck Island* (a book which I intended for children up to the age of ninety) I drew partly upon my memories of that happy place and its vanished poet:

"A song-sparrow piped three plaintive notes where the pines went down to the water. It was too delicious never to have been heard by someone who enjoyed it. It was not the time for bird-song, but it was answered by a remote elfin echo, dying away along the coast. Somebody had listened to that lonely cry, keen and sweet as a pine-needle pricking your heart. But nobody was there now."

XVIII

Princeton Days, and Spring-Rice at Washington

IT WAS at the Aldriches' house in Boston, the spring of 1913, that a new and very happy chapter of my life was opened when a letter reached me from Yale University, offering me the honorary degree of Doctor of Letters. This had a further result in several warm friendships.

I was presented for the degree by William Howard Taft, who, at the end of his term as President of the United States, had joined the faculty of Yale, teaching Constitutional Law.

Among the recipients of degrees on this occasion was President Hibben of Princeton University. When the speech-making was over he asked me if I would accept the Murray Professorship of English Literature at Princeton. The former holder of this chair, Henry van Dyke, had been appointed Ambassador to the Hague, and the Trustees had empowered President Hibben to offer me the vacancy.

Though the invitation was tempting, I hesitated for some time, as I did not want anything to interfere with my writing; but on being told that I should have to lecture only twice a week for half the College year, and that the rest of my time would be at my own disposal, I accepted the offer, and so entered upon a delightful experience.

The Princeton arrangement was completed some months before the outbreak of war in 1914. There were some outstanding men on the English faculty there. The most widely known of these was perhaps Professor Harper, who fluttered the placid atmosphere of Dove Cottage, and indeed all England, by his discovery of Wordsworth's unacknowledged love affair in France, making E. V. Lucas break out into parody: "Wordsworth! Thou should'st be living at this hour."

A small group of students who had literary ambitions used to meet me once a week to discuss their own work in prose and verse. Among these were Scott Fitzgerald and Edmund Wilson, each of whom was destined in his own way for a literary career.

Scott Fitzgerald once told me he thought he had it in his power to choose between writing books of permanent value, or writing for money. He asked me what I thought he should do, and I told him that if he wrote books of permanent value I believed he would have more satisfaction in the long run. He looked doubtful about this, and told me a little later that he had decided to "take the cash and let the credit go." But that was only expressing a mood of the moment; and

I think he was right in supposing he had the power to make the choice.

Scott Fitzgerald had a great many friends. One day, however, he brought me some verses from which my attention was distracted by the fact that he had a black eye. It was explained to me afterwards that at a dance on the previous night Fitzgerald had become a little too hilarious, and had been thrown out by the captain of the football team.

His visit to Galsworthy in England, later on, brought this exponent of flaming youth into amusing contrast with the formal and rather solemn biographer of Soames Forsyte. Dinner was a dignified affair, but when the men had had their conventional twenty minutes with the port and proceeded to join the ladies, Fitzgerald grasped the decanter firmly in one hand and his glass in the other, and took them into the drawing-room. There from time to time he refreshed himself, Galsworthy pretending not to notice but becoming plainly more and more anxious to distract the attention of his other guests. In fairness to Scott Fitzgerald, however, it should be remarked that it was a vintage port and he knew it.

Edmund Wilson, five of whose undergraduate poems I published in an anthology of Princeton verse, came regularly with Scott Fitzgerald and John Peale Bishop (afterwards a source for Fitzgerald's biographer) to the little weekly symposium, or preceptorial as it was called. He made a vivid impression on me, as he had unquestionable literary gifts and a critical flair quite unusual in a young student. He appreciated subtleties of technique in verse that were quite beyond the usual range, and he was very sure of himself. I doubt whether it had ever occurred to him that he could possibly be wrong; and though I strongly disagreed with some of his opinions, I had no doubt whatever of his gifts. In a preface to my *Book of Princeton Verse* (1916) I said, "It contains a considerable quantity of work that would hold its own in any contemporary anthology." One of the poems of Edmund Wilson, for instance, on Dean Swift and Stella, had the true ring in its opening:

> Because I doubted friend and cause and God,
> Proved false to all, lest they prove false to me,

and there was real beauty and a fine sense of literary values in his poem on "A Rose Found in a Greek Dictionary":

> In what dead summer came her petals here?
> By what dead fingers dropped to mark a page,
> Among the little words that live so clear
> Beside this dimness and decay of age?
>
> This heavy tomb, whose walls can only bleach
> Her hue, shall make the lightest leaf to spring
> From the full-petalled flower of ancient speech,
> The frailest epigram, a deathless thing.

I doubt if any student anthology has ever contained a poem of more delicate subtlety than this.

Some quite unusual poems were contributed by John Peale Bishop, James Creese, Hamilton Fish Armstrong and Isidor Kaufman. Two poems by one of these young students, Brooks Henderson, had a quality which promised great things. His tragic death after leaving Princeton was a loss to literature. One of his poems, "Chanteur," which I included in the Princeton anthology, now reads like a foreshadowing of his own departure:

> He came with dawning wind
> Singing, and faced the day;
> Not of the night behind
> He made his lay.
> Because his face was fresh as morning skies
> We asked his bent,
> Because as deep as heaven were his eyes;
> But on he went.
>
> He came with chill of night
> Singing, and faced the cold.
> With weariness of day his eyes were bright,
> His look was bold.
> Because his song was rich as night and day
> And he forspent,
> We hoped he would forget awhile and stay;
> But on he went.

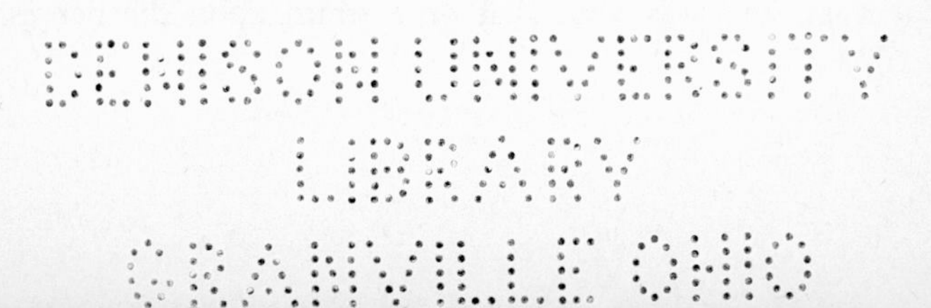

One would have to search very far and wide to find a body of work of so fine a quality by young students; and the memory of the mornings that I spent with these young authors often fills me with nostalgia for the campus where "magnolia boughs embower the halls of old Nassau."

One of my colleagues in the English Department was Professor Duncan Spaeth, a man of tremendous enthusiasms. In his discourses on English, German and American literature his judgment was as sound as his appreciation was keen and inspiring to his students. His wife was French, one of his parents Scottish and the other German. I found him one day in a state of great excitement. He clutched my arm, the tears streaming down his face, and exclaimed, "This European war is raging inside me!"

America at that time had not made up her mind about the war, and the German Ambassador, Count von Bernstorff, had addressed a large audience at Princeton, giving his own side of the case. About a fortnight later President Hibben asked me if I would care to give a talk on the other side. During my talk I saw my good friend Spaeth at the back of the auditorium, and felt instinctively that the war was still raging within him. When I had finished, this became very apparent, for he rose to his feet and in a stentorian voice shouted, "Now I know why the sun never sets on the British Empire. God wouldn't trust an Englishman in the dark!" It is a remark that has frequently been made since those days, but I rather suspect that he was its originator, perhaps on this very occasion. He was too original a man to have expressed his emotion in borrowed words. We all enjoyed the explosion; and it did not diminish the friendliness of the audience towards what I had said. My personal friendship with Spaeth was actually increased from that day.

In addition to his other activities, Spaeth was exceedingly popular as the coach of the Princeton crew, and (possibly because I had rowed in my own College eight at Oxford and Henley) he asked me to act as judge in one of the athletic events of the year, the race between Princeton and Harvard. It was a great occasion, with thousands of spectators, and was somewhat of a strain upon the nerves, for in

America the tension of such events is screwed up to the highest pitch. The office of judge was made all the more difficult by the fact that the race was practically a dead heat in the last hundred yards. First the Harvard boat would shoot a foot or two ahead, then Princeton would do the same, the positions alternating with every stroke. It just happened that Princeton crossed the finishing line first by a yard, though I have no doubt that Harvard in a few more seconds would have drawn level. I gave the verdict for Princeton, and was almost stunned by the uproar that arose. Newspaper reporters, who had not been in position to see the finish as precisely as I had done, wanted to cross-examine me as to whether it was by thirty-five or thirty-six inches that Princeton had won. When I allowed that it might be thirty-five, they asked if I was sure it wasn't thirty or twenty-nine, and my certainty that it was more was taken, with some scepticism, as an affirmation that I knew the distance to an eighth of an inch.

Thirty years later I am told that the legend still exists in Princeton that a poet once acted as judge of the Princeton-Harvard race, and decided that Princeton had won "by the breadth of a butterfly's wing!"

There were two schools of thought in Princeton at that time concerning the policies of Woodrow Wilson, its former President. Spring-Rice, our Ambassador in Washington, had no hostility to Wilson, but one of his closest friends was Senator Lodge who was in disagreement with the President, and when Spring-Rice, with his sparkling Irish wit, remarked that Wilson might be the shepherd of his people, but McAdoo was his crook, Lodge was not likely to hide the scintillation under a bushel. Wit may be a dangerous asset to an Ambassador, but with Spring-Rice the danger was rendered harmless by his own kindly and sensitive nature, which won the affection of all who met him.

When the Ambassador went to see President Wilson to take leave of him, the President shook hands with him and said: "Remember, I am always your friend."

Spring-Rice came to Princeton with Jusserand, the French Ambassador, to receive an honorary degree, and won the regard of the whole university.

The ceremony took place in the open air, on a beautiful summer day, outside Nassau Hall, which during the Revolutionary War had been the headquarters alternately of the British and of Washington himself. The ceremony was very stately and impressive, and the various speeches had been excellent and were greeted with rounds of applause. Spring-Rice watched the proceedings in a kind of trance, as if he were at an absorbingly interesting play. Like many other Europeans, he never quite seemed to feel that the New World could be real. Columbus must have felt something of the same kind. At the end of each speech Spring-Rice clapped vigorously with the rest of the audience. Then, at the climax, after the degrees had been conferred, a Bishop, most magnificently episcopal, swept to the front of the platform to pronounce a closing benediction. He was an imposing figure and looked so very like a Bishop (which of course he really was) that Spring-Rice seemed completely fascinated by his perfection in the part. As the last words fell from the Bishop's lips, Spring-Rice brought his hands together with a resounding clap, and was about to give more applause when George Ellery Hale, the astronomer, who was sitting immediately behind him, seized his elbows with the quick decision of a scientific mind, and saved Princeton from such sensational headlines as "British Ambassador Claps Praying Bishop."

On the old battleground of Princeton a monument was erected to the united memory of those British and American soldiers who had fallen there in conflict with one another and had been buried side by side in the same trench—a symbol of the new friendship that may one day save the world from final catastrophe. At the request of the Trustees I wrote an inscription for this monument:

Here Freedom stood by slaughtered friend and foe,
And, ere the wrath paled or that sunset died,
Looked through the ages; then, with eyes aglow,
Laid them to wait that future side by side.

Mr. Pyne, one of the Trustees, told me that after my death they would add the author's name to the inscription. If they do, my shade will be proud indeed.

The drawing together of the whole English-speaking world, as a nucleus of a wider comity of nations, had been the theme of much of my work at this time, both in my books and on the lecture platform. In the furtherance of understanding between the English-speaking nations the literature of the English language, as a medium for the communication of ideas mutually understood, is of incomparable value, for at its highest and best it stands above all parties and all political conflicts in every generation. It is more important than the spoken language, for differences of idiom sometimes lead to misunderstandings, while the literature of both countries embodies something more permanent.

I had seen an illustration of this at a mass-meeting in the United States to honour the tercentenary of Shakespeare, who belongs to America no less than to England (some of his Elizabethan idioms are still used in the mountains of Kentucky). Materialists may have shaken their heads over Carlyle's declaration that Shakespeare was a greater asset to England than the Indian Empire. During that tercentenary England was fighting with her back to the wall. When Shakespeare's words in praise of England were spoken from that platform, the sight of six thousand Americans silently rising to their feet was of far more than insular significance. It was enough to fill the heart of any Englishman with gratitude to the universal poet who was born on St. George's Day and who by his words could unite nations.

This aspect of art and literature, as a ground upon which all nations could meet, was in my mind throughout my lectures. I found that it worked in actual practice, sometimes quite surprisingly. When America came into the war I was invited by Mr. Lane, Secretary of the Interior, to join a Committee in New York as British Adviser to his Department. The British Ambassador approved of this, and so for a time, although a British subject, I became a civil servant of the United States.

One of the tasks of this Committee was to deal with problems raised by the "foreign language press" in the United States. At that time there were more than a thousand newspapers there printed in German, and proportionally large numbers of Scandinavian and

Italian papers. People at home who talked and thought of America as one vast "New England" had not the slightest conception of what these figures meant in an international struggle.

Various nationalities were represented on this Committee, the Irish representative being Mr. John Quinn, a prominent New York lawyer, who had all the best qualities of the Irish—including their pugnacity.

For some strange reason or other Quinn had a bee in his bonnet about the English uniform, and on one occasion made a remark about it which almost brought him to blows with our military representative on the Committee. (Curiously enough, Augustus John, who met Quinn in Paris at the time of the Versailles Conference, found this bee still buzzing, and records in his autobiography that there was a breeze between them on the same subject.) I remember Quinn at one of our meetings pounding the table with his fist, and saying that while this war was on he was loyal to the cause which America had espoused, but that when it was over he was going to work for war between the United States and England. However, he was a lover of art, and after executing his war dance he compromised by collecting the works of British painters. I found common ground with him on Irish poetry, and after crossing this pleasant bridge we could discuss other matters without acrimony.

One day a British member of Parliament arrived at Princeton with a letter of introduction from Lord Bryce. I was about to give a reading of my poems in New York for the benefit of the Prince of Wales' Fund. It was to be given under the auspices of an influential Committee headed by the British Ambassador, and the chair was to be taken by Mr. Joseph H. Choate, former American Ambassador to England. The member of Parliament, armed with his letter of introduction, approached various members of the Committee and expressed an urgent desire to make a speech of his own from my platform. I could obtain no idea of what he wanted to say, and, as Spring-Rice had lent his name to the occasion, I thought it wise to consult him. He answered:

"I don't know anything about Mr. —— but I have asked F. O.

[the Foreign Office] if he has a special mission for them, which is the main thing for this Embassy. I see no harm whatever in his thanking the American people for relief work, but I hope he won't say anything about Anglo-American relations, at least not officially, because anything which is said on this subject is liable to be misunderstood or misinterpreted. My own rule, which I try to observe as far as possible, is that I avoid all criticism or praise, or (if I can) any mention of our international relations. There are so many dangerous aspects of the question that I think it wiser (for an official at any rate) to avoid the subject altogether. All people who talk our language, whether foreigners or not, are presumed also to think our thoughts. This presumption is of course not realized in experience, because people in America have in many cases quite a different point of view. This leads to bitter disappointment which is really not justified—because life here is so different to life at home that people here must necessarily think differently on very many often vital things. In your line there is much more solidarity of feeling, because poets must always belong to the world at large, and not to any particular people—and an English poet must speak with special weight to people who read him in their own language. Politicians belong to a nation, or a district; and I naturally think as a politician—so presumably does an M. P. This is my humble opinion, for what it is worth. Excuse the observation."

A few days later I received a telegram from Washington to the effect that the "person mentioned represents only himself" and suggesting that I use my own judgment.

The situation was difficult, for the letter of introduction from Lord Bryce had induced the Committee to invite the persistent M. P. to a luncheon which was given a few days before the meeting. I did not feel at liberty to disclose the communication from the Ambassador and could only tell the Committee that I feared there would be no opportunity for Mr. —— to speak. This was communicated to him, and he discovered that, although I was only an English poet, it was actually my platform. (Incidentally, as I wanted the entire proceeds to go to the Prince of Wales' Fund, I was paying the rent of the hall out of my own pocket.) He decided, therefore, to be ingratiating. Sliding an arm through mine, he murmured in my ear: "My dear fellow, I hear that you don't want me to speak at your meeting?"

His persistence, of course, simply underlined the purport of the telegram. I told him it was a merely literary occasion, the hall had been engaged for a definite time, the program had been arranged, and unfortunately there would be no time left. He then had the effrontery to say: "Very well, then I shall speak to Mr. Choate about it. It has been announced in the newspapers that I am to speak, and if I am called upon I shall certainly do so."

There was only one thing left for me to do. I saw Mr. Choate myself before the meeting and he told me that he would take care to bring it to a close as soon as my reading was finished.

The politician, of course, had no particular wish to share the platform of a mere poet, but he would have liked very much indeed to appear in New York under the chairmanship of Mr. Choate. During the reading he occupied a prominent seat in a box, awaiting the call, but in spite of the newspaper paragraphs (for which of course he was responsible), he was not called upon. Mr. Choate brought the proceedings to a close with some delightful remarks upon English poetry, and then, with a humorous twinkle in his eyes, asked the audience to join in the National Anthem.

As we left the building, the politician met me in the outer lobby, and, in the best style of melodrama, muttered in my ear: "We shall meet again, Mr. Noyes!"

He was then taken to tea at the Plaza Hotel by some of the sympathetic ladies of the Committee. Six months later I was told by one of these ladies, Mrs. Junius Morgan, that although at the time they thought I had been unkind, subsequent events had justified me. Meetings had been arranged for him to raise funds for a war charity, and satisfactory accounts had not been rendered.

When Mr. Balfour visited America he relaxed his mind on the voyage with detective stories. Newspaper reporters observed that he was carrying a book when he landed, and a sensation was caused among them when, in answer to their inquiries, his secretary told them it was entitled *The Man with the Missing Toe.*

In connection with a projected visit by Mr. Balfour to Princeton, Spring-Rice wrote to me:

"By great good luck President Hibben happened to be here yesterday, and came in after dinner when we had a party of people to meet Mr. Balfour at the Embassy. They had quite a good talk together, of which President Hibben will doubtless tell you. I feel sure that he would be glad to visit Princeton, if time and strictly professional engagements allow, and I think he realizes, just as much as I do, the far-reaching influence exercised by the great universities of this country."

Spring-Rice felt intensely the strain of those early years of the war. Many traps were laid for him, and there was one attempt at assassination. Sir Valentine Chirol, in his biographical memoir of Spring-Rice, justifies the Ambassador's reserve, with a clear view of the complexities of the situation. Among those who did not share the views of Spring-Rice was Lord Northcliffe who, as the head of a great newspaper organization, believed in propaganda.

My own relations with Lord Northcliffe were always friendly, and he occasionally sent me telegrams of great length. One of these, at a somewhat later date, ran

> I am exiled to this very rainy part of Wessex I have watched your journeying with much interest and should like you to see Sir Campbell Stuart at The Times He and I are deeply concerned at increasing demonstration of anti-British propaganda in United States which can only be frustrated by people like you, Galsworthy, the best men from the Universities and by methods which Stuart and I discuss almost daily when together Would you write to me
>
> NORTHCLIFFE Parkstone-on-Sea.

One of the difficulties, which perhaps Northcliffe (like most people in England) overlooked, was that many of the best Professors at the American universities regarded one or another of the German universities as their Alma Mater. They had taken post-graduate courses in Germany in order to obtain their Ph.D., and had naturally formed many close friendships there. One of these men, with a nation-wide reputation, told me with some emotion that Germany had given him all that he had, and, as in the case of Duncan Spaeth, a civil war was raging within him.

That so many Americans went to Germany for their post-graduate work was partly because a considerably longer time was required for obtaining a similar degree at Oxford or Cambridge.

In 1916, when I was doing some temporary work at the British Foreign Office, I wrote a memorandum on this subject, suggesting, with considerable urgency, that English universities should ease the conditions for American graduates. This was approved by Sir Edward Grey, who took the matter up successfully with the English universities, and it has had happy results in the academic relations of the two countries. I like to think that I at least planted one acorn out of which forests may be whispered "to tower against the sun."

Few Ambassadors have left more affectionate memories behind them than did Spring-Rice in Washington. On his premature death in Ottawa there were many who felt the truth of the saying that a man's worth is realized in the gap made by his departure. I wrote some lines at the time expressing my own sense of a very great loss, and I have some pride in the fact that Sir Valentine Chirol quotes them in his memoir of Spring-Rice, saying:

"The following lines, though written by an English Poet, were first published in the *New York Times,* and afterwards so widely reproduced all over America that they may stand for the epitaph placed by the American people themselves upon the grave of one who had held the banner of England high amongst them at the most solemn hour of their national fortunes and our own."

From Government House, Ottawa, Lady Spring-Rice wrote:

"I cannot say at all what I feel about your poem. No tribute could be more fitting than one from your pen. You understood what he was and what he stood for and you have given me the most precious memorial and the children an inspiration for their whole lives. You have—with your vision—revealed him to the public who only knew him as the professional diplomatist.

"He assuredly gave his life for his country, and the end was so beautiful that I could not wish it otherwise. He passed away absolutely peacefully—no struggling, no lingering agony, and it seemed like a calm and noble transition from this world. With his over-sensitive nature he would have suffered terribly in this most acute stage of the war—he has been spared much. I need not tell you how much he valued his intercourse with you. . . .

"Again thanking you with all my heart, believe me,

"Yours sincerely,

FLORENCE SPRING-RICE"

He wrote his own noblest epitaph in the verses which, after his death, were sung in Westminster Abbey about that other country:

"And all her ways are gentleness and all her paths are peace."

XIX

Theodore Roosevelt

SHORTLY AFTER the outbreak of war in 1914 I had written some verses about the invasion of France which were printed in the London *Daily News* and had a wide circulation in the American press. I sent these lines to Theodore Roosevelt, and he replied in a letter which was one of the earliest and most outspoken expressions of American opinion on the side of the Allies from the foremost American of the day. The United States was officially neutral, and I did not then feel at liberty to publish the letter. I think now that this was a mistake, and that he must have intended me to do so. It was not until 1923 that the letter was printed in Lord Charnwood's biography of Roosevelt:

November 28, 1914

"MY DEAR MR. NOYES:

"I am greatly pleased with your letter and with the poem. I very sincerely believe in peace. I hold the man who, in a spirit of levity or wantonness or brutality or mere fancied self-interest, goes to war, to be an abhorrent brute. But, as the world now is, I am convinced that peace will only come on the same terms on which we get it in great cities—that is, by doing everything to cultivate justice and gentleness and fair dealing between man and man, and at the same time having a court backed by physical force, that is, backed by the police power, to which one can appeal against the brutal, the disorderly, the homicidal. I believe your verses will be of benefit here; for too many of our peace people have degenerated into the ultra-pacifist type. None of our peace bodies, for instance, have ventured to denounce Germany for her destruction of Belgium, which is, on the whole, the most hideous crime against peace and civilization that has been perpetrated since the close of the Napoleonic wars. They hold little futile peace parades, and send round peace postage-stamps with a dove on them, and get up petitions for peace in the public schools; but they do not venture for one moment to condemn any man who has done wrong, or to do more than raise a feeble clamor to the effect that peace must be obtained by tame acquiescence in wrong.

"Sincerely yours,
THEODORE ROOSEVELT"

"P. S. I am not anti-German; I am anti-brutality. I should protest as quickly against wrong-doing by England or France or Russia; and more quickly against wrong-doing by the United States."

In January, 1919, Mr. Pyne, one of the Trustees of Princeton, invited me to motor with him to Roosevelt's house at Oyster Bay. We arrived early in the afternoon and were hospitably welcomed by Mrs. Roosevelt, who gave us tea and told us (apparently without any anticipation of the blow that was to fall) that unfortunately her husband was not well enough to leave his room. She went upstairs for a minute or two, and we heard his voice in a room above. On her return to the drawing-room she gave me a jovial message from him: "Tell him I'm a pacifist, but I do believe in common sense."

From Oyster Bay I went to New York, where I stayed that night in an hotel. Early in the morning a newspaper was sent up with my letters. The front page had heavy black lines around the announcement that Theodore Roosevelt had died during the night. The message that he sent down to me must have been his last words to the outside world.

XX

Mount Wilson Observatory

At noon, upon the mountain's purple height,
Above the pine-woods and the clouds it shone
No larger than the small white dome of shell
Left by the fledgling wren when wings are born.
By night it joined the company of heaven
And, with its constant light, became a star.

THIS OPENING of *The Torch-Bearers* was my first impression of the great Observatory on Mount Wilson seen from "rose-crowned Pasadena" among her orange groves and palm trees far below.

Some months before the first trial of the 100-inch telescope in November 1917, I had the great privilege of meeting George Ellery Hale, who had done more to advance astronomical science than any man since Galileo. This at least was what the British Astronomer Royal told me at a dinner of the Astronomical Society in London, to which I was invited after the publication of *The Torch-Bearers*. The opening scene of this poem was laid in the Mount Wilson Observatory.

Hale's friendship was inspiring. It was through him that I was invited to the Observatory on that great opening night when we were to see something more in the gulfs of space than had hitherto been seen by human eyes. After more than a third of a century Hale is still to me one of the most vivid and living of all the men I have known. It is in no conventional sense that one uses the word "brilliant" of his intellectual qualities, for it is the exact and only word to describe the radiant intensity of a mind that seemed to shed light on everything that came within its wide horizon.

He was a specialist, of course, in his own line of work, but, like all great men, he rose above specialization and "saw life steadily and saw it whole." He read widely on many subjects and was especially interested in biography, which, at its best, opens all the doors to history. He could pass from the discussion of an astronomical problem to the antiquities of Egypt. He thought of poetry as the "flower of the mind" and could have capped quotations with Macaulay. His humour was of the kind that makes life worth living.

The mountain trail up to the Observatory in those days was a rough and, as it seemed to me, a perilous one, winding sometimes along the edge of a precipice with a sheer drop on one side into forests half a mile below. Hale diverted my mind from the danger of the way by quoting from the hymn "Shall I be wafted to the skies on flowery beds of ease," with an amusing story of an earlier visitor on whom those lines had had a soothing effect.

To me that night on the mountain-top was indeed memorable. While various adjustments were being made in the mechanism Hale spent some time walking about with me on the plateau outside the Observatory. One could see the lights of the city twenty miles away, like another constellation in the gulf below us. He talked of Dante and of what may be called the astronomical passages in the *Paradiso,* from the opening lines which Shelley translated in Adonais, "That light whose smile kindles the universe," up to the final line, perhaps the greatest in all poetry, *"l'amor che move il sole e l'altre stelle."*

He made a remark that night which cost me ten years' work. We had been talking about the way in which science was being harnessed to the war chariot. Even the astronomers were not exempt, and it was partly through methods analogous to those of astronomy that the first effective detectors of those deadly undersea planets, the submarines, were perfected. "The poets have written too much about war," he said. "Isn't there a subject for a poem in this other fight, the fight for knowledge?" We discussed the possibility of a poem dealing with the great moments in science—the passing on of the torch from the Greeks through all the generations down to the present day; and *The Torch-Bearers,* upon which I spent the next ten years, owes a profound debt to his inspiration and encouragement.

Pasadena was where I saw most of him. It was through Hale that

I was invited to give a series of lectures at Pasadena to a college which later on became the famous California Institute of Technology, under the presidency of Dr. Millikan. Some very remarkable work in science was being done at this institution, and Dr. Millikan won the Nobel Prize for Physics in 1923. A great deal of the work upon the 100-inch and later on the 200-inch telescope was developed there.

I had met Hale at Princeton University when he came to receive an honorary degree together with Sir Cecil Spring-Rice and Jusserand, the British and French Ambassadors to Washington. On this occasion Hale's alertness (as I have described in an earlier chapter on Princeton) averted what might have become almost an "international incident."

In 1923 Hale visited us at Rottingdean. He wanted me to give another series of lectures at "Cal-Tech," for he thought it was a good thing to open a few windows upon literature and poetry in an institution which specialized in science, and he was eager in turn to give me any scientific help that might be needed for the completion of my *Torch-Bearers.* In a letter on this subject he said: "I do hope you are cabling an acceptance to Millikan, partly because we are so anxious to see you again in Pasadena and also because I feel confident that you would find there just what you need for the second volume of *The Torch-Bearers.*"

Messages of this kind helped to offset the view of one literary critic, who smartly declared that "this poem will interest everyone but the astronomers." In the same month the Astronomer Royal wrote an article recommending it to students of astronomy; a Professor of Astronomy at Harvard University wrote to the same effect; and Sir Oliver Lodge, whom I did not know then, wrote a letter to *The Times,* commending it as an interpretation of modern science. Passages from the book were read at the opening of the next meeting of the British Association.

Eight years later came one of the most interesting letters of all, in which Hale spoke of the great project that, on its completion, became his memorial—the Observatory on Mount Palomar, with its 200-inch telescope.

"How well I remember that night we spent on the mountain so

long ago! And how beautifully you recorded it in your admirable book!

"Since 1928 we have been struggling with the problem of building a telescope of 200 inches aperture, which should collect four times as much light as the 100-inch telescope. In fact, because of various new developments, it should have fully ten times the effectiveness of our present largest instrument. We are making good progress, but the task is a very long one, and the 200-inch telescope cannot be completed in less than five or six years."

It was through Hale indirectly, and through Mrs. Hale directly, that in 1948 my wife and I were invited to the dedication of this Observatory to his memory. It was a noble ceremony. The natural grandeur of forest and mountain which formed the setting was matched by the grandeur of man's achievement. The dome of the Observatory seemed to crown the mountain with a new splendour, and within the building science and religion found that there was a height at which their paths met. We were warned again, in a most impressive speech, that even this great weapon of scientific precision might serve a destructive purpose in the acquisition of technical knowledge which again might be used in war, if we lost sight of higher values.

In the tone of these speakers there was a real reconciliation between science and the ultimate values; men were building, not a Tower of Babel, but a temple of beauty comprehending all values, great and small. And for me there was an exquisite symbolism in the fact that while the dedication of this great scientific achievement was taking place and the sunlight streamed over the forests and the mountains, somewhere in the dome of the Observatory the song of a wild bird rang out sweet and clear, adding its own little note of praise to the Lord and Giver of all.

XXI

The News Department

IN 1916 Garnett and I left our pleasant quarters in Princeton and returned to England. One or two surprises awaited me. I found that my poem "A Song of England" was being given nightly at Drury Lane Theatre by Madge Titherage, with an ingenious arrangement of scene changes for the different stanzas, from white cliff to thatched cottage and winding lane. The second surprise was a letter from Hubert Montgomery at the Foreign Office, asking me to come and see him there. Sir Cecil Spring-Rice had suggested to Sir Edward Grey that my "American contacts" might be of some use in a newly formed department of the Foreign Office. The News Department, as it was called, was really the nucleus of the later Ministry of Information. At this time it consisted of a very small group occupying only two or three rooms. The four colleagues in my own room were Miles Lampson, who afterwards distinguished himself in China and became High Commissioner in Egypt, John Buchan, who later became Governor General in Canada, and two Cambridge Dons—Stephen Gaselee who afterwards forsook Trinity College to become Librarian at the Foreign Office, and Geoffrey Butler, one of that amazing Cambridge family who could quote Sophocles in their cradles. R. C. Lehmann's natal ode to one of them, a brilliant piece of versification, will be remembered by all lovers of the Cambridge Horace:

> Dr. Butler, may I venture without seeming too officious,
> To congratulate you warmly on a birthday so auspicious?
>
> . . . . . .
>
> The son! With two such parents this small member of our college
> Must be, unlike the ruck of us, a paragon of knowledge.
>
> . . . . . .
>
> At three he'll take a tripos class in Aryan mythology,
> And at four confute all Germany in Roman archaeology;

And if his Teuton rivals print huge quartos to suppress him, oh!
I'll back this cyclopaedic child, this English duodecimo.

Geoffrey Butler afterwards became Director of the British Information Services in New York, and ratified his Anglo-American theories by marrying a very charming girl from Philadelphia.

Buchan, characteristically enough, in addition to his work at the F. O., was doing staff work at the War Office. He would turn up in uniform at the F. O., looking tired and grey after some mysterious expedition to the front, in which I could picture him playing the part of Richard Hannay. He was one of the sincerest men I ever knew, and there was something in his bearing which made one think of the young Caesar. He was keenly interested in the results of modern science, and often spoke with enthusiasm of the great French savant Henri Poincaré. Buchan realized more fully than most of his contemporaries the gravity of the world situation, in which the war was merely an irruptional symptom of a far wider and deeper disorder. The faith by which civilization stood or fell, as he wrote in *Pilgrim's Way,* was being attacked along a world-wide front, and at present the attack was succeeding. Sometimes, in ethics as in aesthetics, it seemed as if all the standards were being furiously assaulted by hordes of half-witted and vicious children. At the outbreak of the second world war he wrote to my friend Ferris Greenslet, "We are entering a long dark tunnel, and nobody knows when we shall emerge."

One of the treasures in my library is a copy of his *Greenmantle,* which he gave me with an inscription recalling those earlier days at the Foreign Office.

Many interesting telegrams awaited us every morning on our desks in that room, some of them referring to persons suspected of working for the enemy, and others quite amusing. One morning telegrams that had passed between Winston Churchill and his American publishers were brought in for our delectation. Some lively bargaining about fees for articles was in progress, and Hubert Montgomery, who brought these telegrams to us, obviously had the traditional Foreign Office disapproval of all such goings on. He did not say so, but there was a look of pained superiority on his handsome face as he laid them on the table. His clear-cut nose was slightly lifted—that was all.

Personally, I did not see why Churchill should not increase the dollar reserve, since everything he wrote was of service to the cause.

In another case, not amusing, but symptomatic of the disordered thought of the time, Scotland Yard was asked for the dossier of a certain English writer whose books had been greatly admired in "advanced" circles and had received rather absurd attention in the literary columns. He was then living in Sicily. The dossier, as presented to the News Department for private circulation, was long and horrible, and included most of the vices and some of the crimes, with more than a suspicion of murder. That Scotland Yard should have been able to produce this record at a moment's notice was a little startling. We surveyed one another uneasily.

There were interesting visitors to that room from time to time. Once or twice a day our Chief, Lord Newton, then Assistant Under-Secretary of State for Foreign Affairs, would appear, usually giving vent to dismal expressions about the progress of the War. Butler called him our little ray of sunshine, and on two occasions he really was enlivening. The first was when he entered radiant with a victory which he had won in an action for libel against the *Daily Mail.* The verdict had brought him £1,000 and costs, and his smiles were unclouded. He thought the war was going very well.

The second was when he entered in high indignation to enquire who that bald-headed man was who sometimes walked up and down our corridor. Lord Newton had asked him where Lord Robert Cecil's new room was, whereon the bald-headed one had replied,

"How the hell should I know? I'm not a doorkeeper!"

Gaselee said he thought the offender must be the mad Librarian.

"A mad Librarian in the Foreign Office!" exclaimed Lord Newton. "Do you mean to say a fellow like that is in charge of—"

"Oh, yes, secret documents and all," said Gaselee cheerfully.

Lord Newton blew up. When he had calmed down a little, Gaselee asked him whether he had made any reply to the affront.

"He went into the Library," said Lord Newton, "and I merely put my head inside the door and asked, 'How do you like being bald?' "

One of our collaborators in the News Department was Lord Eustace Percy, who surveyed the proceedings (including his own)

with a cheerful cynicism which once broke into verse. The lines he laid on my desk one morning indicated that he might have been the Locker-Lampson of his generation if he had so wished.

Âmes damnées of the attic,
  Your toils my spirit stir,
Hierophants erratic
  Of things that don't occur.
Hymn, Muse, their versatility,
  Their Tartarean wiles,
The bland deceit of Butler,
  The inventiveness of Miles.

This Don-debauched Department,
  Which does not care for truth,
Weaves the same web for nations
  As snared the Cambridge youth.
Ho! swallow it, ye guileless ones!
  Be cautious, O ye wise,
When Gaselee writes his epigrams
  And Noyes his lyric lies!

But I don't think this really represented the still small voice of the News Department. Perhaps in retaliation an incident of the satirist's own visit to the United States may be recorded. The New York *Sun* at the time was running a comic strip on the adventures of two young men-about-town, one of whom was named Percy and the other Eustace.

On arriving at his New York hotel, the distinguished visitor naturally signed his name in the register with a single lordly word, "Percy." The young woman in charge surveyed it for a moment, then, unacquainted with the ways of the peerage, she asked rather sharply:

"What's your other name?"

"Eustace," the visitor murmured softly.

And with the icy look of one accustomed to repelling all advances, the damsel replied over a haughty shoulder:

"Fresh, aren't you!"

The series of articles which I wrote for the Admiralty Press Bureau, on methods used by the Navy in trapping submarines, appeared simultaneously in all the leading English newspapers (*The Times, Daily Telegraph, Morning Post, Daily Chronicle, Manchester Guardian,* and many others), and led to certain difficulties within the Admiralty itself, on the ground that they were too truthful.

The articles were issued to the Press by the Chief Naval Censor, Rear-Admiral Sir Douglas Brownrigg, who tells the story in his recollections.

Facilities had been given to me for seeing at their work the "Mystery Ships," as they were popularly called, and my problem was to write about them without dispelling the mystery. It was not until the articles were issued in book form by Messrs. Hodder & Stoughton (1916) that the trouble began. It was a trouble for comedy, because while one department of the Admiralty was furiously insisting that every copy of the book should be recalled from English readers, another department was having it translated into foreign languages and circulated, at great expense, in large numbers among the nearest neighbours of Germany.

The publisher, Ernest Hodder Williams, and I were summoned to the Admiralty and seated at a table before four stern-faced men in refulgent uniforms, who wanted to know what we meant by publishing what the Admiralty itself had sent out for publication through the Chief Censor and the Admiralty Press Bureau to almost every newspaper in England.

The publisher was extremely nervous, because a letter had recently been received from South Africa saying that it might be a good thing to have him shot for another publication, and I noticed that he was shivering slightly. I might have been nervous myself but, strong in the fact that every article had been issued by the Chief Naval Censor, I ventured to ask if our examiners knew that another department of the Admiralty was at that very moment having the book translated, and sending the articles to newspapers abroad. The answer was gloriously official: "It has not been brought to our attention." All they were concerned with was the publication of the book in England.

As the articles were absolutely identical with it, I then ventured to ask whether the objection was to the binding and the string that fastened the pages together. The publisher kicked my foot, indicating that he would be thankful to get out of the room alive, so I surrendered. He obtained a knighthood for his services.

Sir Douglas Brownrigg says, in his book *Indiscretions of the Naval Censor,* under the chapter headed "Authors, Publishers and Some Others,"

> I have pleasant recollections of my dealings with each and all of the above classes. . . . The first who looms large in my memory, perhaps because he was, I think, the first author to be employed by the Government to write naval matter into propaganda form, is Alfred Noyes. He was sent pretty well everywhere he wished to go in order to obtain material for writing up the Auxiliary Patrol Service, &c.
>
> He produced a lot of fine stuff, though perhaps we weren't trained to appreciate it at its real value at the time. His next effort on the Navy's behalf was a bit more risky (not risqué), so to speak. "Mystery Ships, or Trapping the U-Boats" I believe it was called. I fought the cause of that work, though I don't believe Mr. Noyes ever believed me when I assured him of this. I suppose that a poet *can* be sceptical as to the truth of a statement when it is made by a Chief Censor. Anyhow, I fought the cause of that book right up to two separate First Sea Lords, got it past one, and bumped it into another, had it, so to speak, thrown back at my head, and, still fighting, finally got an unwilling consent for its publication in a very expurgated form.

His memory fails him here on almost every point. Apparently he was not quite certain even about the title of the book, also it was the first and not the second book I had written for the Admiralty. The second book was entitled *Open Boats.* The only "expurgation" was in a line of my poem "Kilmeny," in which I described a trawler as carrying a gun from the Bethlehem Steel Works. The Censor altered Bethlehem to Newcastle, "She'd a gun at her bow that was Newcastle's best"—thoughtfully giving me a three-syllable word so that the metre was not disturbed. What Newcastle would have said if, on the advice of the Censor, it had been immediately bombed by the enemy, I don't know.

His memory also fails in the next paragraph, for the picture of which he speaks had been completely cancelled on his own suggestion, as may be seen by the few surviving copies of the book which I possess.

It should also be noted once again that the text of the book was that which the Chief Censor himself had actually sent out to newspapers all over the world, and had already been printed in them. His "recollections" continue:

> Presently it appeared on the bookstalls without my having seen it in final proof form, and (from the artists' and publishers' and bookstalls' point of view) with a beautifully illustrated cover showing in colour what the artist conceived to be a "mystery ship."
>
> That tore it!
>
> The first that I knew of it was when I was sent for and "put on the carpet" before various high and somewhat querulous, not to say peevish, officials who asked me—well, it may be guessed what the trend of the crisp questions was. All I could say was that it had been understood between Mr. Noyes and myself that I was to see the book in final proof form before it was let loose "in time for the Christmas sales." (That ghastly expression haunts me yet!)
>
> There were hurried and hectic interviews between Mr. Noyes and myself, and, I suppose, between the poet and the publisher. The net result was that the book was taken off sale and, I suppose, involved one or the other, or both of them, in considerable monetary loss, which I regret. I believe they will both admit, however, that it was due to a misunderstanding between *them* that this regrettable incident took place. But it cost me the regard of Mr. Noyes, and, as I have not many poets among my acquaintances, the case sticks in my mind and somewhat rankles.

He was quite wrong in saying that it had cost him my regard. I had always a great liking for Sir Douglas. Incidentally it may be remarked that I was immediately entrusted with another series of articles in a room at the Admiralty, where hourly reports of ships sunk by the submarines came pouring in on the telephone. These articles were also syndicated and translated into several foreign languages, and were also published in book form. The Admiralty distributed a large number of these books abroad.

In the autumn of 1916, before I left England, I had a talk with Mr. Walter Hines Page, one of the very best of a long line of highly gifted American Ambassadors to the Court of St. James's. He was greatly distressed about our blacklisting of American firms who had been dealing with Germany. He was quite in agreement with the grounds of our action; but he thought the measures taken were unwise; he feared the possible result upon American opinion of what he called the "long arm" of England reaching out into the United States (at that time neutral) to penalize her citizens.

There was a further matter that distressed him. He sympathized intensely with our cause in Europe, but he found it difficult to make people in England understand that thousands upon thousands of American citizens had left Europe to escape her age-long conflicts and to find peace as they hoped in a new world. "How can we throw them back into that furnace?" he said, and there were tears in his eyes as he said it.

It was a complete refutation of the charge sometimes brought against him in America that his point of view was too English to represent the United States. He was convinced of the rightness of the cause, but he was an American, and a very great American.

Occasionally members of the News Department had to take charge of small groups of writers and journalists, who wished to see something of the western front. We were put up at a G. H. Q. guest house and taken from there to various observation posts to watch operations.

On one of these expeditions I accompanied a party which included W. J. Locke, the novelist (who gave me his *Wonderful Year* as a souvenir); James Douglas, editor of the *Sunday Express;* and a well-known American journalist whose fire-eating courage very nearly got us all into serious trouble. I call him Bill, though that was not his real name. He was not content with our observation posts, from which we could watch the shells dropping along the enemy lines and little fountains of brown earth rising in the dust as the shells burst. Nor was he satisfied with the sound of the enemy shells going overhead like so many express trains. Even when one of them burst in the wreck of a French Cathedral exactly one minute after we had left it he wanted something more exciting. A drive at eighty miles an hour along a road past a particularly hot spot known as "Hell Corner" because it was constantly under German fire, left him still thirsting for more; and since I was nominally in charge of the party (though of course we were under military supervision during the whole of our stay) he kept on asking me to obtain permission for us to enter the trenches and go to a point from which he understood it was possible to throw a hand grenade at the Germans. I was not enthusiastic. In the matter of hand grenades I am a complete amateur. He appealed to Locke and Douglas. "Didn't the idea of throwing a hand grenade at the Germans stir their blood?" They looked doubtful. W. J. Locke said he had quite a large public in America, also that he had promised his wife that he would never throw any hand grenades at Germans. James Douglas' nose grew rather red, perhaps with the secret fire to which Bill was appealing; but he said he owed a certain responsibility to a great Sunday newspaper.

However, Bill, whose eyes did look fighting mad, was so pertinacious that at last I asked the officer in charge if it could be arranged.

An hour or two later he told me that there was a point where it was possible for our visitor's wish to be fulfilled. The Germans were in possession of one section of a trench and the British of another, separated by only a few yards. As a concession to transatlantic fervour he had obtained permission but (greatly to my relief) for only one of the party to enter that trench. He explained that if the enemy spotted civilians in mufti entering the trenches they would immediately conclude that the visitors were persons of great importance, possibly the Prince of Wales and members of the Cabinet, and would begin an intensive bombardment which might be very hard on our own troops.

I made up my mind at once that, as I was in charge, if I couldn't be in Paris, I could at least remain in the observation post. Of course none of us mere amateurs wished to disappoint our American friend. W. J. Locke looked fierce for a moment, but almost immediately remembered his promise to his wife. James Douglas remarked that he had to go to press on the following Saturday afternoon.

Arrangements were made accordingly. Bill set off, walking rather stiffly, between two silent duplicates of Colonel Bramble, but looking very grim and determined in the steel hat which had been lent to him for the occasion.

Major ——, who remained with our party and took us to our

observation post, began to have misgivings. "If anything happens to him," he said, "there'll be trouble."

About half an hour later a terrific bombardment began. "That's torn it!" said the Major. "They probably think it's Lloyd George encouraging the front line." The infernal din continued most of the afternoon. It had been arranged that Bill should meet us at five o'clock at a point on the road where cars were waiting to take us back to G. H. Q. The rest of us were all there at the time appointed, but there was no sign of our friend. We waited nearly an hour before we saw in the distance the two silent duplicates of Colonel Bramble with their guest, who was still walking a little stiffly between them.

As they drew nearer one saw that Bill's face, unusually pale, was pitted with small red spots by the sand that had been blown into it. His escort saluted and left us. "You didn't miss much," muttered Bill savagely. "They started that darned barrage, and I spent most of the afternoon at the bottom of a dug-out. I had the parapet blown over me twice and I had to be dug out—with spades!" He repeated this several times. He never explained what other implements he thought should have been used.

During dinner that evening at G. H. Q. guest house, Bill, who had hitherto been the most communicative member of the party, maintained a grim silence. But indignation was still sizzling within, and just as we were turning in for the night I heard him muttering: "Dug out! With spades!"

XXII

Sir Roger Casement

THERE IS only one moment in my association with the News Department which I look back upon with regret.

Sir Roger Casement had been in the British Consular Service for some years. He first came into prominence through his protests against

The author in 1912.
Photo. by Lewis-Smith, Chicago

Lulworth Castle, Dorset.

Mary Noyes and the children at Hanover Terrace.
Photo by Lenare, London

The author, right, appearing in an amateur performance of Bulwer-Lytton's play, NOT SO BAD AS WE SEEM, in 1921. Others in the cast were, *l to r,* John Brett Langstaff, Lady Jean Douglas Hamilton and the Duchess of Hamilton.

the atrocities in the Belgian Congo, and later by a similar campaign against the brutalities of the Peruvians in a Putumayan rubber concern. He accepted a knighthood from the British Government and, when he retired, a pension he continued to draw quarterly until the quarter in which the world war of 1914 began. In September, 1914, he left untouched the quarterly payment in William Deacon's Bank, apparently because he had decided that, with the help of Germany, he could now free Ireland from what he regarded as the yoke of England. Accordingly he made his way to Norway and from there went on to Berlin. With the approval of the German Government he visited a number of Irish prisoners of war in Germany, and tried to induce them to form an Irish Brigade for service against England. Later he was landed on the coast of Ireland from a German submarine, and was arrested within a few hours by the British.

England conceded to him a State trial, and allowed him the benefit of Irish and Welsh counsel; and even, in the words of Dr. Maloney, one of his defenders, "went so far as to concede his sister's request for American counsel." On May 17, 1916, the following cable dispatch appeared in the American Press: "London, May 16. The Foreign Office announced tonight that in response to a request from Casement's sister permission would be granted for the appearance of Michael Francis Doyle, of Philadelphia, as one of the attorneys for Casement."

The trial ended in Casement being sentenced to death for treason. Lord Birkenhead was counsel for the prosecution, and Lord Darling was the presiding judge at the appeal, which was dismissed and followed by Casement's execution.

It was reported that a diary, recording the loathsome experiences of a sexual pervert, had been found among Casement's effects. It was accepted by John Redmond and other Irish leaders as genuine and in Casement's handwriting. The diary was not brought up at the trial, and therefore it should not have been used at all.

Shortly after the execution of Casement I was asked to write an article on the Irish troubles of that year. A typed copy of Casement's alleged diary had been shown to me in the Foreign Office by Gaselee. In common with others to whom it had been shown, I accepted it as genuine, and found it so repulsive that in my article, praising the great traditions of Ireland, I suggested that Irishmen should be on their guard against a very real danger—the danger that the anti-English element in Ireland would make a hero of Casement despite those acts which necessarily had brought him into conflict with a law that holds good throughout the world. The regrettable brief paragraph in my article was one in which I spoke of the diary that had been shown to me, saying that if the foul record came to light it would disgust any possible hero-worshippers. It was a very brief paragraph of eight lines in a long article, and it never occurred to me for a moment, any more than it did to John Redmond, or to Bernard Shaw, or to Michael Collins, that a document so attested could be anything but genuine. Whether it was genuine or not there is apparently now no evidence, but in the circumstances it should never have been circulated. My article was sent out from the News Department with others on different subjects, *after* the execution of Casement, which took place on August 3, 1916.

A few weeks later I was giving a lecture in Philadelphia on a purely literary subject to an audience of nearly two thousand when a very painful incident occurred: The chairman had just finished his introduction, and I was already on my feet, when a lady of distinguished bearing rose in the audience and asked if she might say a few words. I at once made way for her, and, to my horror and that of the audience, she announced that she had come for the express purpose of exposing the speaker of the evening as a "blackguardly scoundrel." Fortunately her next sentence clarified the matter. "Your countrymen," she cried, "hanged my brother, Sir Roger Casement." Then, her tall spare figure quivering and her face white with anger, she poured out a torrent of invective against England. Chairman, audience and lecturer sat listening helplessly for some minutes. Overwrought and distraught as she was, there was a strange irrational nobility shining through all her wild charges and accusations. The men in the audience remained quite silent, but at last the women began to interrupt and hiss, and with that unhappy accompaniment (which I can honestly say I longed to silence) she left the auditorium.

I made no reference to the incident in my address, but asked the audience to let me preface what I had to say by reading them something that I had written about England in happier days.

Twenty years later the *Irish Press* printed a series of articles which were afterwards published in book form under the title of *The Forged Casement Diaries*. In almost every chapter of this book I was portrayed as one of the men who brought Casement to his death, others being Lord Darling, Lord Birkenhead, General Sir John Maxwell and Sir Basil Thomson of Scotland Yard. The single paragraph in my article (which had first appeared some time after Casement's death) was repeated again and again in such a way as to suggest that I had both written and spoken all over the United States before and after the execution, and on innumerable occasions, on that subject alone; whereas that single unfortunate paragraph, in an article sent out by a Government agency *after* Casement's death, was the only comment in all those years I ever made on the subject, and I never on any occasion either repeated it or spoke on the subject at all.

Dr. Maloney's book, *The Forged Casement Diaries,* was illustrated by photographs, carefully chosen to represent us as "smiling damned villains." That of myself was a masterpiece of horror. The author of the book had secured—Heaven knows where—an awful newspaper snapshot in which I looked like a cross between Jack Johnson and Crippen, and wore a ghastly cynical grin, the brutality of which was emphasized by a context dealing with the trial and execution of a fellow-creature. It was probably snapped when some reporter was asking me what I thought of modern poetry.

W. B. Yeats indeed broke into some extraordinary verses about this matter, which were featured in the *Irish Press* under the heading "Irish Poet's Striking Challenge." In the second stanza he introduced a cockney rhyme with a startlingly comic effect:

> I say that Roger Casement
> Did what he had to do,
> He died upon the gallows,
> But that is nothing new.
>
> Afraid they might be beaten
> Before the bench of Time,

They turned a trick by forgery
And blackened his good name.

I found myself in good company, however, for in the fourth stanza he relates:

For Spring-Rice had to whisper it,
Being their ambassador.

In a letter to Lady Dorothy Wellesley, Yeats stated that he wanted this ballad to be sung by the undergraduates of Oxford and Cambridge. I must confess that if this had taken place I should very much like to hear what kind of music they would have made of the closing lines (which he altered later):

Come, Alfred Noyes and all the troup
That cried it far and wide,
Come from the forger and his desk,
Desert the perjurer's side;

Come speak your bit in public
That some amends be made
To this most gallant gentleman
That is in the quick-lime laid.

I did not think verse an appropriate medium in which to answer Mr. Yeats, even on a charge of perjury. Accordingly I wrote an open letter to him, and it is only fair to say that the *Irish Press* gave it full prominence, and wrote generously of it in a leading article:

"DEAR YEATS,—

"You have appealed to me publicly and personally, in your poem on Roger Casement (which *The Irish Press* described as 'a challenge to a brother poet') to retract certain statements about Casement, circulated, 'wittingly or unwittingly,' by myself and others, twenty years ago.

"Those statements, as *The Irish Press* and Dr. Maloney have said, were based on information offered by representatives of the British Government of the highest reputation, and on a diary, of which the original was admittedly in Casement's own handwriting, and guaranteed by the Attorney-General. This diary, as Professor Eoin Mac-

Neill now tells *The Irish Press,* and as Dr. Maloney shows, was accepted 'in all honesty' by many Irish-Americans and even personal friends of Casement, to whom copies were shown, as one was shown to me. I knew nothing of Casement, and I accepted it as they accepted it, on exactly the same grounds.

"Michael Collins accepted the authenticity of the original; and the explanatory suggestion now made by Dr. Maloney that Casement had transcribed, with his own hand, the diary of a Peruvian criminal; that he had sent it on to the British Foreign Office for use against that Peruvian; and that it had been used against himself instead, by the heads of Scotland Yard, was not then forthcoming.

"If there had seemed to be any room for doubt at the time I suppose that those of Casement's own friends who accepted the diary must have thought—as I did—that it was the work of a disordered mind. It would seem more conceivable that one man (Casement) should have been mentally unbalanced, than that a large number of men of high reputation should have deliberately conspired with Scotland Yard in so appalling a manner, even in the feverish and abnormal conditions of the 'Great War.' You will hardly, on reflection, sustain your suggestion that your own countryman, Spring-Rice, the Ambassador to Washington, deliberately aided and abetted a foul trick of this kind. His Irish friends, as well as his English, all knew Spring-Rice as a man of the most sensitive conscience and highest integrity and, moreover, as Mr. Stephen Gwynn's finely proportioned biography shows, a poet who would be the first to feel the tragedy of his own countryman, Roger Casement. Spring-Rice would have understood the magnificence of the words in which Casement (without knowing it and while writing as an enemy of England) attacked the whole sordid and bestial business of modern war. He would have felt all the desolate splendour and bitter poetry of those words, which move me to-day, as I know they move you, 'there is not a glint or a gleam of chivalry in all their battle-line.'

"The verses in which Spring-Rice expressed his own love of England ('I Vow to Thee, My Country') have all the devotion with which the Irish are acquainted in their passion for their own land. He was a chivalrous as well as an upright man, and I believe that he was probably the moving spirit behind the appeal made for Casement's reprieve in the name of Senator Lodge; for Lodge was Spring-Rice's closest friend in America. Spring-Rice would never have lent himself to an abominable slander of the kind now suggested. If the diary was not Casement's then Spring-Rice and many other men of honour, like those Irish-Americans, and friends of Casement himself, mentioned by Dr. Maloney and Professor MacNeill, were simply misled by an unspeakably wicked fabrication. But they believed the diary to be genuine.

"And here, let me say that Dr. Maloney makes one or two mistakes (natural enough in the circumstances) with regard to myself, and these have in turn misled you. My only reference to Casement was in the one paragraph (about twelve lines) of an article which was written shortly after a typed copy of the diary had been shown to me in circumstances which then seemed to preclude all doubt of its authenticity. The article containing this paragraph was issued through a Press Bureau, and it appeared in the Philadelphia *Public Ledger* some weeks after Casement's death. Headlines, prefatory editorial notes, and the machinery of publicity (for which I was not responsible) gave my dozen lines about Casement a disproportionate prominence, which naturally misled Dr. Maloney as to the real extent of my allusions to the matter. It will be noted that, in his own book, though he refers to me again and again, all his quotations are repetitions of one or two sentences from that paragraph of twelve lines; and that, once or twice, he uses one of those sentences in support of his own argument as to the real nature of the 'diary,' *whoever its author may have been.*

"His references to my 'two hundred lectures' in America may give the impression that these also were about Casement. They were on entirely different subjects, and they were arranged, not by Sir Gilbert Parker, as Dr. Maloney suggests, or by any other British Agency, but by the well-known American agent who had always arranged lecture tours for me since 1911. This agency (Wm. B. Feakins, Inc.) has a complete record of every lecture engagement I ever made in America, and they were all made by that agency except a very few which I made myself.

"None of my lectures dealt with Casement or with Irish affairs (most of them were addresses on the case for English civilization which, you will agree, has produced some of the greatest poetry of the past; they were based on that poetry and, in some cases, they were readings of my own poems on purely English subjects). I cannot be sure that at one or two lectures, out of a total of more than five hundred, questions were not asked about Ireland and Casement. At one of my lectures, shortly after my article had been printed in the *Ledger,* Casement's sister appeared in person and asked to be allowed to speak. I made way for her, and I think I may say that I enabled her to secure a thoughtful hearing from an audience of nearly 2,000, which, at one moment, showed signs of resentment at the bitterness of her attack on England.

"I realized, as fully perhaps as you would have done, the natural cause of that bitterness and the tragic stress by which she was torn while she was speaking, and when she had left the hall I made no reply or comment on what she had said, but continued my address on the great English poetry of the past.

"Newspapers, of course, 'featured' the interruption in large headlines and omitted most of the address, so that the Casement affair was once more to the fore, and a false impression created of my own part in it. So far as Casement's sister was concerned, even while she spoke, and despite all the bitterness of what she was saying, I was conscious of that lady's own innate nobility.

"Though I had accepted the 'diary' as (I must repeat) some of his own Irish friends had done, I had no longer any thought but of the tragedy of it. I had known nothing of Casement personally; and the appearance of his sister was a tragic revelation to me of the distinguished race from which he sprang, and the blood that ran in his veins.

"I wished 'from the deep heart's core' that the whole miserable affair of the diary could have been undone, and I could think of no explanation of it, but the possible mental disorder of its writer. He ought never to have been executed; and, genuine or not, the diary should never have been brought up at all, though we must remember —if we are to be fair to everyone concerned—Dr. Maloney's own explanation of the handwriting; the strikingly *un*Irish explanation that *Casement had transcribed another man's diary, for use by the British Government against that other man's character.*

"This does introduce an entirely new explanation; but it is obviously not entirely satisfactory on the point as to what should be done with such a diary, if it was indeed genuine. Those who had seen a copy of it might wonder whether the transcription of so loathsome a thing at such length—it ran to many pages—was a very much better explanation from Casement's point of view than the former suggestion that it was the work of a temporarily disordered mind.

"On the other hand, if it really was a 'forgery' I can only say, at once, that I can imagine no more wicked imposture, and no more detestable crime.

"But you will realise that, in such a case, the matter can be settled, and there is only one way of doing it.

"In view of Dr. Maloney's new theory of the provenance of the 'diary' it seems imperative that the diary itself, and the evidence pertaining to it, should be re-examined with a view to establishing the truth once and for all.

"As long as information and access to the documents are refused, deep feeling on the one side can only be met by helpless and irritating inadequacies on the other, and our national relations will continue to be embittered.

"It cannot be said that because these things happened twenty years ago there should be no attempt to establish the historical truth, in a matter of justice involving two nations. New evidence has been brought forward. It is only right that it should be critically examined with reference to the original documents.

"If a critical historian like Dr. G. P. Gooch, with expert experience in the examination of documents, could be associated with you in such an enquiry, I would gladly join in an appeal for the usual facilities accorded to the historian in such cases, and I do not see how it could be justly set aside. Casement will certainly be remembered in history, if only by the moving eloquence of his last speech to his judges, that superb and tragic utterance which may or may not be compatible with noble reason partly overthrown, but has elements of greatness rare in this or any age.

"Of one thing we may be sure. The tribunal of history is not mocked. It has righted many a wronged man, and occasionally it has vindicated a great nation.

"The appeal of Casement was not to the High Court of England. But neither can it be to Ireland. It was to a greater tribunal than he knew, when as a condemned man he spoke from the dock certain sentences which will not easily die, and may live for centuries, waking echoes in innumerable hearts and minds:

> 'I hope I shall be acquitted of presumption if I say that the Court I see before me now is not this High Court of England, but a far greater, a far higher, a far older assemblage. . . .'

"The final appeal is not to England nor to Ireland but to the truth; and all who make it, as I said in that article twenty years ago, make it 'at their peril.' But, if it can indeed be made in the spirit of the impartial historian, for whom 'patriotism' is not the final law, I am wholeheartedly with you, whatever the judgment may be."

To this Yeats replied, to the Editor of the *Irish Press:* "DEAR SIR: I accept Mr. Alfred Noyes' explanation and I thank him for his noble letter. I think, too, that the British Government should lay the diaries before some tribunal acceptable to Ireland and to England. He suggests that Dr. G. P. Gooch, a great expert in such matters, and I should be 'associated' with such an inquiry. I have neither legal training nor training in the examination of documents, nor have I the trust of the people. But I thank him for his courtesy in suggesting my name.

"I add a new version of my song. Mr. Noyes' name is left out; but I repeat my accusation that a slander based on forged diaries was spread through the world and that, whatever the compulsion, 'Spring-Rice had to whisper it.' He was an honourable, able man in the ordinary affairs of life; why then did he not ask whether the evidence had been submitted to the accused? The British Government would have been compelled to answer.

"I was dining with the wife of a Belgian Cabinet Minister after

Casement's condemnation, perhaps after his execution; somebody connected with *The Times* was there; he said they had been asked to draw attention to the diaries. I said that it was infamous to blacken Casement's name with evidence that had neither been submitted to him nor examined at his trial. Presently Roger Fry, the famous art critic, came in, and the journalist repeated his statement, and Roger Fry commented with unmeasured fury. I do not remember whether *The Times* spoke of the diaries or not. Had Spring-Rice been a free man he would have shared my indignation and that of Roger Fry."

(Here follows revised poem.)

For some weeks there was a spate of controversy in the *Irish Press*. Some of the letters were from irreconcilables, who simply put their fingers in their ears and refused to listen to any rebuttal of their own wild charges.

Count Plunkett wrote:

"SIR— The case against Mr. Noyes and his colleagues awaits the final judgment. Mr. Noyes repeated, over and over again, throughout America, and elsewhere, his slanders against Casement and Ireland.

"It is not enough to say of the concealed forger, in the words of Dante, 'Galeotto fu il libro, e chi lo scrisse.'—the diary was scoundrelly, and he in writing it. The gentle apologist for Voltaire could repeat only slanders against the heroic souls in Ireland; struggling, under God, for their nation's liberation, they were to be led to the culmination of false charges, justifying the murder of a man for his virtues.

"Mr. Noyes in a manner withdraws his offence against the honour of Casement. What about his charges against the honour of Ireland? How can he explain away the 'reasoned' method of his continuous attack?

"A smooth Canadian novelist was commissioned to win America to 'come into the war,' and Belgium should be satisfied for the charges made against her regarding the Congo. And England should be justified for her holocaust of all the leaders of the Irish rising.

"In this connection Mr. Noyes was an agent of the British propaganda—he cannot repudiate his own words. How can he pretend that the scoundrels who were answerable for the brutal inventions—Ministers, Ambassadors, public representatives of England—were honorable men? How can he explain away his own ready acceptance, without enquiry, of these lies intended to defame Irishmen who had earned respect at least?

"We in Ireland, who know our own history, know that such crimes against humanity have followed our people whenever it was England's policy to defame our nation.

G. N. COUNT PLUNKETT"

To this I replied:

"*To the Editor of* The Irish Press,

"SIR— Mr. Yeats responded in a spirit of generous recognition of my own desire to establish the truth in this controversy once and for all; and your own editorial comment on my open letter to Mr. Yeats exactly expressed my intention. It is only in the truth that we can find peace on either side.

"Mr. Yeats and *The Irish Press* have convinced me, as I said before, that the new evidence adduced about Roger Casement makes it imperative that there should be an investigation of original documents by competent historians; and, as I said when I made the suggestion, I am ready to join in an appeal for such an inquiry.

"Other correspondents have now taken up another ground, and raised another question with regard to that one article in the Philadelphia *Public Ledger* of twenty years ago. First, let me emphasize once more that all your correspondents refer to that one article, quoted by Dr. Maloney; that they all quote only his quotations from it; and that one or two of them still suggest that it was one of a multitude written by myself on Irish affairs. It was the only article I ever wrote on those affairs. Your correspondents not only ignore the fact that all their references are to this one article, but they imply and even directly affirm that in their quotations from it they are referring to a long series of attacks upon Casement and the honour of Ireland by myself. Is this, honestly, in the interests of that truth that we all desire? What possible service can it do to their own cause to demonstrate to me, as they do, at the very outset, that on the very few facts of which I have direct and complete knowledge, they are asserting what is simply not true. I gave the facts in my letter to Mr. Yeats.

"The article from which all your correspondents quote contained eight lines (not twelve, as I said in my former letter) about Casement. (None of my lectures dealt with Ireland.)

"I am quite ready to add that the whole of that one article on Irish affairs was based upon the report issued by an authorized Press Bureau in England, during a world upheaval, when emotions and thoughts were not easily checked.

"I knew nothing beyond those official reports of conditions in Ireland. I did not impugn the honour of Ireland. Indeed, in that very article, I paid my tribute to the only Ireland I knew, the Ireland which has contributed so much to our common literature. But I did believe, on the strength of those authorised reports, that individuals (of whom I knew nothing, not even the names) had been criminally shedding the blood of their own Irish countrymen. My article was an appeal to an honourable Ireland not to look at murder through a mist of romance, and not to canonize those who I believed were wronging her.

"I am now told that the facts which I then accepted had not the slightest foundation. If that be so, and men of honour in Ireland tell me it is so, I say that the story of the Easter Week Rebellion should be investigated by historical experts and that the truth should be established once and for all.

"I agree that Dr. Maloney has brought forward evidence that demands enquiry; but it is absurd to say that because I see difficulties, from Casement's own point of view, in one or two details of Dr. Maloney's explanation of the diary, this impugns my own sincerity. After all, Dr. Maloney's explanation must be the basis of the enquiry; but it is not yet, in every detail, an essential part of the Athanasian Creed. I wrote to *The Irish Press* in all good faith, and in answer to Mr. Yeats who (like *The Irish Press* itself) has met me in the same direct and straightforward spirit. I must point out to one or two of your correspondents, however, that their implications are now demonstrably incorrect, and that some of their statements are simply untrue. A copy of the Casement Diary was shown to me, as it was to others, for a few minutes; but I never had either the original or a copy in my own possession. A correspondent who seems to be writing as a novelist rather than as a historian, says that I went to America 'armed with the Diary' in order, I suppose, to 'hawk it around' there. This is simply untrue.

"Moreover your novelist correspondent has no right to say that I am known only as a very bitter enemy of Ireland, or that I persist in accepting a report which I did once accept twenty years ago. These statements also are simply untrue. I have already publicly affirmed that in view of Dr. Maloney's book a proper historical investigation into the Casement documents is imperative in the cause of justice, and I also regard the report upon which I based my single article as utterly unreliable.

"The alleged facts in both cases were sent out, as Dr. Maloney has shown, in a stereotyped form from sources that, at the time, caused them to be accepted without hesitation by thousands. Supposing the facts to be true, my comment on those facts would have been absolutely justified. But your correspondents have not seen the article and they miss one important difference between my comment and the stereotyped report, which is that I did pay my tribute to Ireland herself, and that I took it for granted that the alleged crimes must have been committed by individual wrong-doers. Even at that time I emphasized this; and of those alleged wrong-doers I did not even know the names.

"It is in this way, I suppose, that nations are led to engender bitterness; and the experience of those years should certainly prevent most of us from accepting such reports in future without verification. But does it? Even in Ireland?

"I have not touched upon any Irish questions from that day, twenty years ago, to this; but I have often expressed my disgust at the falsehoods which we were all led to believe about many matters during that time of world upheaval. Millions of people believe the story of the Russian Army crossing England, and believed it on rumours which have never been traced to their source. It is surely a little absurd, then, to single me out in this way, and to ask me why I once accepted a direct report from an authorized Press Bureau.

"But let me again point out, in turn, that your later correspondents, even with the facts before them, do now accept and persist in statements which are equally without foundation as to my own very slight and indirect part in this matter twenty years ago, and my own attitude now. Let them look into their own consciences and ask themselves whether this is in the interests of the truth which we can secure only in one way—by being exactly truthful ourselves. Falsehoods on either side will only obscure the whole matter.

"For Count Plunkett's letter I have no criticism. I know from what a depth of personal tragedy it arose. I suppose he will not believe me when I say that although he accuses me of all the misdeeds against humanity and justice which the powers of evil can conceive, his letter did really move me. He must find someone on whom to direct his feelings; and so it happens that I, who only a few days ago heard the story of his own tragic experiences for the first time, must now incur the whole of his concentrated indignation.

"In circumstances like these, what is the use of our bandying words with one another? If in my ignorance of Ireland I accepted once, twenty years ago, from official sources, an untrue report, I had absolutely nothing to do with its origination, and I am equally ready to co-operate in an appeal for a thorough investigation by scientific modern historians, so that the truth—in all these matters—may be established finally, and that where wrong has been done to any man's memory it may—so far as lies in human power—be righted."

I may say here that, while Yeats withdrew his charge against me, and also withdrew from doing anything practical to clear the matter up, I did make a personal effort, first through Stephen Gaselee, Librarian of the Foreign Office, who had originally shown me the transcript, but he could give me no further information. I then applied to a Cabinet Minister, who made additional enquiries. These were finally brought to an end by the following letter from the Permanent Under-Secretary of State for War, which was addressed to the Cabinet Minister in question and forwarded to me by him:

MY DEAR ——,

It was nice to see you again and in such good form.

I had our archives searched, but apparently we have nothing in our registry which throws any light on the Casement Diaries.

There was nothing more that I could do; and, so far as I could discover, no one else took any practical steps at all.

Bernard Shaw wrote a characteristic letter, exonerating John Redmond and myself, but apparently condemning everyone else, including Casement, the British Government, and Queen Victoria. This chapter, however, may very well end with the wisdom of Touchstone:

"*To the Editor,* The Irish Press

"SIR,— Dr. Maloney's book entitled *The Forged Casement Diaries* is probably making a very superfluous addition to the bad blood still existing between England and Ireland. As bad blood between near neighbours does nobody any good, may I point out that there was no forgery in the business and no villainy. I remember the circumstances quite well; and I had some personal acquaintance with the late Lord Birkenhead, who, as Attorney General, was prosecutor at the trial, and Admiral Sir Reginald Hall, who exhibited the documents pretty freely at the Admiralty. Now I cannot imagine either of these gentlemen as the villains they would certainly have been had they known that the documents found among Casement's belongings were memoranda of Putnamayan cases made by Casement in his famous campaign against horrible atrocities in that region as Britannic consul there. Galloper Smith Birkenhead was hated as the boldest and most unscrupulous political reactionary of his day; and as Casement's prosecutor he was in the predicament of having notoriously committed the very offence with which Casement was charged; that of levying arms against the Crown. And he was not in the least put out by it. Later on, he stepped brazenly and cynically down from the woolsack into the City. He drank shamelessly. Yet he was an irresistibly likeable man. I never met anyone who knew him personally who disliked him; and I found it impossible to dislike him myself.

"As to Admiral Hall, there is no evidence in his record and no suggestion in his personality that he is a melodramatic villain. That these two men were capable of committing a diabolic fraud on public opinion to secure the conviction of a distinguished public servant of their own class, whose pardon would not have done them the slightest harm, is too improbable to be believed without overwhelming proof.

"There is, so far as I can see, no proof. The trial occurred at a time when the writings of Sigmund Freud had made psychopathy grotesquely fashionable. Everybody was expected to have a secret history unfit for publication, except in the consulting rooms of the psychoanalysts. If it had been announced that among the papers of Queen Victoria a diary had been found revealing that her severe respectability masked the day-dreams of a Messalina, it would have been received with eager credulity and without the least reprobation by the intelligentsia. It was in that atmosphere that Casement was accused of keeping a psychopathic diary; and though innocents like Alfred Noyes and John Redmond were shocked, the rest of us were easily credulous; but we associated no general depravity with psychopathic eccentricities; and we were determined not to be put off by it in our efforts to obtain a pardon. The Putumayo explanation never occurred to us.

"Why, then, should it have occurred to those who wanted to have Casement hanged? Smith, who apparently did not want to have him hanged, proved his complete sincerity, as Dr. Maloney's book reveals, by characteristically disregarding his obligations as Crown Counsel and advising the defence to plead insanity and use the documents to prove their plea. This seems to me to settle the question of Smith's good faith and good nature. He made no use of the documents in court. And as the members of the cabinet and civil and military services chiefs were no cleverer, to put it moderately, than F. E., it is reasonable to suppose that they also believed the current misinterpretation of the documents. For they did not invent the documents. The documents existed and were authentic. What were they to think of them?

"As to the notion that a British Cabinet is capable of an organized conspiracy in which every member knows all that his colleagues know and all that their departments are doing, Mr. Lloyd George's memoirs have made an end of that. No Cabinet Minister seems to have known what his own department was doing, much less what his colleagues knew; and the war would have gone to pieces had not Mr. Lloyd George been made dictator. Mr. Yeats calls on Mr. Alfred Noyes to repudiate a forgery; but, I repeat, there was no forgery; the documents were there; and Casement was dead long before the clue he gave to their real nature was followed up and brought to light. Then there was nothing to be done officially; for as the Government had made no use of them at the trial there was nothing for them to withdraw.

"Nevertheless, as the supposed Diary had been busily gossiped about and exhibited to discredit the petitions for clemency which were being rained on the Prime Minister (Asquith) at the time, and Casement's high reputation is still befouled by a slander with which not only his relatives, but the whole Irish nation are deeply concerned, some opportunity should be taken by a responsible British Minister to declare that the Government has no documents in its possession which reflect on Casement's personal character, and that all rumours to the contrary were based on a misunderstanding which has since been cleared up.

"A question in the House of Commons could elicit this easily enough, but only on condition that the declaration could not be mistaken for an admission of the guilt of deliberate forgery and intentional calumny. If Casement is to be used by the enemies of England as another stick to beat her with, it will be impossible for England to do him justice. If his case is reasonably and frankly put, there should be no difficulty in obtaining the only reparation that is now possible and now a long time overdue."

Under the critical microscope this epistle disintegrates, but as there appeared to be a general shrinking from the scientific instrument, one must accept the conclusion of the "sage in motley," who looking on his dial, said very wisely, "It is ten o'clock."

XXIII

President Wilson, Colonel House and Admiral Beatty

SHORTLY AFTER the close of World War I, Garnett and I were invited to a week-end house-party given by Admiral and Lady Beatty at Esher, a house they had taken for a year or two. Among the guests was the mysterious Colonel House, whom everyone had supposed to be the personal adviser of President Wilson on matters too subtle for the ordinary channels of diplomacy.

At dinner one evening another guest (I think General "Tom" Bridges) asked Beatty how he would like to die if he were given the choice. He replied that he would like to break his his neck in the hunting field. By a curious coincidence, about ten years later I heard Jellicoe give his own answer to the same question at a dinner party in his Isle of Wight house. The question was asked quite casually by one of the guests, who knew nothing of the former incident. Jellicoe answered, "I should like to die on the last green of the golf course, after holing out." The replies were curiously characteristic of the two men and their actual achievements. Beatty, who in some ways was more like a cavalry officer than an Admiral of the Fleet, very gallantly lost a considerable number of ships at Jutland; while Jellicoe (the man who by a single incautious move might have lost the British Empire in half an hour) "holed out" successfully.

On Sunday morning of the Esher week-end I went for a long walk with Colonel House. On that walk, at least, he was by no means as reticent as he was reputed to be. In fact, the strong silent man made some surprisingly weak statements. He was certainly right in regretting that Wilson had left the secure Olympus of Washington for the general *mêlée* of Versailles, but his explanation of the reason for

Wilson's decision to come took one's breath away when one considered how much was at stake.

He said that Wilson was extremely touchy, and might have taken great offence if he (House) had sent him a message advising him to stay at home. House had therefore sent him a carefully composed cable, half of which was intended to indicate that House personally was longing to see Wilson at Versailles, while the other half was intended to suggest that in his more impartial judgment it would be far wiser for Wilson to stay in Washington. Wilson, according to House, misunderstood the cable, and took the more cordial part of it as an expression of House's real wishes. With the fate of whole nations trembling in the balance, Wilson therefore adopted a course which his subtle adviser accepted without any attempt to clarify the situation; though, as he told me, he felt it would lead to disaster. It was extremely important at this time that Wilson should stay at home. In Washington he was perhaps the most powerful figure in the world. When he came to Europe he was merely an honest professor in a gang of card-sharpers. It is no discredit to Wilson to say that he was no match for them. In fact it is a compliment, and one that was aptly illustrated by Max Beerbohm in a cartoon depicting Lloyd George and Clemenceau engaged in a furtive conversation, with Wilson off in the background. "Between you and I," says Mr. Lloyd George, stealing a sly glance at the idealist; and the barb was not entirely in the grammatical solecism.

But Wilson's adviser apparently could do nothing to explain what he meant when his advice was misunderstood. Nor did he even take the trouble to find out what Wilson meant in one of his most completely misunderstood phrases, though House could have done so by the very simple process of reading the context. He told me (raising the subject himself) how he deplored Wilson's phrase "too proud to fight." I asked him if he knew the rest of the sentence, and to my amazement he said that he had not the slightest notion! And this was a man who was helping to mold the destinies of nations. The phrase had been cabled over and used in thousands of journals, public speeches and on the music-hall stage, as if some demoniac imp in the minds of men was urging them to abuse and alienate their best friends, the only friends who could save them from ultimate disaster. If our enemies had been able to choose what we should do, they could have chosen nothing more helpful to their cause. "Too proud to fight" was bandied about as a cheap sneer from end to end of England, and not a soul in England could supply either the subject or the verb that accompanied the phrase.

Later, at an English-Speaking Union dinner in London, General Dawes (the American Ambassador), Lord Reading and one of our Archbishops were present, the phrase was again deplored by one of the speakers. In my own brief speech I asked the same question: "Could anyone in the room give the rest of the sentence, or even the subject or the verb which gave meaning to the sentence?" Although at least half of those present had probably been repeating the phrase for months past with that awful parrot-like iteration which sometimes obfuscs even the intelligent, and has something in common with mob-emotion, not one of them could give the answer. Here was a single phrase torn out of a passage from which all the significant words had been omitted, yet used like a blank cheque to be filled up at the user's will with all the malice at his command.

The sentence occurred in a speech made by Wilson at Philadelphia when there were threats of attack across the border from Mexico. It was the period known as "watchful waiting." The sentence referred, not to Germany, but to the petty provocations of Mexico—the sparrow pecking at the eagle.

Wilson did not say that the United States was too proud to fight Germany. He said, with reference to Mexico:

"The example of America must be the example not merely of peace because it will not fight, but of peace because peace is the healing and elevating influence of the world and strife is not. There is such a thing as a man being too proud to fight. There is such a thing as a nation being so right that it does not need to convince others by force that it is right."

Later, with obvious reference to the larger question, he said that *America must not be looked upon as a country that would not fight.* Had this latter statement been cabled over with the same emphasis as that other phrase in its meaningless detachment, it is no exaggeration to say that the war might have been shortened, if only by the heartening of the Allies, and thousands of lives might have been saved.

XXIV

A Debate with Hardy

ALTHOUGH SOME of Thomas Hardy's letters to me are included in the volume *The Later Years of Thomas Hardy* by Mrs. Hardy, and we corresponded frequently, I met him only once, not in Dorset, but in London, at a small afternoon party given by Mrs. William Sharp. The only other guest was Robert Hichens, who was then regarded as one of the "younger generation" of novelists. It was a very hot summer afternoon, and I remember that Hardy introduced what might be called a Wessex note into the picture when the urbane younger novelist was presented to him; for, by way of comment on the heat, he gave so vivid an imitation of a field worker wringing the sweat from his brow with two fingers that for a moment London melted into Froom Vale.

Afterwards he talked of an Earthly Paradise which he would have liked to provide for horses, cows, sheep and other animals on which he thought mankind inflicted unnecessary suffering. I asked him quite innocently if he was a vegetarian; and he replied in a tone so dismal that it seemed to imply the very desperation of pessimism about his own character, "Oh no, I'm not consistent." For some days afterwards I felt a sense of remorse as if, like some *enfant terrible,* I had unconsciously split the great man's personality. However, when *The Dynasts* appeared I tried to make up for it in an article in the *Daily Graphic.* I did not send it to him, but Hardy wrote me:

"I have come across your review of Dynasts III in the *Daily Graphic* and I must write a line to say how very generous I feel you to have been in writing the article. My own sense of the shortcomings of the book tells me that the lightning of your imagination has met me half-way in the presentment, and more. My usual experience is, and yours also no doubt, that the poor writer of verse is left to do all his own imagining and his reader's likewise."

What I admired most in *The Dynasts* was not the verse but the grand architectural design and the masterly prose descriptions, which take the place of stage scenery and form the background of the action. I expressed my admiration wholeheartedly, at a time when many critics were in doubt about his works in verse.

However, Hardy formed a less favourable opinion of my critical abilities when I was a little less enthusiastic about a much slighter work which he published later, *The Queen of Cornwall.* He wrote to me:

"How kind of you to take the trouble to write an article on my little play—53 years in contemplation, 800 lines in result, alas!

"Thank you very much. I envy you the dispatch by which you could do it in a few hours."

Alas for human consistency! By this time it was the fashion for everyone to praise the verse of Hardy indiscriminately, but I could not sincerely burn incense before a work which to-day everyone would regard as a quite negligible part of Hardy's achievement. Apparently it did not occur to him that a critic might form a very sound opinion of a picture if he contemplated it for a single hour. I had in fact praised *The Queen of Cornwall* far more highly than would his most devoted admirer to-day, but there was an obvious petulance in his letter.

In a lecture given to a London audience in 1920 I ventured to say that one could admire the mastery of his art without necessarily accepting a pessimistic philosophy which regarded the Creator as an imbecile jester. Hardy read a newspaper report of the lecture, and somewhat to my amazement he wrote a rather tart epistle asking me in what part of his work such suggestions were to be found. As they pervade almost everything he wrote, I was somewhat embarrassed by the riches of the treasure house upon which I could draw. In *Time's Laughing-Stocks,* for instance, Hardy had called the universe a "vast imbecility" and had made many allusions to the power behind the universe as blind, "unweeting" and making cruel sport of its creatures.

I began to feel that I had really split his personality. Of the correspondence that followed, only Hardy's letters were printed in his biography:

"13th December 1920

"DEAR MR. NOYES,

"Somebody has sent me an article from *The Morning Post* of Dec. 9, entitled 'Poetry and Religion,' which reports you as saying in a lecture, that mine is 'a philosophy which told them [readers] that the Power behind the Universe was an imbecile jester.'

"As I hold no such 'philosophy,' and, to the best of my recollection, never could have done so, I should be glad if you would inform me whereabouts I have seriously asserted such to be my opinion.

"Yours truly,
THOMAS HARDY"

"December 17, 1920

"DEAR MR. HARDY,

"Your letter of December 13th has just reached me here. I am exceedingly sorry that the abbreviated report of my address did not also contain the tribute which I endeavoured to pay to yourself as the acknowledged head of our literature. There was a suggestion of this in the *Morning Post,* but I went much further than was there indicated, and I emphasized the fact that the pessimistic philosophy of which I spoke was in all of your works the outcome of a profound sympathy with human suffering.

"I then went on to say that the pessimistic view was one with which I felt bound to disagree, and I tried to show how, in my opinion, it led logically to the conclusion that the Power behind the universe was malign. I put it into a nut-shell by using the phrase to which you refer in your letter.

"It has always seemed to me that the four lines at the end of *Time's Laughing-Stocks,* although they were entitled 'A Young Man's Epigram,' fairly represented the philosophy of the whole book, which is implied again in the title. The last stanza, for instance, of 'The Unborn'; the poem entitled 'New Year's Eve,' the last stanza of which describes the 'unweeting way' of the Power behind the universe; the next poem entitled 'His Education'; the desire for nescience to be reaffirmed; and the last stanza on page 88 expressing 'clear views and certain' on the final worthlessness of existence; these are the passages which I would quote on the spur of the moment in accordance with your suggestion that I should tell you whereabouts you have expressed the opinion I attributed to you in my address.

"I need not say how grateful I shall be if you will tell me whether I have misinterpreted these passages. I am publishing the address in a volume of essays very soon, and I shall be only too glad to revise it if I am wrong. In former articles published in the press (and in the *North American Review*) I made the same distinction between the philosophy and the artistic mastery, which everyone acknowledges.

"Yours sincerely,
ALFRED NOYES"

"December 20, 1920

"DEAR MR. NOYES,

"I am much obliged for your reply, which I really ought not to have troubled you to write. I may say for myself that I very seldom do give critics much trouble, usually letting things drift, though there have been many occasions when a writer who has been so much abused for his opinions as I have been would perhaps have done well not to hold his peace.

"I do not know that there can be much use in my saying more than I did say. It seems strange that I should have to remind a man of letters of what, I should have supposed, he would have known as well as I—of the very elementary rule of criticism that a writer's works should be judged as a whole, and not from picked passages that contradict them as a whole—and this especially when they are scattered over a period of 50 years.

"Also that I should have to remind him of the vast difference between the expression of fancy and the expression of belief. My imagination may have often run away with me; but all the same my sober opinion—so far as I have any definite one—of the Cause of Things, has been defined in scores of places, and is that of a great many ordinary thinkers:—that the said cause is neither moral nor immoral, but *un*moral:— 'loveless and hateless' I have called it; 'which neither good nor evil knows, etc. etc.'—(you will find plenty of these definitions in *The Dynasts* as well as in short poems, and I am surprised that you have not taken them in). This view is quite in keeping with what you call a pessimistic philosophy (a mere nickname with no sense in it), which I am quite unable to see as 'leading logically to the conclusion that the Power behind the universe is malign.'

"In my fancies, or poems of the imagination, I have of course called this Power all sorts of names—never supposing they would be taken for more than fancies. I have even in prefaces warned readers to take them as such—as mere impressions of the moment, exclamations, in fact. But it has always been my misfortune to presuppose a too intelligent reading public, and no doubt people will go on thinking that I really believe the Prime Mover to be a malignant old gentleman, a sort of King of Dahomey—an idea which, so far from my holding it, is to me irresistibly comic. 'What a fool one must have been to write for such a public!' is the inevitable reflection at the end of one's life.

"The lines you allude to, 'A Young Man's Epigram,' I remember finding in a drawer, and printed them merely as an amusing instance of early cynicism. The words 'Time's Laughing-Stocks' are legitimate imagery all of a piece with such expressions as 'life, Time's fool,' and thousands in poetry, and I am amazed that you should see any *belief* in them. The other verses you mention, 'New Year's Eve,' 'His Education,' are the same fanciful impressions of the moment. The poem called 'He Abjures Love,' ending with 'And then the curtain,' is a love poem, and lovers are chartered irresponsibles. A poem often quoted against me and apparently in your mind in the lecture is the one called 'Nature's Questioning,' which contains the words 'Some vast imbecility,' etc.—as if these definitions were my creed. But they are merely enumerated in the poem as fanciful alternatives to several others, having nothing to do with my opinion. As for 'The Unborn' to which you allude, though the form of it is imaginary, the sentiment is one which I should think, especially since the war, is not uncommon or unreasonable.

"This week I have had sent me a review which quotes a poem entitled 'To My Father's Violin,' containing a Virgilian reminiscence of mine of Acheron and the Shades. The writer comments: 'Truly this pessimism is insupportable. . . . One marvels that Hardy is not in a madhouse.' Such is English criticism; and I repeat, why did I ever write a line! . . . And perhaps if the young ladies to whom you lectured really knew that, so far from being the wicked personage they doubtless think me at present to be, I am a harmless old character much like their own grandfathers, they would consider me far less romantic and attractive.

"Yours sincerely,
THOMAS HARDY"

I am not sure from what passage Hardy took his quotation of "Time's fool," but even if it was from *Henry IV* Shakespeare answered it himself in the greatest of his sonnets:

Love's not Time's fool, though rosy lips and cheeks
Within his bending sickle's compass come.

Moreover, Shakespeare, far from suggesting that this was an irresponsible exclamation, ended:

If this be error, and upon me proved,
I never writ, nor no man ever loved.

Shakespeare here, of course, was speaking in his own person, and not through a character in a play. However, I tried to be tactful in my reply, though I had to stick to my guns on the foundations of my own belief that the universe has a meaning and a purpose.

"DEAR MR. HARDY,

"I must thank you very much for your letter and must write at once to say that when my book of essays is published I shall make some alterations in my references to your opinions. I sincerely hope that these alterations will make amends for any trouble that you have been caused.

"I think that the chief reason for my inability to understand many passages in your works was the fact that I have never been able to conceive that the cause of things could be less in any respect than the things caused. Of course I never for a moment thought that you yourself really believed the Prime Mover to be a sort of King of Dahomey, and I must frankly confess that the phrase which I used was not even down in my original manuscript, so that I hope you will forgive it as one of those extempore exclamations which, as you say in your letter, do not represent one's opinions as a whole, especially as it was intended to refer to the conclusion readers might draw rather than to your own views. I believe that I had the privilege, when the *Dynasts* appeared, to write of it as 'one of the greatest poems of modern times,' even when the field included works like Goethe's *Faust;* and I have had some pride in the fact that an extract from this notice appeared at the end of the first edition of *Time's Laughing-Stocks*. I hope, in fairness to myself, therefore, my opinions also may be considered as a whole. I have also suggested elsewhere in print that the kind of negation that one finds in great poetry from Ecclesiastes to *Macbeth* often postulates far more than it denies, casting off the temporal for the eternal; and I have quoted from your own works in illustration of this. I could not help, and never shall be able to help, expressing my personal belief (which is very far from orthodoxy of any kind*) that life proffers to fulfil eventually, and not to deny. I should be very sorry indeed if you thought this a proof of my feeble intelligence, for, in common with most people at the present day, I am confronted by what must appear to be blind cruelties, and it is just because I can see no solution here that I am forced to seek the explanation beyond. It may be an intellectual weakness on my part, but it is inconceivable to me that this whole universal process should be meaningless to its victims.

"There is just one more point which I should like to mention.

* This was written before I had fully accepted the perennial philosophy of Christendom.

My chief reason for raising this question at all was my feeling that, as you say in one of your poems, Voltaire is an extremely moderate man compared with the orthodox of to-day. I find myself surrounded at the present moment in London by people who misinterpret my 'superficial optimism' almost as completely as the superficial critic you mention in your letter misinterpreted the lines on the violin. There seems to be a destructive spirit abroad which would misapply texts taken from your own work, for instance, for its own purposes; and I was striking at this spirit in my address and not at the texts themselves. Perhaps I ought to have made this clearer; but much of what I said was extempore, and the abbreviated report you saw threw everything out of proportion. English criticism, of course, has sunk about as low as possible from every point of view. It may amuse you to know that a writer in *The Athenaeum* furiously demanded that my books should be burned. Nothing would distress me more than to think that anything I had said or written had given a moment's pain to yourself or led you to believe that I belonged to that contemptible fraternity. I was trying to express certain things which I sincerely believed and it would be a matter of lasting regret to me if I thought I had so blundered in a single sentence.

"I hope you will accept the very best Christmas wishes from both myself and my wife, who wants me to tell you that she has not forgotten the overworked horses' paradise which we once discussed together at Mrs. William Sharp's house in London.

"Believe me, sincerely yours,

ALFRED NOYES"

As I have noted in a later chapter, Voltaire, affirming his belief in God, declared it was better not to believe in Him at all than to believe in one who had no care for His creatures.

The final missive from Hardy was a card which reached me on Christmas Day:

"Dec. 23, 1920.

"Many thanks for letter. Yes, the whole scheme is incomprehensible, and there I suppose we must leave it—perhaps for the best. Knowledge might be terrible. TH. H."

I could not help chuckling over this last missive. It could hardly be regarded as the most optimistic of Christmas cards. However, peace was restored. Mrs. Hardy, in *The Later Years,* remarks: "It should be stated that Mr. Noyes had always been a friendly critic of Hardy's writings, and one with whom he was on good terms."

The editor of *Punch,* Mr. E. V. Knox, attributed to us a charming duet, which was afterwards reprinted in his *Parodies Regained.* By his kind permission I am allowed to give it here. In this duet Mr. Punch skated very charmingly over the surface:

THE TWO SHEPHERDS

(I have tried to imagine in these lines a sort of idyllic meeting between Mr. Thomas Hardy, the doyen of English letters, and Mr. Alfred Noyes, who came back to visit us this year, wearing so many laurels, from the U.S.A. It takes place, I suppose, somewhere in Dorset, and grazing or lying under trees near by must be imagined a quantity of sheep, half of them wearing expressions of sentimental joy, and half of deep though philosophical gloom.)

MR. ALFRED NOYES (*gently touching his Arabian zither*): Shade is here, and hedge-rows trailing.

MR. THOMAS HARDY (*coming in with the bass viol*): Rest, methinks, were not amiss. (*They sit down.*)

MR. ALFRED NOYES (*brightly*): I have a song to sing O.

MR. THOMAS HARDY (*rather gloomily*): Sing me your song O.

The opening solo attributed to me, however, was quite rightly dismissed by Mr. Hardy:

MR. THOMAS HARDY: . . .

Let me sing something to you of my own,
Rayed with eternity and Time's deep moan.
A little satire of obliterate life,
Such as outlooms in Wessex:

The False Wife

The ghost of the man who had killed his new-got bride
On their wedding-eve, and had wived the gibbet-tree,
Crept, as his wont was, close to her grave's side,
In the moon's apogee.

She had said, "I loved another prior to you,
Whom I met at a watering-place on the southern coast."
So he drew his rusting sabre and stabbed her through,
And now he was ghost to her ghost.

But to-night he found her not. And to his unsight
It seemed that this was perhaps a bitterer pain
Than when he had found her false, a new-wed wight,
That she should be false again.

For he knew, not knowing, yet sure that the spectre jade
Who had tricked him so in her blooth with a woman's guile,
Far off from the charnel vault and the tomb had wayed
To a different domicile.

Down the eweleaze she had fared and passed the door
Of the Old Green Man to the hollow that was beyond,
To house with the ghost of her former paramour,
Who had fallen, for spite, in a pond.

MR. ALFRED NOYES: It seems to me your song is much too sad.

MR. THOMAS HARDY: Life is like that. Ghast, weariful and bad.

MR. ALFRED NOYES: Well, let's try something then in unison to make things cheerful—something with a run.

MR. THOMAS HARDY: Illuding through the woof of tears.

MR. ALFRED NOYES: *Robin Hood's in Sherwood, in Sherwood, in Sherwood.*

MR. THOMAS HARDY: A nescience unfriends the years.

MR. ALFRED NOYES: *And Friar Tuck's in Sherwood.*

MR. THOMAS HARDY: Perfectly rotten!

MR. ALFRED NOYES: Well, let's try once more.

MR. THOMAS HARDY: And keep together.

MR. ALFRED NOYES: And please mind the score.

BOTH TOGETHER:

Through the shady glens of Ida buds of amaranth are peeping,
And a pirate fleet's a-sailing on the sunny purple main,
But Corporal Henry Tullidge lies in Mellstock Churchyard sleeping,
Out of pain,
Out of pain.

O it's good to lie at Mellstock when the moon is on the tombstones
(Falling silver on the tombstones)
Falling silver on the tomb of Corporal Tullidge,
Who'll never go a-vlirting or a-vighting
With Boney again.

. . . .

(*They are left singing.*)

XXV

Not So Bad As We Seem

THE SECOND time I met Mr. Asquith was at an amateur performance at Devonshire House of *Not So Bad As We Seem.* This production of Bulwer-Lytton's play took place exactly seventy years after the original performance in the same room, when it was directed by Charles Dickens. The cast, in 1921, was composed very largely of descendants of the original cast. Queen Victoria and the Prince Consort had attended the original performance, and the cast had then included Wilkie Collins, Sir John Tenniel, Douglas Jerrold, Mark Lemon, John Forster (the biographer of Dickens and Landor), Charles Knight and Mrs. Henry Compton.

The 1921 revival was organized by Brett Langstaff, and was featured in the Press for almost two months, with what Brett called "murder headlines." Not only was it taking place in the same room, but the players wore the identical costumes of the original performance. My own participation in the revival was limited to writing an epilogue, and reading it in Dickensian costume. The overture was specially composed by Ivor Novello.

The council with whose enthusiastic support the scheme was carried out included a remarkable variety of names: Barrie, Galsworthy, Lord Dunsany, the Duchess of Hamilton, the Archbishop of York, the Bishop of London, Robert Bridges, Edmund Gosse, Kenneth Grahame, H. G. Wells, Kate Douglas Wiggin, General Sir Baden-Powell, Sir Frank Benson and the Marquess of Cambridge. The producer was Nigel Playfair, fresh from his masterly production of *The Beggar's Opera.* The cast included descendants of both Bulwer-Lytton and Charles Dickens. The Earl of Loftus was played by Neville Lytton; Mr. Goodenough Easy by Henry Dickens, K. C. (son of the novelist); "A Watchman" was played by Compton Mackenzie (a descendant of Mrs. Henry Compton); "Sir Thomas Timid, a frequenter of Will's Coffee House," was played by A. A. Milne; Sir William Orpen played Paddy O'Sullivan; Sir Gilbert Parker played "Lord Strongbow, a Fashionable Gentleman"; W. H. Davies (who insisted on arriving by the kitchen door, on the ground that he was a tramp poet) played "A Newsman"; G. L. Stampa, of *Punch,* appropriately enough took the part of "A Drawer"; while Ian Hay, H. V. Esmond, E. Temple Thurston and W. B. Maxwell, though only four in number, were more than equal to "Half a Dozen Fashionable Gentlemen" in walking-on parts.

Two of the women's parts were played by Miss Tennyson Jesse and Miss Rebecca West; but the third woman, "The Silent Woman of Deadman's Lane," a non-speaking part, presented a problem. Mrs. Henry Compton had played it in 1851, and it was hoped that Fay Compton would now take it, but she was unable to do so. Nigel Playfair could think of no one suitable, when a brilliant though an obviously paradoxical idea occurred to Brett: Why should not "The Silent Woman of Deadman's Lane" be played by Mrs. Asquith, who was about to talk in America?

Accordingly Brett wrote her a polite little note, in some trepidation lest the paradox be too palpable. To his surprise, he was immediately bombarded with urgent messages from the prospective star—telegrams, telephone calls, and notes by express messenger, asking him to come and see her without delay.

Leaping into a taxi with the agility of Peter Flower, Brett hurried to her house. An agitated butler in shirt-sleeves (for the hour was early) ushered him into a dignified drawing-room where Mrs. Asquith was restlessly walking up and down with an air which did not

Alfred Noyes and the children on the coast of Maine, 1942.

Lisle Combe, the author's home on the Isle of Wight.

The author and his wife at Vista del Arroyo, Pasadena, California.

In the garden at Pasadena.

at all suggest a dumb woman. She explained that she was intensely busy, every moment was occupied; but that THIS—her proposed part in *Not So Bad As We Seem*—was so important that it took precedence over everything (the eight weeks of "murder headlines" had evidently done their work. For some time there had been rumours that the part was to be played by a personage of great importance, the name being kept secret—for the excellent reason that nobody knew it).

A little optimistically, perhaps, Brett assured her that she would have no difficulty as there were no words to learn for the Silent Woman of Deadman's Lane.

"Do you mean that I am actually to say nothing?" exclaimed Mrs. Asquith.

"Nothing at all," said Brett, adding tactlessly, "moreover, you will be at the back of the stage and veiled when you do appear."

"I am quite sure," said Mrs. Asquith with some asperity, "that if Nigel Playfair was clever enough to revive *The Beggar's Opera,* he is quite clever enough to write something in it for me to say. I shall certainly not remain at the back of the stage, and I don't think a veil at all suitable."

Still trying to make things easy for her (and perhaps for himself), Brett volunteered that it would not be necessary for her to attend any of the rehearsals but the last.

"I shall attend them all," said Mrs. Asquith crisply.

And she did.

In the play itself at one point, a character on the stage is supposed to be startled by catching sight of the Silent Woman peering at him through a window, and exclaims to be a companion, "Hideous apparition, avaunt! I will go home to my mother!" Asquith, who was sitting in the front row, shook with silent and appreciative laughter for the next ten minutes.

The illustrated programme, produced somewhat in the style of a special edition of *Punch,* may still be a collector's item, for it included contributions by Owen Seaman, Stephen Leacock, Augustus John, Wilfrid Scawen Blunt, Mrs. Belloc Lowndes, W. L. George, Henry Dickens, Compton Mackenzie, Claude Shepperson, St. John

Lucas, Pett Ridge, Frank Reynolds, H. M. Bateman, L. Raven Hill, G. L. Stampa, Justin McCarthy, W. H. Davies and George Belcher.

The object of this revival was to endow a Children's Library in the little house at Somers Town where Dickens, in his own poor childhood, had discovered a few old books in a garret, and so entered upon the road that led him to a place in Westminster Abbey.

And he sat him down among the tattered volumes;
 And, with one foot under him curled,
His dark eyes blazed above the pages,
 And he woke, in that great new world.

The night was grim, and dark, and growing darker,
 He sat there, stiller than a stone—
A small boy, reading in a garret,
 A great king, seated on a throne.

The Children's Library, thus founded by the revival of *Not So Bad As We Seem,* directly led to the establishment, in many cities and towns throughout the United Kingdom and the Dominions, of Children's Libraries—little havens from which the young imagination could set sail to undiscovered ends. They owed it all to Charles Dickens. In the epilogue (printed in the programme) I imagined him—a little lonely perhaps—leaving his resting place in the Abbey for the poor little house where he had found that hidden treasure:

For he stole like a shadow up the dark street;
 And there—through a window—he could see
Not a room, but a harbour, bright with lanthorns,
 And tall ships casting from the quay.

To every ship a watchman in the crow's nest,
 With one foot under him curled;
And a crew of urchins crowding on the canvas
 For adventure to the ends of the world.

. . . . . .

And the shadow at the window stood and wondered,
 "Oh, who can the harbour-master be?
For his pilot-lights are shining on the waters
 As they never shone for me."

Then he saw—a crooked stair behind the harbour.
He stole through the open door;
He climbed to a little room, and entered
Like a thief, in the night, once more.

It was narrow as his house in the Abbey.
It was dim with smiles and tears;
And he groped for the master of the dream-ships
Through the mists of a hundred years.

He groped there, silent as a shadow;
For he saw him, stiller than a stone—
A small boy, reading in a garret,
A great king, seated on a throne.

XXVI

Barry Pain Puts on His Pince-Nez

BETWEEN 1908 and 1929 I saw a great deal of Barry Pain, a writer whose best work in the short story never received the recognition it deserved, partly owing to the fact that publishers and public insisted that he must continue in the vein of light humour in which he made his first popular success. He had a profound insight into character, and a more subtle art in delineating it than most of his contemporaries. Lord Charnwood, the biographer of Lincoln, described Barry Pain's *The Exiles of Faloo* as the best of all novels for a young man to read—and for this book Barry had considerable difficulty in finding a publisher!

It is the story of an island in the Pacific, to which a number of scoundrels of various kinds, together with other men not entirely scoundrels but broken by the law, had escaped "beyond the law's pursuing." They establish a Club, with rules designed for the circumstances, one of which naturally was that no credit should be given. Gradually, through the original flaws in character, the society ends disastrously in conflict with the native population. There is humour and heroism, beauty and tragedy in the tale and, like all great stories, it is a parable.

For several summers Barry Pain and his wife were our near neighbours at Rottingdean, and I had many long walks with him over the Sussex downs. At that time he was a great admirer of Huysmans. Though his own strong critical sense had nothing in common with the eccentricities of that writer, the morbid power of *Ā Rebours,* and the dawning of a finer philosophy in *L Cathédrale,* drew him, I have sometimes thought, a considerable distance towards the final solution discovered by Huysmans.

There was sadness, and a really deep wisdom, behind the mask of Barry Pain's continual flow of light humour—but it is hardly true to call it a mask. It was more like the sparkle of the sun on deep waters.

I have never enjoyed any conversations more than those I had with Barry on some of our long walks, with the thyme underfoot and the skylark singing overhead. He had all Belloc's "Four Men" in him, with the wisdom of Grizzlebeard the predominant note. We used to choose a village from eight to ten miles distant as the goal of our walks, with cold beef and good ale in prospect for lunch at one of those immortal Sussex inns.

On one occasion we had been planning a walk from Rottingdean to Lewes, where E. V. Lucas had a house. A few days before, Barry had sent me the MSS of the novel upon which he was working (*The Exiles of Faloo*). He was sixteen years older than I, and it pleased me enormously that he should care for my views upon it. We were to discuss it on the walk to Lewes, which, however, had to be postponed for the reason given in the following letter:

"I clean forgot, a parson relative of mine comes here to-day. He's a co-trustee with me, and has trust business to discuss.

> O Lord, how joyful 'tis to be
> With such an one a co-trustee!
> For trust accounts like psalms resound,
> And mortgaged pubs are holy ground.

Explanatory note to last line. The estate of which we are trustees has a mortgage on a public house and the public house has been scheduled for compensation, and we've got to look into it.

"The main point is that once more I shall not be able to walk to Lewes—that Paradise which we've striven so vainly to enter. But as soon as the Rector goes back to his flock, I'll come round and see if some minor walk can be attempted. It might be three of the clock or it might be four. There is even the hideous possibility that he might stay on for tea, but I believe that his train back won't let him.

"Don't stop in for the purpose if you want to go out—I'll just take my chance. *Send along that novel.* No, I'll pick it up when I come." This referred, not to *Faloo,* but to something that I had been writing myself.

A few weeks afterwards he wrote from his London house:

"The ill-fated *Faloo* has arrived safely— Many thanks. But if you don't procure and forward full details of the negress and the padded cell, you are no man." (This refers to a macabre newspaper story of which I thought he might make use.)

"When are you coming to see my books? It's very quiet here at present. But there is a prospect that a big house opposite will be turned into a Steam Laundry for Fallen Women of the Repentant Type and the Roman Catholic Persuasion. This is not an effort of our genial humourist—it's the actual fact.

"Three men I know have committed suicide this year, and one of them was a poet. Are you insured?"

The next letter is partly concerned with a new book of poems I had sent him. The "Two Painters" was afterwards set as a cantata by Coleridge-Taylor, under its sub-title *A Tale of Old Japan.* It was produced with great success at the Albert Hall by the Royal Choral Society, and since then has been performed on innumerable occasions. The rather savage conclusion of the poem, of which Barry Pain approved so highly, was, however, omitted entirely from the cantata. Possibly this was right from the musical point of view, but the satirical note at the conclusion was intended to emphasize the point of the poem, that human affections are more important than art. The death of O-Kimi-San is depicted in the music of Coleridge-Taylor with more beauty than I could hope to give it in verse; and there the cantata closes. But the point of the poem, in the omitted conclusion, is that the great painter Sawara, with complete unconcern, makes a picture of the dead girl who had loved him, and wins the master's approval for it,

> "Hokusai is not so great.
> This is art," said Tenko.

Barry was a true artist, but as between life and art he always put first things first.

"Many thanks for your book, which I'm delighted to have. I've been reading in it all the morning. Some fine things in 'Lucifer.' I liked 'The Newspaper Boy' also, particularly. But I don't know that I wasn't keenest of all on the 'Two Painters,' the end of which is beyond words good. But I haven't finished the book yet, and have still the 'Enchanted Island' to read.

"We shall be very glad to see you both next week. I can't sell *Faloo* serially, which is rather damnable, especially as I've sold a lot of stuff that's much worse. . . .

"I hear with some joy that the attempt to bring the Roman Catholic ladies within the sphere of my refining and elevating influence is likely to go pop. But don't let this stop you from coming to see us."

In the following summer Barry Pain arrived at Rottingdean before his wife, and took bachelor lodgings in the little house of a retired Sergeant Rose, whose rubicund complexion fully justified the surname. The establishment was run by the Sergeant's three daughters, one of whom had an unfortunate predilection for playing hymns on a piano immediately under the sitting-room where Barry Pain was trying to write *Stories in Grey.* The only effect upon his good humour, however, was to plunge him into some verses of which he sent me a copy:

THE THREE ROSES

In this poor lodging where I stay,
Three Roses deck the parent spray,
Mona and Marjorie and May.

Dark May with her lagoons of eyes,
Pale face, red lips, and low replies,
Mary in Martha's lore made wise!

At nothing practical she stops,
Counts wash, makes beds, lays table, shops—
My God! She empties out the slops!

Marjorie, buxom and more ruddy,
Acts sometimes as May's understudy,
And when she does it's simply bloody.

Yet bloodier far it seems to me
When ceaselessly from nine till three
She plays the hymn for those at sea.

Mona, a blithe but knowing kid—
A bud these roses blown amid—
Does nothing, as she always did.

If it be so, as I suppose,
And she'll do nothing till life's close,
Would God that I were Mona Rose!

By the way of contrast, on the other side of the village green lived Lady Burne-Jones, the widow of the pre-Raphaelite painter, an old friend of Barry Pain and his wife. Her son, Philip Burne-Jones, was an occasional visitor. My book on William Morris, for the *English Men of Letters* series, had not taken very seriously some stories told by Mackail (son-in-law of Sir Edward Burne-Jones) about the author of *The Earthly Paradise.* In the official biography of William Morris, Mackail had described the irascible temperament of the poet, and quite solemnly affirmed that in a moment of annoyance at a dinner party he had bitten his fork into a fantastic shape, and upon another occasion he had actually bitten through a solid oak window-frame! Swinburne had told me at The Pines that Rossetti had invented these stories for the sheer fun of astonishing the grave scholar, and Rossetti had been doubly astounded to find that Mackail had swallowed them, hook, line and sinker. A young writer could hardly resist the opportunity of having a little fun with the official biographer.

Some of the elderly critics of that day were very severe on my scepticism about Morris' dental prowess, and my still greater scepticism about Mackail's suggestion that Morris was a greater poet than

Tennyson. Andrew Lang, however, came to my rescue in the *Spectator,* declaring that what had been said required saying and had been well said. Thirty years later C. S. Lewis wrote that my book had given a true picture of the real Morris. But for a time I had an uneasy feeling that I must be out of favour with Mackail's in-laws; so it was an unexpected pleasure to find that the ice had been broken by Barry Pain and his wife. A little later Philip Burne-Jones, who looked like one of his father's Arthurian knights pale and wasted with the search for the Holy Grail in the mazes of London society, came across one of my poems entitled "The Shadow," and surprised me with a letter very straight from the heart and so full of a personal sadness that I will not quote it here. *Mentem mortalia tangunt.* But he refers to it in the letter which follows:

"DEAR NOYES,

"Let us dispense with formalities in addressing each other (if you agree)—a line to thank you for that interesting book of essays which you have so kindly sent me.

"I shall read you on the tendencies of modern art with the greatest interest—and I expect I shall agree with every word of it. The man who wrote 'The Shadow' is not likely to have formed opinions on this subject with which I should be disinclined to agree.

"I look forward greatly to seeing you in October when you get back again to London. I myself shall probably be going abroad soon.

"I never go to Rottingdean now— There is something so inexpressibly sad about the survival of the outward and material aspect of a place in which one has had great happiness, when the soul and spirit which made that happiness is no longer there—and I shirk the experience in this case.

"Yours gratefully,

PHILIP BURNE-JONES"

In the winter Barry Pain and his wife occasionally took rooms in Brighton (four miles from Rottingdean) and our walks were renewed. One morning he wrote with a whoop of joy:

"The enclosed cutting from a local paper was sent to me. Knowing that you are interested in poetry I send it on to you. But return it—it is very rare and beautiful.

HARVEST HYMN

How shall we thank the giver
For the blessed gift of fruit?
Now let our hearts be thankful
We dare not now sit mute.

For God expects our praises
He wishes for gratitude
For all his blessings given,
Especially for our food.

Let us not take God's blessings
So much as a matter of course.
If he withheld the gift of wheat
That perhaps would make us think."

Some months later Barry Pain sent me a remarkable poem of his own. His wife had died of cancer in 1917 and he was still expected to play the humorist. The sadness which had grown upon him was clearly expressed in the poem, though in the title, "Nocturne of a Poor Old Man," he seems still to be smiling at himself:

'Tis no joy to lie abed, cold, sleepless, lone and thinking—
Watch the sneering moon, precise in regulated flight—
Hear Time's little feet mince by
In arid clock-ticks ceaselessly
While thoughts like midges sting and fly.
Night denies me charity? I'll up and rob the night.
There's a little in the cask, a stoup of pleasant drinking,
Fire still lingers in the logs beneath the ashes white;
Tomorrow let the tap run dry,
And fierce winds scour a frosty sky;
Tonight, once more before I die,
The blaze shall set my blood aglow and good wine make delight.

"Fool, who waits for you below? Whose heart for you beats quicker?
You have none for company but such as memory brings.
Wood you burn and wine you pour,
And of both you've scanty store,

Nor any gold to buy you more;
Therefore spare, and calculate, and save for happenings."
Wisdom speaks, but never yet have I spared love or liquor;
Vainly, at my heart's back-door, trade-wisdom knocks and rings;
Often has she knocked before—
Made her old blue knuckles sore.
Tonight there's wood and wine galore:
Empty hearth and empty cask concern the king of Kings.

Now the fire leaps up apace, and struck logs volley glories,
While the cask, well-tilted, yields no niggardly supply;
All those mad thought-midges slain,
Sleepless fever leaves the brain,
Warmth and life come back again;
I raise my glass in silence and I drink to memory,
For, 'tis true, I sit alone with unforgotten stories,
I who, far too weak to live, seem yet too strong to die.
That old reaper, they explain,
Chooses out the better grain;
Scribbling sensualists remain;
For the gleaner no great prize; and such derelict am I.

Wine, thou friend of weary men whose life has passed its middle!
Youth has love—that only spell more magical than thine—
Manhood is on work intent,
Ignorantly confident;
Age has only to repent
All its works and all its loves and drown them deep in wine.
Wine, illuminant of us who have not guessed the riddle,
Cannot leave the question, yet no answer can divine!
Where all faiths and knowledge blent
Weave their fine-spun argument,
Wine, far more benevolent,
Wipes the problem off the slate with her red anodyne.

Ah, the grudging clock strikes three! But three's a sacred number;
And there's mercy in the air and quiet in my heart,
Golden flames and chalice red
Breed the wild thoughts in my head
That may grow to dreams in bed,
Dreams of purple birds that purr and drag me in a cart.
Welcome, you mad arabesques that strut the stage of slumber!
Tune, you frantic orchestra, 'tis time for you to start!

In dreams I'm loved and wed;
I'm young; I'm great; I'm dead—
Applause prohibited.
The world's a stinking greenroom; I go on to play my part.

In answer to my letter thanking him for it he wrote:

"So glad that you liked that gay little poem. It expressed me when I wrote it. I don't suppose it's *my* metre. I've not seen it before, but it must have been done. In any case, if you like it, you'd be paying me a very great compliment if you wrote in it. Do. I wouldn't like the general public to know, but it's hell on rhymes."

His "Nocturne" rather haunted me, but there were still moments when his growing despondency broke into the joyous humour of the day when he edited *The Granta.* I wrote a column in the *Daily Express* about his work, and began by saying that Barry Pain belonged to no group or school, he was "big enough to be independent." The printer gave this as "big, rough and independent," but fortunately I caught the mistake in proof just before it went to press.

When the article appeared he wrote:

"21.9. 21.

"DEAR ALFRED,

"At 7.20 a.m. this morning on stepping from my bath I heard the arrival of letters through the slot in my front door, and went down just as I was to collect them.

"Here a note of explanation is needed. Mrs. Ray, my middle-aged and excellent housekeeper, does not arrive until 8 a.m. and leaves at 5 p.m. Between her departure one day and her arrival on the next I am absolutely alone in this house. This totally disposes of your allegations of immodesty. Besides, I always put on a pince-nez to read the letters. Also, by the time I've read them I am generally dry by natural processes, thus saving wear and tear of one towel, bath, large, author for the use of. We will proceed.

"At 8 a.m. Mrs. Ray arrived; and, being clothed indifferent well, I went as my daily custom is down the road to the news-agent. He that has fixed newspapers makes monotony for himself. Every morning I select as the mood takes me, and this morning the lot fell upon the *Daily News* and the *Daily Express.*

"At 8.20, again as my daily custom is, I sat down to eat bread and honey and drink excellent coffee in my garden. I opened the *Daily Express* and the first thing I saw at the head of a column was

The Genius of Barry Pain. By Alfred Noyes.

"Yes, it was the article whereof your letter spoke.

"I thank you very much for it. I keep that article to read in moments of depression. And meanwhile I'm too proud to do any work this morning.

"But do you realize what you have done?

"It is the Magna Charta privilege of all English critics to adopt a very superior attitude in dealing with the work of Barry Pain, because he writes funniments at times, which is low of him. These critics will all get up and go for you—not the less because you rather use your boots on some of them. There will be six letters in the *Daily Express* to-morrow, stating and proving that Barry Pain is a reptile of a low order and that Alfred Noyes has become insane. You will be hounded into an asylum and reduced to abject poverty. The rest of your career becomes a subject for the film. I can see some of the titles on the screen—"Garnett pawns her wedding-ring"—"Over the Cliffs at Rottingdean"—"Part Three will Follow Immediately"—and similar trenchant phrases. It will feature Douglas Fairbanks and Mary Pickford. Yes, and Mr. Fatty Arbuckle (if released) will play ME!

"Haud Angli sed Los Angeles!

"Seriously, your outspoken generosity will get you into a lot of trouble. My gratitude increases directly as your martyr's crown. There are, I think, about two people in this country who would more or less agree with you about my work, and neither of them dares to say so. There's a hard, cold, bitter time coming for you.

"I remember that I promised you 'Going Home.' I also recall that the witness neglected to fill in the lines stating Occupation and Place of Residence.

"I had reserved a copy for you. It is a copy in a special form of which Laurie did some to please me, and better than the ordinary edition. The only reason I have not sent it is that I shirk doing up parcels. But your self-sacrifice in the *Daily Express* settles it, and the book goes to you to-day.

"I fear I can't get down to Rottingdean for the week-end. I can't leave this house absolutely unoccupied, for there are burglarious people about here, and I've not yet been able to fix up a care-taking arrangement. Mrs. Ray, my housekeeper, says that she simply dare not be alone in a house all night, and she thinks it 'hardly right' for me to do it. (This was not intended as an invitation.) But I will come to see you when you are in London.

"Also you will come to see me here and to inspect the small box in which I live as a hermit. The question is whether Garnett and you have the moral courage to face a cold supper. Also, as I have no servant at all in the evening, it's rather a picnic. Still, strong people have done it and have not only survived but have been through the ordeal again. . . .

"For sheer length and nothing but length this letter beats the Epistle to the Hebrews.

"And again very many thanks for that article. It should do me a lot of good.

"Yours ever,
BARRY PAIN"

Shortly after this *The Bookman* devoted a special number to his work, and the editor, St. John Adcock, invited me to write the chief article in it. I had done a series of special articles for them on Landor, Carlyle, Swinburne and others, and it seemed that something should be done about a master of the contemporary short story, who in his best work challenges comparison with the best of Daudet, and in several instances goes considerably deeper.

My wife and I spent the summer at Veules-les-Roses in Normandy. At that time, and I hope it may still be so, it was a tiny unspoiled village with a stream running through it, and with the wild-flowers that Linnaeus called *tectorum* growing on the roofs of the cottages. It was a haunt of artists, and there was a group of these who used to gather on the beach in the forenoon, while one of their number, chosen by lot, went into the primitive little casino to try his luck at the roulette table. If he was successful enough they all had lunch in the casino dining-room. If unsuccessful they took bread and cheese on the beach.

I tried to persuade Barry to visit us. His reply contained better news about his work:

"*Nash's Magazine* editor has now gone definitely mad. But I don't want this to be generally known, as the good man has gone mad about my work; he has also managed to infect to some extent the editor of the American *Cosmopolitan.* The result is that I'm commissioned to write six stories of 6,000 words for *Nash's* and the *Cosmopolitan* is to have the option to take any of them. It won't take any of them, for I don't understand the American public, have never suited it and am not likely to begin now at my advanced age. But if it did take one I should get £165 from the two magazines for it. Which has never happened to me before.

"The result is that I sit wondering whether I'll have a Rolls-Royce or a Daimler, when I ought really to be doing the work.

"A further proof of the editorial insanity is that the excellent idiot commissioned me to write a serious poem of sixteen lines on Christmas for his Christmas number. Nobody ever commissioned me to write a serious poem before. I did the thing and sent it off by return of post, for fear he'd change his mind or be put into an asylum.

"The six stories also are all to be serious. This temporary change from the horse-collar to the harp is pleasing. The only thing that worries me is the question whether I can do the stuff now I've got it.

"On Thursday Eva presented me with my first grand-daughter Sylvia Eckersley.* I have very good news of both of them. I imagine each one pointing at me and screaming '*Tempus abire tibi est!*'

"I was ass enough to give my good housekeeper a fortnight's holiday, and her sister has taken on the job until her return. The sister has the highest heels and the lowest intelligence known to science.

* Barry Pain's daughter Eva had married Thomas Eckersley, grandson of Thomas Henry Huxley.

She has a good heart. But she also has a plaintive voice, and I find that a plaintive voice gets on my nerves. She can make 'Will you have it poached or boiled?' sound like a funeral oration, and does. I mention this so that if I do stick a fork into her giblets, as I am daily tempted to do, you will be able to give evidence that I acted under extreme provocation. However, Mrs. Ray returns next Sunday.

"I shall have to cast a critical eye over you on your return. You will obviously be saturated with cider. You will be laden with wealth —acquired by neglecting your work and gambling at the casino. You will be an authority on Art, caused by association with painters at the said casino. Your French will be nearly perfect. I fear I must expect some moral laxity.

"This last you will be able to correct to some extent by visiting Barry Pain at his hermitage, partaking of his frugal fare and spiritual uplift, and so home by the useful though prolix Bakerloo. I have four half-tame sparrows that fly into the room. I have enough damsons on one tree to keep an entire Sunday-School in stomach-ache for six months. My pear-trees are laden. And—God forgive me!—I'm going to make sloe-gin as soon as the sloes are ripe. But that's not what I mean by spiritual up-lift. . . .

"This is such a long letter that it will be much the same thing as if I had come to Veules-les-Roses in person. I'm quite sure I should have liked it immensely, but, alas, it's not possible for me."

In spite of Barry's talk about frugal fare, he liked good wine and was something of an epicure, in the best sense of the word. On one of his birthdays a friend sent him a haunch of venison which Barry found a little too "gamy" for his taste. Knowing that another old friend enjoyed things rather gamy, Barry had it carefully repacked and sent off to him by special delivery.

By the time it arrived of course it was a little further advanced, and this friend also decided to bestow it on yet another friend who had a reputation as a gourmet. On opening the package the gourmet, disorganized even to his French, exclaimed:

"C'est plus fort que moi!"

He determined that only a real connoisseur like Barry Pain could possibly appreciate it. He sent it by express messenger, but it was too late.

Barry decided to bury it hurriedly under his damson tree, which rewarded him the following year by producing an enormous crop of fruit.

Barry Pain told me on one occasion that when Clement Shorter, Editor of the *Sphere,* was married, George Meredith, who did not know him at all well, sent him a cheque for five guineas, asking him to buy himself a wedding present. Clement Shorter added a great many more guineas of his own, purchased a handsome silver cup, and had a very affectionate inscription engraved on it, from George Meredith to his "dear old friend."

Anyone who is tempted to think that Barry Pain's inability to concentrate on his best work was entirely his own fault might well study the following letter:

"16.1.24.

"We really *must* meet soon, and after this week-end I shall fix it. You are not the only one who has much to discuss. For example:

"(1) I climbed Yorkshire hills last heat-wave, and over-strained my heart. No organic disease and normal blood pressure though I have to go slow.

"(2) My play has been turned down by most of the managers in London by now. Vedrenne very nearly did it but changed his mind at the last (he has since lost £5000 on two failures and got a nervous breakdown).

"(3) I guaranteed an overdraft for another person two years ago. The other person having failed to do as promised, I was up to be shot at. I've arranged with the Bank to the Bank's satisfaction. As this sops up my small private income, it should be a stimulus to my worst work—the only kind that sells.

"Also other things. 'My head is bloody,' as W. E. H. remarked. But I'm keeping my end up so far. And hope to continue."

About this time Barry Pain wrote to me:

"Laurie published an eighteen-penny dollop of funniments for me about a fortnight ago, but the secret has been kept splendidly. No advertisements, no reviews, and no sales. If you should see on the bookstall a little book of which the cover alone makes you sick at the stomach, that will probably be a copy of mine which has leaked out. Don't buy it, for I shall send you a copy. And when I send it, don't read it."

When I published a volume of short stories, about this time, Barry Pain wrote me a letter from which I transcribe a few sentences that I value greatly as containing the friendly criticism which certifies the sincerity of the encouragement.

"Most of these stories depart very far from what the magazine editors have decided that their public wants. They" (the editors) "have the fixed recipe for the magazine story, and would not depart from it though one rose from the dead. They are rapidly driving me mad—not because I ever read the rot they print but because I write stories for a living and find it so hard to keep within the groove prescribed. That your collection does depart from the worn-out magazine merchandise is a great attraction.

"I think 'The Wine Beyond the World' one of the best in the book. It keeps exactly in its own atmosphere throughout. Gayley and the German inn-people are life itself. It also makes a setting for a delightful poem. But on one point I would be critical—as follows:

"I have often said (not for a lust for paradox but from conviction) that nowhere is a strict accuracy of fact more essential than in a fantastic allegorical or symbolical story, just as a keen sense of humour is essential in writing the pathetic scene. So it must be true of course, for I am not a liar about work, though I do what I can about other things.

"Now about the wine itself. It is described as a red wine, also as a sparkling wine, and as very old. I know of no red sparkling wine which has repute. The life of port and of some hocks is about fifty years. The life of a sparkling wine is about twenty—perhaps a little more if the wine's robust and the corks have professional attention.

The wine that went beyond that period would probably be as nasty as Gayley and his wife found it. But you speak of 'costly bubbles,' 'bursting and evaporating'! There would be no bubbles in a sparkling wine that had exceeded the age limit—it would be dead flat.

"All of which you can put right in the next edition by very slight alterations. Alternatively, you can tell B. Pain to go to the devil.

"The last story in the book, 'The Parson's Tale,' has a curiously 'human document' effect, as if some of it at any rate were a transcript from real life. The 'Red Rat' amused me terrible—I use the verses in it to read out to people."

The only defence I could make against this criticism was that the wine in the story was not only described as very nasty, but—and this was the point of the story—a fraud.

The next month he wrote again. My book of essays, *Some Aspects of Modern Poetry,* was published at about the same time as the book of stories. He said in his letter:

"Your *Some Aspects of Modern Poetry* reached me three or four days ago but it is not a book to be read hurriedly and I have now only just finished the first reading of it. There is much to which I shall return. On most points I am in agreement with you. Poetry and every other form of art must grow as the tree grows. That which has been is essential to that which is and will be. These moderns would saw through the trunk and bring the tree down, though they have nothing whatever to put in its place. It does not scare me because the saw won't cut.

"It is an understatement to say that I look with profound suspicion on anything which would make art easier. If it makes art easier it seems to me to require no other condemnation. Why should the fences be lowered till even the donkeys can jump them?"

XXVII

The Judgment of Solomon

IN THE early twentieth century there was a time when a solitary poet, plodding his way homeward, might suddenly find he was being attacked by a furious flock of strangely coloured birds, frantically trying to peck off his nose. Perhaps it was in the hope of some fantastic excitement of this kind (with box-office results) that a Hospital Committee invited me, late in 1923, to debate, at the London School of Economics, with Miss Edith Sitwell on the comparative values of the older poetry and the "new." It seemed a worthy cause and I consented.

Sir Edmund Gosse was in the chair. He took me aside before the affair began and said he hoped I was not going to make fun of the "new" poetry: "Do not, I beg of you, use a weaver's beam on the head of poor Edith." He told me that she was in a highly nervous condition and already on the point of fainting. I assured him that nothing was further from my thoughts than to make fun of writers who had been described as "artists to their finger-tips." Gosse seemed rather nervous himself. For my own part, I was quite at a loss to understand why so much heat had been generated before a word had been said on either side. There was a general sizzling all around us.

The first open crackle was a somewhat challenging question before the proceedings began, as to whether the Sitwell supporters might all sit upon the platform. This would have made me feel a very solitary Daniel in the lions' den, since my only support could come from those who, *ex hypothesi,* were dead. I therefore said I had no objection but that I rather wished my supporters could sit there too. The answer to this was a scornful "And who are yours, pray?" I could not resist the reply: "Oh, Virgil, Horace, Dante, Chaucer, Shakespeare, Milton, Wordsworth, and a few others." It was decided, therefore, that only the speakers and the chairman should occupy the platform.

Everything about this debate was delightfully topsy-turvy. Miss Sitwell, the champion of modernity, wore a gold laurel wreath and looked remarkably like a female Dante; while I, the champion of antiquity, appeared to be "a typical American professor, wearing the horn-rimmed glasses of the New World." So said a newspaper reporter who had heard a vague rumour that I had once lectured at Princeton. I must confess that I almost felt I owed an apology to the audience for my commonplace modernity.

Miss Sitwell, remaining seated, read her address from a formidable manuscript and, through no fault or merit of mine, handed me the whole debate in her opening sentence. "In their day," she began tremulously, "Keats and Shelley were the most persecuted of poets, and" (bitterly) "Tom Moore was the most popular. In our day my brothers and I are the most persecuted of poets, and" (pointing an accusing forefinger at myself) "Mr. Noyes—" the rest was drowned in a roar of laughter from the audience. After this I had no trouble.

I punctiliously kept my promise to Gosse, and refrained from any criticism of the new poetry, confining myself simply to the thesis of Sainte Beuve that true poetry is a contemporary of all the ages.

One of the "new" theories (which I did not discuss) was that in poetry the impressions received by one sense, of sight for instance, might be rendered in terms of the other senses, hearing, taste, etc. It seemed to be a wonderful thing to be able to make a sunset neigh like a horse, or a donkey's bray smell like a rose. It was forgotten that the method had been used by much earlier poets in a more subtle way and often with great beauty. Sydney Dobell, in the nineteenth century, had likened a faint streak of colour in the evening sky to a hunter's horn heard in the distance. Swinburne had spoken of a transcendent world where "the song sung shines as a picture wrought," a really beautiful comparison. The trouble begins when something that is right and beautiful in its proper place is exaggerated into a principle for use on all occasions. It has been remarked that nearly all the heresies arise from the exaggeration of a partial truth. In a good many of my own earlier poems I had played with these transmutations:

> Music of the star-shine, shimmering o'er the sea,
> Mirror me no longer in the dusk of memory. . . .

There are five distinct transmutations in that juvenile experiment. I too, in my adolescence, had written of "meadows of dim blue grass";

> There the roses flutter their petals;
> Over the meadows they take their flight.
> There the moth that sleepily settles,
> Turns to a flower in the warm soft light.

I had intended in the debate to explain why I gave up some of these things, but in deference to Gosse and to the nervousness of Miss Sitwell, I refrained from all criticism of her school.

When it was over Edmund Gosse, with that peculiar mixture of rosy benevolence and glittering malice of which he and Anatole France possessed the secret in perfection, offered his arm to the laurelled exponent of modernity, remarking: "Come along, Edith. I have no doubt that in his day Shakespeare was thought to be mad."

A touch of comedy ensued. A man with a keen intellectual face, who had been sitting in the front row, approached and offered me his card, saying, "I thought you might like to know that I came here this afternoon to have a good look at some of your opponents. Many of my patients . . ."

Here I glanced at his card, and discovered that he was one of the most distinguished of living alienists, Dr. Norman, who presided over the institution in which poor Dan Leno had been confined.

. . . "Many of my patients," he resumed, after I had composed my countenance, "have been turning out work which I find quite indistinguishable from some of the stuff which is called modern art and poetry. Very often it seems to me an expression of what may be called mental deliquescence. Of course what we have heard this afternoon is nothing like that. But I have been interested—I really have."

A shrewd and highly intelligent Scot (Mr. J. G. Wilson, Director of Bumpus's Book Shop in Oxford Street) was standing at my elbow when this conversation took place. He gently nudged me afterwards, and remarked, "If you ever want a witness to that conversation I shall be very happy to confirm it."

A curious illustration of the topsy-turvyness in all this, and one which is quite typical, occurred in the report of the proceedings given in the *Morning Post* on the following day. Miss Sitwell had read her entire address from manuscript. I spoke, according to my usual custom, without notes of any kind and quite extemporaneously. The newspaper, however, evidently thought this was a quite improper reversal of what the public should expect, so it reported that the old-fashioned Mr. Noyes read from a ponderous manuscript, while Miss Sitwell, the champion of modernity, delivered a bright and sparkling speech.

I got a good deal of fun out of this debate. It gave me an even more cheerful moment when I left the hall, to overhear a remark made by Harold Monro, proprietor of the Poetry Bookshop and at that time an apostle of what was then believed to be the very latest. He was surrounded by a scowling little group of his own clan. "I told you how it would be," he was saying. "He is an old hand at this kind of thing."

Perhaps this explains an incident which a little later was reported to me with delight by one of the Princeton Professors. He had made the awful mistake, during a visit to England, of enquiring for some of my books at Harold Monro's Poetry Bookshop. "Have you any of Alfred Noyes' works?" he innocently asked the young woman attendant. She surveyed him from head to foot with an icy stare. "It is possible," she answered coldly. "We are broad-minded."

The Sitwells continued the debate for some time afterwards by controversial letters in the Press. Kipling referred to one of these letters as one of the most impertinent he had ever read. The fact that I refrained from criticizing any of their school was so contrary to the theory of persecution that they really could not get over it; and apparently to make up for the deprivation, a Sitwell book was advertised as "the kind of thing that will rouse Mr. Noyes to fury." But I did not take the bait.

A diverting letter from St. John Adcock describes his visit to the Women Writers' Club, where he intervened to prevent the literary proceedings developing into a free fight. He had succeeded Lobban in the editorship of *The Bookman,* and was one of the most unselfish men that the "Street of Adventure" has known, continually helping lame dogs over stiles and sometimes working himself to death for very little worldly reward. He loved literature for its own sake, and united shrewdness of judgment with a tolerance which enabled him to view the foibles and absurdities of the hour with the amusement of an impartial spectator. Something of this appears in the letter which follows:

"I'm just back from the Women Writers—an amusing evening. I had heard Edith Sitwell was to be there, but had not realised that she was guest of the evening and was to deliver an address. I was introduced to her and she was reasonably affable. I was asked to speak, but excused myself as I was not prepared, and said also I knew Miss S. was touchy and I should probably be led into saying things that would annoy her, and I did not want to spoil the atmosphere. Her address was sad nonsense. She spoke of herself as a great poet, others of her school were ditto, but the critics could not recognise it—they had not recognised great poets in any age, and out came the quotations about Keats and Shelley which you once heard.

"Well, one or two women got up (there were only five men there—and some sixty women) and were non-committal. Then a tall, shrewd-looking woman, a Miss Solomon, rose and walked into Edith with considerable ferocity; said the so-called new poets thought too much of themselves, too little of any who were not of their school; that their poetry did not deal with human beings but with puppets, things of paint and sawdust that had no life, but were moved with strings; their scenery was not of this world, but resembled nothing so much as the toy trees and such that came out of Noah's Arks; that Miss Sitwell had contradicted herself by first saying that she and the new poets imitated nobody, and later said that critics could not understand them because the critics were unacquainted with 17th and 18th century poetry, and the free-verse writers were derived from Marlowe, Dryden and Pope.

"All the while she was speaking Edith was in a state of growing rage, and kept interjecting . . . . [censored]

"Miss Solomon made no bones about accusing them (Miss S. and her followers) of crudity, vulgarity, primitive childishness, suggesting that most of what they had done might have been written by raw cave-men if they could write. When she sat down Edith was shaking with wrath and exclaimed, 'I shall not reply to that speaker, I never answer rude and insolent remarks.' There was discomfort all around. Margaret Woods, the Chairman, said she was certain Miss Solomon had not intended to be at all discourteous, that it was customary in the Club for all to speak frankly. When she sat down Edith said, 'I agree that no writer is entitled to attack others merely because they write in a different style and on different principles,' and fell sternly silent.

"So I repented and rose to point the moral and pour oil on the troubled waters. Said I had not meant to speak but felt I must say how glad I was to hear those words from Miss Sitwell. I had never been able to understand why she and her school were so bitter with and made such attacks on those writers who preferred to write mainly in classical metres. She had complained that she and her group had been called mad, but surely it looked as if they were mad when they made *that* a cause of quarrel, and they could not complain if peaceful observers thought they *were*. I hoped from her admission that she and they were coming to see that poetry might have form as well as formlessness; that the new poetry was not new, but, from the days of those ancient poets before Chaucer, had been written by this, that, and the other man all down the ages. That to say the new poetry derived from Pope amazed me, for no poet had been such a formalist, and if, as she had quoted some couplets by a brilliant unnamed new poet she meant that they had derived the couplet from Pope I was still amazed [Chaucer, Marlowe, Shakespeare, Dryden, and innumerable others had written couplets]. The whole argument seemed ridiculous—there was really nothing to argue about. Here were all the metres that ever were, invent new ones or use which you liked of them, and leave others to use one or other of them unblamed. This attacking men who use a metre or metres you could not or did not use yourself was the greatest nonsense. A poet could write poetry in any metre and should be free from attack by those who did not want to use many but just some particular one of the many poetical forms. All such squabbling was wrong and silly and ought to be ended. Why on earth all poets could not live in peace together and allow each to choose his own forms and go his own way I could not imagine. As for the critics—I noticed that some of them had been very kind to

Miss S— 'Oh, yes,' she laughed, 'some.' Well, said I, she could not be so unreasonable as to expect all of them to share her views and praise her. And when she said that no great poet had been recognised while he was alive I felt she was speaking at random, for the fact was that, with one or two exceptions, every great poet had been recognised as such by his contemporaries before he was dead, and those that had been dug up later had never been more than second to fourth rate men. It was no use thinking you could prove your own was the only way by jumping on and quarrelling with everybody who thought there were other ways, we should lose nothing by being tolerant of views and ways that were not ours and I hoped from her admission that we were going to be a little more just to each other than we had been. I said it placidly and without wrath, and she now and then nodded approval. At the finish she merely said she agreed with several things I had said, but denied that she quarrelled, said that only occasionally when somebody hit her on the head she bashed him in the face. Which I remarked was misleading and to some people looked like quarrelling, and she joined in the laugh. The Chairman made another attempt to smooth over Miss Solomon's speech, said again she was sure no offence had been intended and she apologised if Miss Sitwell had been hurt at all, but Miss Solomon always spoke frankly, it was usual in the Club, and was certainly not in intention unkind or insulting. When Edith got up to acknowledge the vote of thanks . . . [censored]."

Apparently his wise words fell on somewhat stony ground, for later the following report appeared in *The Granta* (May 22, 1925), the organ of the younger generation at Cambridge, though the younger generation appear not at all modern in the Sitwellian sense:

NOR SITWELL OUGHT IN MALICE

"Miss Sitwell's address to the 'Cam' Club on Thursday was a great social event. All the low-brows of all sexes were present, including 'Aristotle' Hale of Johns and *The Gownsman;* and a gentleman who had had the honour of being introduced to Sir Rabindranath Tagore. The former, brimming with wise saws and modern instances, was able to readjust several of Miss Sitwell's rash opinions by means of his notorious critical skill.

"Miss Sitwell concluded her paper with the words, 'I've had a lovely grumble'—an understatement, to say the least of it. She lashed right and left with her scorn, and held up to contemptuous ridicule poor Mr. Coward, that 'flapper,' that 'writer of salacious revues'; while Mr. J. C. Squire and Mr. Alfred Noyes were also among those castigated.

"In addition Miss Sitwell proved conclusively that she and her brothers are geniuses, because Keats, too, was called insane by his contemporaries.

"A most enlightening evening."

XXVIII

Shadow-of-a-Leaf

IT MAY not be always true that "the days that make us happy make us wise," but I am quite sure that from an autobiographical point of view the moments in which poetry was born were those in which I felt I was really living in the fullest sense.

From the early days in my nook above the fir woods, those moments were often associated with an imaginary character, an invisible friend, whom I called Shadow-of-a-Leaf—a kind of Ariel who could open doors into unseen worlds for me. He began simply as the companion who is often invented by children who are much alone. His name I think was derived from the leaf-shadows that flickered over the pages I read in my nook above the fir woods. He was known only to myself—a playmate in childhood, but the curious thing was that he never altogether left me; he matured as time went on, and became a companion who sometimes played the part of an invisible Touchstone. He enabled me to say with Jaques:

"Invest me in my motley; give me leave
To speak my mind."

He suggested a little series called "Touchstone on a Bus." In *The Torch-Bearers,* more seriously, he lent me his wings to pass from scene to scene through space and time. There was something fey about him, which lifted ideas out of the ruts of the work-a-day world.

I have spoken elsewhere about the curious way in which poetry sometimes anticipates events, and again and again I have found that my Shadow-of-a-Leaf was something of a prophet. It would be taking him too seriously to compare him with those indwelling daemons whom so many writers have regarded as their source of inspiration and a kind of guardian of the artistic or philosophic conscience. Perhaps his chief aid was in relieving me from the egoism, or the inhibitions, of speaking in the first person. I felt freer when he guided the pen.

It was perhaps inevitable that as a defender of tradition I should run the risk of being labelled merely *laudator temporis acti,* but this was very far from my own point of view. When Shadow-of-a-Leaf was on the scene I wanted to make all sorts of metrical experiments. I had always believed that there were unlimited possibilities for the invention of new and beautiful metrical forms, and that this was the true line of development in English poetry, as opposed to the idea that originality could be found in formlessness or by breaking the first principles of good writing. It was natural enough that my own metrical experiments should have been overlooked, even when Shadow-of-a-Leaf prompted me to put the rhyme at the beginning instead of at the end of the line, as in "Astrid." From "The Burial of a Queen," in *Tales of the Mermaid Tavern,* the lyrical passage beginning, "Many a red heart died to beat . . ." where the short lines are caught up into the longer, is perhaps the most successful of my own metrical experiments. In *The Torch-Bearers* there are others at the opening and closing of the section on Linnaeus, for instance, and in the section on Pasteur; many of them were written in the moods when I could evoke Shadow-of-a-Leaf.

The opening of Linnaeus and many other passages are in what is now called "sprung rhythm," a phrase that has been used a great deal lately, though there is really nothing new about it. The trouble is that when "sprung rhythm" occurs rightly and naturally it escapes notice, as indeed the technician should desire. When the mother of the child Linnaeus walks through her garden calling

"Carl! Carl! O, Carl! Now where is that elfkin hiding,"

the stresses are not those of the ordinary iambic line but they fall within the compass of the metrical law. Some of the modern theories about "sprung rhythm" are quite right. They are wrong when they claim that it is new. From the time of Shakespeare onward these metrical effects have entered into the technique of English poetry. The great verse, "the multitudinous seas incarnadine" certainly does not count its syllables in any mechanical fashion, but its stresses are marked by the vital pulse of poetry, which has a precision of its own. A placid sea breaking into storm does not, for all its clashing breakers, lose the great pulse of the ocean.

Shadow-of-a-Leaf entered, as an actual character, into many of my poems, the earliest of these being "The Progress of Love," which I omitted from later collections because neither I nor anybody else could understand it. This might have made it fashionable to-day, but though there were some parts of it which still please me, I was very conscious of its immaturity. There is one curious and incomprehensible passage about Shadow-of-a-Leaf in which a host of shadows call upon him to lead them through the night of intellectual doubt.

He appears again in my play *Sherwood,* of which he is in fact the chief character, asserting the final triumph of Creation over the cruelties of the conqueror, and giving up his life in order that two lovers might enter the "shining glen."

In 1924 I published a book entitled *Songs of Shadow-of-a-Leaf.* The most complete portrait of him is in a lyric which I append here as a psychological curiosity. Looking back on it now, I feel that in its final prayer it anticipates something of which I was unconscious at the time, since it was written long before I became a Catholic.

Elf-blooded creature, little did he reck
 Of this blind world's delights,
Content to wreathe his legs around his neck
 For warmth on winter nights;

Content to ramble away
Through his deep woods in May;
  Content, alone with Pan, to observe his forest rites.

Or, cutting a dark cross of beauty there
  All out of a hawthorn-tree,
He'd set it up, and whistle to praise and prayer
  Field-mouse and finch and bee;
And, as the woods grew dim,
Brown squirrels knelt with him,
  Paws to blunt nose, and prayed as well as he.

For, all his wits being lost, he was more wise
  Than aught on earthly ground.
Like haunted woodland pools his great dark eyes
  Where the lost stars were drowned,
Saw things afar and near.
'Twas said that he could hear
  The music of the spheres which had no sound.

And so, through many an age and many a clime,
  He strayed on unseen wings;
For he was fey, and knew not space or time,
  Kingdoms or earthly kings.
Clear as a crystall ball
One dew-drop showed him all,—
  Earth and its tribes, and strange translunar things.

But to the world's one May, he made in chief
  His lonely woodland vow,
Praying—as none could pray but Shadow-of-a-Leaf,
  Under that fresh-cut bough
Which with two branches grew,
Dark, dark, in sun and dew,—
  "The world goes maying. Be this my maypole now!

"Make me a garland, Lady, in thy green aisles
  For this wild rood of may,
And I will make thee another of tears and smiles
  To match thine own, this day.
For every rose thereof
A rose of my heart's love,
  A blood-red rose that shall not waste away.

"For every violet here, a gentle thought
To worship at thine eyes;
But, most of all, for wildings few have sought,
And careless looks despise,
For ragged-robins' birth
Here, in a ditch of earth,
A tangle of sweet prayers to thy pure skies."

Bird, squirrel, bee, and the thing that was like no other,
Played in the woods that day,
Talked in the heart of the woods, as brother to brother,
And prayed as children pray,—
Make me a garland, Lady, a garland, Mother,
For this wild rood of may.

XXIX

Some London Friends

BETWEEN 1918 and 1926 Garnett and I spent many months of the year in London, at 85 Cadogan Gardens, where we had taken a flat immediately opposite St. Mary's Catholic Church. From the balcony of the flat we occasionally saw religious processions entering the doors of the Church where, little as I knew it then, I was later to be received.

I think that in those years at Cadogan Gardens we saw the last and best of a London life that was finally disrupted by the second world war. The recovery from the first world war had been quicker than anyone supposed possible. The pathological symptoms which followed the second, in art, music and literature, had not yet appeared to any serious extent. Grief and bitterness were there, bound up in many hearts and minds, but not the cynical despair of to-day.

Many good friends came to see us in those days at Cadogan Gardens, among them Wilfrid and Alice Meynell, Claude Shepperson, Barry Pain, Lord and Lady Charnwood, the Dowager Lady Jersey (who had reminiscences of her visit to Stevenson in the South Seas), Lord and Lady Hewart, Shane Leslie, Sir Owen Seaman, Edmund Gosse, Sir Alfred East, J. C. Squire, W. B. Maxwell, Sir Frank Dicksee, and Ambrose McEvoy.

I greatly admired some of McEvoy's work, but his method of finishing some of his water colours, however effective it might be in the mystification of his admirers, seemed to me too fortuitous for art. It amused me one day in his studio to find him "finishing" one of these water colours by holding it under a tap of running water. "For me the mists of Turner swim," said Andrew Lang, speaking of his own short sight; but he would hardly have wished them to swim under the tap.

I had very pleasant "contacts" at this time with several members of the *Punch* set. Claude Shepperson, at whose house in Chelsea we dined to meet Gerald du Maurier, made a delightful portrait of Garnett, and I wrote a preface to the catalogue of one of his exhibitions. Dum-Dum was among the writers in *Punch* whose criticism I greatly valued. He wrote a long article in *Blackwood's Magazine* on my first collected volume of poems. He had a peculiar gift of writing humorous verse in the "grand style," and I have always thought that the opening of his ode to his own sense of humour had the authentic touch:

> Come not as thou wast ever wont to come,
> Making a scandal of thy saving grace.

I could have made that appeal myself, perhaps, when *Punch* discovered a misprint in one of my peace poems in the *Irish Times*. My verses had depicted a family dreaming of the home-coming of their soldier from the wars, while

> All night he lies beneath the stars,
> And dreams no more out there.

The *Irish Times* printed it as

> All night he lies beneath the stairs,

and made matters worse by adding, "Only a true artist could achieve this effect of quietly hopeless tragedy." *Punch* seized upon this, and said that if I could express a wish for the New Year, it would probably be to meet the Editor of the *Irish Times.* Oddly enough, a week or two later I found myself sitting next to him at a public dinner, and, as an opening gambit in our conversation, remarked that we had recently met in *Punch.* To my surprise he blushed violently, and said something about having dismissed two printers, that it was the fourth time during the last month or two he had found himself in *Punch.*

The misprint, however, was not so affecting as one that happened to my friend Hermann Hagedorn, the American poet and biographer of Theodore Roosevelt. One of the best magazines in America published a poignant little poem by Hagedorn in which two lovers part forever on a hill-top. The pathetic last line, which should have read, "And left me alone with the dusk," was transformed by the change of a single letter into a masterpiece of modernity:

And left me alone with the duck.

In September 1927 I was elected President of the Johnson Society. The gathering at Litchfield, his birthplace, was a large one. In my address (afterwards reprinted in my book *The Pageant of Letters*) the "originality" of Dr. Johnson was the main theme. No character in history had been more individual and none had made a more pregnant criticism of the mere hunters for novelty. Of those who preferred superficial novelty to sincerity or the deeper things of the spirit, he said: "It will readily be inferred that *they were not successful in representing or moving the affections.*" One of the most striking characteristics of certain classes of literature of the present day is that you may search them from end to end without finding a hint that any human affection ever existed.

Once or twice during this period I lectured at the City Temple, which gave me two of the best audiences I have had in England. Each numbered about two thousand. Several times I also gave readings of poetry at St. Martin's-in-the-Fields, when Dick Sheppard and Pat McCormick successively presided. Both of these men had great kindly hearts and a rich sense of humour. Pat McCormick told me someone had been spreading a rumour that he was about to divorce his wife, and one of his lady parishioners had written to the Bishop asking him, in view of this promising event, to suggest her own eligibility for the vacant position.

These two parsons followed to the letter Chaucer's description of a good pastor:

> Christès loore, and his Apostles twelve
> He taught, but first he folwed it hym selve.

In 1926 the tercentenary of Francis Bacon was celebrated, and I was invited by the *Sunday Times* to write an article for the occasion. It happened that while I was writing *The Torch-Bearers* I had carefully read his works, including the *Natural History,* which I suppose few even of his keenest admirers read to-day. The article I wrote was therefore extremely sceptical about his claims to be regarded as the "father of modern science," and the inventor of what he called the "New Organ"—the very ancient method of inductive reasoning.

My article drew some interesting letters. Rather to my surprise Edmund Gosse (who was in full agreement) sent me a blessing from George Moore, of all people in the world. Lord Darling wrote: "I spent yesterday in reading about Lord Bacon—and it seems to me that you are right in thinking he has been too much revered. I didn't find that he depreciated Harvey—but he seems to have completely ignored him—and he died only half suspecting that frost will retard putrefraction. For all that, I admire his essays—which is about all that I had hitherto read of his works—of course I omit *Hamlet, A Midsummer Night's Dream,* the *Sonnets,* and such unconsidered trifles."

Belloc was in cordial agreement and amused me by writing (as if he had actually seen and known Bacon through and through), "I like your chiding of Bacon. He was a dreadful skunk, and no one ever underlines that. You do well to emphasize his eyes."

For this detail I had relied on the report of Harvey himself, who, after an interview in which Bacon had dismissed his perfectly sound theory, remarked, "He had the eye of a viper."

The apotheosis of Bacon by Macaulay (he quite seriously compared Bacon's beneficence with that of the Deity) seemed to me a typical illustration of the way in which a great public position may create false values, endow its holder with gifts that are not his own, and make a great philosopher out of a corrupt lawyer.

The fact that Bacon had actually dismissed the greatest scientific discoveries of his own day, ridiculing Galileo's telescope; declaring that the earth could not move since this was against the general opinion of mankind; dismissing Harvey's "circulation of the blood" for the same reason; and affirming that warts could be cured by nailing a piece of mutton-fat outside your bedroom window—all these things had been overlooked in the acceptance of a famous name, and some harm had been done to modern thought by Macaulay's suggestion that the methods of Bacon had somehow made an end of deductive reasoning, reasoning from those first principles or postulates without which all thinking is chimerical. It was just here, in fact, that the world took its most fatal step in the direction of universal scepticism. For immediate practical purposes the inductive method is valuable. Its beneficent results, as Lord Macaulay pointed out, include the invention of gunpowder—and we may now add the atomic bomb. But when Macaulay dismissed the whole of Greek philosophy as worthless because deduced from first principles instead of ascending from particular facts (like Lord Bacon's warts, which diminished as the mutton fat melted in the sun), he was rendering a great disservice both to humanism and the higher intellectual life of mankind.

All this had a direct bearing on my final acceptance of the *philosophia perennis,* a philosophy in great part "deduced" from the most certain of all postulates.

XXX

Conversion

WHEN IN 1927 I was received into the Catholic Church it was no sudden "conversion" but the end of a long process of thought, something of which is recorded in my book *The Unknown God,* and in some sections of *The Torch-Bearers.*

In early days I had unconsciously adopted from a Protestant environment a feeling that there was something sinister about the Church of Rome. John Noyes, a direct forebear, was burned at the stake in the reign of Mary Tudor, for denying the Real Presence. Two of my father's three brothers were extremely Low Church Anglican clergymen, and each had presented me with a photograph of John Noyes' tomb, by way of encouragement; while the third, who was rather High Church (at St. George's, Hanover Square) also presented it to me, perhaps by way of warning. Both the Low Church uncles, in their letters, would strike little ominous notes about the views of their High Church brother, in terms which made me feel that there must be something very dangerous in his ritual.

One of the Low Church uncles was for fifteen years chaplain to the British Embassy Church in Paris, and preached several times before King Edward VII. The first occasion was shortly after the Boer War, when the English were not at all popular in Paris. The *Figaro* gave a somewhat startling account of what it called King Edward's visit to God: *"Le roi de la Grande-Bretagne et d'Irelande et des possessions britanniques d'outremer, defenseur de la foi, empereur des Indes, va faire-visite à Dieu."* There was an even more astonishing remark about the Lord's Prayer: *"C'est la prière que nous ne savons plus."* More serious, apparently, was what appeared to the *Figaro* the failure of my uncle to observe the Real Presence: "*. . . Enfin les chants ayant cessés le Rev. Dr. Noyes se lêve et prononce le sermon dominical. . . . et l'office termine . . . par un dernier cantique, sans que aucune allusion aie été faite à la presence du Roi.*"

In spite of this, and the sermons to King Edward VII, my uncle's second son, Major-General Eric Noyes, became A.D.C. to King George V.

My uncle took great pleasure in showing me a small metal figure of Our Lady which opened in front like a cupboard, revealing a number of sharp spikes within. He explained that this was a miniature model of a figure in which the Inquisition used to incarcerate its victims. The subsequent crushing and spiking process, he said with some gusto, was known as "the embrace of the Virgin."

Although my uncle had shown me this awful effigy, his sons had no clerical inhibitions. One of them, Cyril, felt no qualms at becoming a godfather of my daughter Margaret, though the christening was at St. James's Church, Spanish Place. In crisp military language, Cyril expressed the opinion that it was better for me to be a good Catholic than a bad Protestant. I don't know what he had done with the effigy, but when he and his wife visited us at Lisle Combe he showed me nothing worse than the battered old diary* of another Anglican forebear who had served as chaplain in Marlborough's army in Flanders. Its very terse and practical entries were more concerned with night marches and military manoeuvres than with any religious views.

Cyril died on his way home from India in 1946.

The Times in its obituary memoir (Mar. 12, 1946) said:

> General Sir Cyril Dupré Noyes, K.C.S.I., C.B., C.I.E., M.C., third son of the late Rev. H. E. Noyes, D.D., . . . saw active service in the Naval Operations, Persian Gulf, 1912-13, and during the 1914-1918 war he served on the Suez Canal and in Mesopotamia. . . . He also fought in the Third Afghan War, and took part in the Mohmand operations, 1933. . . . He was a graduate of the Imperial Defence College, and held many important appointments in India. . . . In the 1939-45 war he . . . became G.O. C.-in-C., Northern India.

A further note in *The Times* said:

> Noyes was a big man in every sense of the word . . . efficient, unassuming, imperturbable and tireless. Disloyalty, jealousy, self-advertisement and self-indulgence were abhorrent to him. Devotion to duty was his watchword. He always played for the cause—for himself never. In his long and varied Army career, Noyes rendered notable service, [particularly] the remarkable contribution that he made in pre-war days towards the development of the tactics of close support between the Army and Air Force which served us so well in the late war.

My uncle Robert Noyes, who became Archdeacon of Achonnry, Ireland, in 1902, seldom wrote a letter without expressing his Calvinistic convictions. His wife, Mary Rowley, was a sister of my mother. The Rowleys were proud of the fact that, like the man in Belloc's poem, they bore their "father's grandfer's father's father's name." They traced their descent from the Rowleys of Rowley, who had

* This diary of Dr. Noyes, Fellow of King's College, Cambridge, is quoted by Winston Churchill as one of the MS. sources in his *Marlborough: His Life and Times,* Vol. II.

retained lands in Shropshire from before the Conquest. One of them, William Rowley, was "inclined to the tenets of Puritanism," and was sequestered by the King's party in 1638 for high treason. Perhaps in atonement for this, in 1747 another of my mother's forebears, Roger Rowley, an out-and-out Roundhead, is recorded as having purchased from the sequestrators appointed by Parliament the estates of Sir William Whitmore, who was of the King's party. This is one of those curious coincidences in the pattern of life; for Frances, sister of Sir William Whitmore, was married to one of my wife's ancestors, Sir John Weld, who raised a troop of horse for King Charles and matched my Roundhead at his own game by writing a Catholic treatise on certain divine principles, the manuscript of which is now in our library. The portrait of Frances, by Janssen, hangs at Lisle Combe next to that of her cavalier husband, but I fancy sometimes that she looks at me with a rather cold eye.

William Rowley is spoken of by Richard Baxter as "my very dear friend Mr. William Rowley, a gentleman of Shrewsbury." Richard Baxter lent him books on non-conformity, "which had the effect of indisposing him still further to the establishment."

The east window in St. Leonard's Church, Bridgenorth, is dedicated to the memory of one of my mother's forebears, Thomas Rowley, D.D., Master of the Bridgenorth Grammar School, by subscriptions of his former pupils. During Dr. Rowley's time the grammar school had a great reputation. Among these former pupils were two who became Anglican Bishops, one of whom, Bishop James Fraser, had won the Ireland scholarship in 1839 and a fellowship at Oriel in 1840.

Despite the Protestant feelings engendered by this background, there were certain curious contradictions in my innocent hostility to Catholicism. When I was about fourteen, my Aunt Anne, my godmother (whom I always regarded as a real saint), sent me various religious books, including the *Confessions* of St. Augustine, Thomas à Kempis, and Dean Goulburn's *Thoughts on Personal Religion*. These three books were like three gates into that walled city of whose existence I had hitherto been only dimly aware. I remember feeling a certain shock of surprise that so devout a Protestant as my Aunt Anne should have sent me Dean Goulburn's book, for it had passages in which I seemed to detect the smell of incense. But there was something else—a rich illumination of ideas which had hitherto lain dormant, though they were implicit in the Creed which I heard every Sunday. The little edition of *De Imitatione Christi* (the Latin text) which she sent me was edited by P. Cælestinus Wolfsgruber, *presbyter monasterii Benedictinorum,* and I marked many passages in it, one of them for a striking resemblance to lines in Shakespeare's *Tempest:*

> The powers, delaying, not forgetting, have
> Incensed the seas and shores, yea, all the creatures,
> Against your peace.

This conception of the divine governance of the universe impressed me as almost a paraphrase of *"Quia autem frequenter et graviter peccavi tibi, merito armatur contra me omnis creatura."*

I soon became aware of something that has been expressed to perfection by Walter Pater:

"There is a venerable system of sentiment and idea, widely extended in time and place, in a kind of impregnable possession of human life—a system which, like some other great products of the conjoint efforts of human mind through many generations, is rich in the world's experience; so that, in attaching oneself to it, one lets in a great tide of that experience, and makes, as it were with a single step, a great experience of one's own, and with great consequent increase to one's sense of colour, variety, and relief, in the spectacle of men and things."

Biologists tell us that each individual recapitulates in little the whole evolutionary process, and I suppose this may be true to a certain extent in the mental life. Of this process, in the perennial philosophy of the Catholic Church, Pater said in another passage, which quite early made a great impression on me:

"In a generous eclecticism, within the bounds of her liberty, and as by some providential power within her, she gathers and serviceably adopts, as in other matters so in ritual, one thing here, another there, from various sources—Gnostic, Jewish, Pagan—to adorn and beautify the greatest act of worship the world has seen. It was thus the liturgy of the Church came to be—full of consolations for the human soul, and destined, surely, one day, under the sanction of so many ages of human experience, to take exclusive possession of the religious consciousness.

Tantum ergo sacramentum
Veneremur cernui:
Et antiquum documentum
Novo cedat ritui.

Looking back I can see now that in little I was experiencing this process within myself.

My reading had been extremely "eclectic," and I had no difficulty in adjusting the focus of my mind to the very different fields of vision offered by Darwin and the Bible, St. John and Voltaire, Baudelaire and George Herbert.

A great man of science once remarked that when he said his prayers he locked the door of his laboratory. He did not mean that science and religion were irreconcilable, but simply that the focus of the mind must be adjusted to entirely different fields of vision. The not very profound truth of the anatomist that there is a skull beneath the skin is not a contradiction of what one sees in the face of a friend.

With all this varied reading, I seemed to be increasingly conscious that, with due allowance for differences in the field of vision, there were many truths that at first sight appeared to be contradictory, yet in a complete synthesis might be perfectly compatible. The pessimist who insists that dust returns to dust is in complete accord with Ecclesiastes and the ritual of Ash Wednesday on that particular point.

All this time I was moving along the road to the perennial philosophy of the *Civitas Dei.* There are indications of this not only in "Acceptances" (with which I have dealt in a previous chapter), but also in "The Burial of a Queen" (in *Tales of the Mermaid Tavern*) both of which were written in 1911.

In the first volume of my *Torch-Bearers,* published in 1922, there were many lines leading in the same direction, and a suggestion of the way in which the discoveries of science were all eventually brought into harmony with the acceptances of religion. There were many of these in the section on that Canon of the Church, Copernicus, and also in the section on Galileo. In the former I made Copernicus answer those who thought that his new Universe, glittering against the still unfathomed darkness, would destroy the *Civitas Dei:*

> . . . If the poor light we win
> Confuse or blind us, to the Light of lights,
> Let all our wisdom perish. I affirm
> A greater Darkness, where the one true Church
> Shall, after all her agonies of loss
> And many an age of doubt, perhaps, to come
> See this processional host of splendours burn
> Like tapers round her altar.

There were many other milestones on the road, and one very clearly marked, when in 1926 Garnett and I visited the Monastery at Roncesvalles a week before she died. We had been staying at St. Jean de Luz. As we left the Chapel at Roncesvalles she said: "It has almost made me wish that I were a Catholic," and she said it with a depth of feeling that made a lasting impression on me, for she came of a New England Puritan stock and when we were in England she had gone regularly to communion at an Anglican church. Occasionally, though not often, she had been troubled by a doubt, inculcated, I think, by certain Anglican waverings on the central clause of the Christian Creed. Once she asked me if I myself felt certain of that central clause, and asked me as if she wanted my poor help to confirm her own faith. I have always thanked God that I was able to answer in the affirmative.

A week later she died very suddenly. She knew that the end was near, but she had kept this knowledge from me, and it was not until some months later that I discovered she had known.

The house in which we were staying at St. Jean de Luz was on a little hill-top overlooking a valley. It belonged to Catholics, and in the untended wilderness of its garden there was a small household chapel. On the side of the house facing the sea there was a niche in which there stood a statue of Our Lady; and I have always felt that these things were not accidental, and that one half of my life was intended to close there.

It was several years before I could record something of this in the lines appended to *The Last Voyage,* at the end of *The Torch-Bearers:*

Under the Pyrenees,
  Where the warm sea-wind drifts thro' tamarisk boughs,
There is a lonely house upon a hill-top
  That I shall never forget or see again.

I shall not see that garden, filled with roses,
  On the high sun-burnt plateau, girdled round
With that low parapet, on the lonely hill-top,
  By sunlight, or by moonlight, ever again.

In that lost garden stands a little chapel,
  And the strange ship wherein we made our voyage,
Our little mortal ship of thoughts and visions
  Hangs there, in chains, before the twilit altar.

The doors are locked. The lamp is quenched for ever;
Though, at one corner of the house, Our Lady
  Looks out, across the valley, to the sea.

And, on the landward side, across a valley,
  Purple as grapes in autumn, the dark mountains,
With peaks like broken swords, and splintered helmets,
  Remembering Roland's death, are listening still.

Look down, look down, upon the sunlit valley,
  Over the low white parapet of that garden;
And you shall see the long white road go winding
  Through the Basque vineyards. . . .

But you shall not see
One face, nor shall you hear one voice that whispered
  Love, as it died. . . .
Only one wooden Image
Knows where she knelt, among the lonely mountains
  At Roncesvalles, in one last prayer for me. . . .

A year later, I was received into the Catholic Church.

XXXI

Reception into the Church

OF THE year that followed Garnett's death I can add nothing to what I have said in *The Last Voyage,* which unconsciously embodied, in a transmuted form, much of my own experience at the time.

The scene of the poem was a ship in mid-Atlantic, on which all the resources of science were being used to save the life of a child on whom an operation had become necessary. The ship's surgeon was receiving advice by wireless from other ships and from a great hospital on the mainland. Various sections of the poem dealt with the scientific discoverers in past ages who were contributing their own aid through the distances of time, as these others were contributing through the distances of space. They did not save the child's life, and this led to the final question of the book, on the ultimate haven of man's last voyage, so that what had been begun as a poem on the great moments of scientific discovery ended where all the lines of human thought end—in the Supreme Reality which transcends all human science.

The dedication of this poem records my final acceptance of the *philosophia perennis.*

I went first to see the Dominican Father Vincent McNabb, and had several long talks with him. I was not sure how far certain scientific doctrines which I believed to be true might be accounted heretical by Catholic theologians; and when I discovered that the best Catholic theologians believed these doctrines themselves, with just that something more that allows the mind to make sense of the universe, I saw my way quite clearly.

A few weeks later, I was received by Bishop Bidwell at St. Mary's, Cadogan Street, immediately opposite the flat where I had spent so many happy years.

On the morning when I was received the door of the Presbytery was opened to me by the sister of Joseph Conrad, and as I passed from the Presbytery into the Church, the striking of a clock seemed to emphasize for me the decisive finality of the step I was taking.

Algernon Cecil once remarked that when he became a Catholic he expected to feel a certain isolation in England, but to his great surprise he found himself a member of an immense army. That army is composed, of course, not only of the great company on earth, but of the much wider communion of the *Civitas Dei.*

My own experience was of the same kind. On earlier visits to Canada and the United States, for instance, I had spoken in many cities which apparently belonged to an almost exclusively contemporary world. When I visited these countries as a Catholic, I became aware for the first time of a great world behind the superficial scene, a world that belonged to the ages and held the keys to the treasure-house of history. I found a great Cathedral in New Orleans packed five times a day between the frescoed walls, that told the history of Saint Louis and breathed not "the last enchantments of the Middle Ages" but the ever-living spirit of a continuing city embodied on earth in Christendom.

It was like recovering one's memory after a long period of aphasia; and it was also the recovery of the road that not only ran back through history, but went forward to the ultimate end for which man was made. There was a sense in which it rejuvenated the whole world, and brought to life a thousand characters that had hitherto been only faded figures in a historical tapestry.

In England it gave a new significance to the ruins of Glastonbury and Tintern, a new meaning to Westminster Abbey itself, and even to Christmas, for modern England has forgotten that the Abbey once implied an Abbot, and that Christmas was once the Mass of Christ. It was a renaissance of the mind, in which the literature and philosophy of all the ages acquired a new and vital beauty. As Alice Meynell wrote:

> All joy is young, and new all art,
> And He too, Whom we have by heart.

There is a sun around which the whole universe moves. It does not try to be original, for it is itself the origin. It does not need to be modern, for it is older than time, and new every morning.

XXXII

Science and Credulity

AN EMINENT English Judge once suggested to me that an interesting book might be written on the Credulity of Unbelief. Those who believe in the perennial philosophy may have this advantage over the contemporary world: they can afford to be completely sceptical about most of the fashionable ideas and superstitions, even those which are sometimes labelled scientific. Mr. W. B. Yeats wrote some very fine poetry, but when he described in detail some of the remarkable things he saw in a crystal ball, I was completely sceptical.

Much ridicule has been poured upon the mediaeval scholastics and their debate as to how many angels could stand on the point of a needle. Very little cross-examination, however, has been inflicted on the modern scholastics who talk of the millions of planetary systems that can revolve within the head of a pin. If they are right, as they probably are, it might at least have occurred to them that there was something to be said for the mediaeval scholastics, who had the excuse that spiritual beings, like thought itself, are not conditioned by spatial dimensions. The modern scholastics, on that point (the only one that seemed ridiculous to the critics of the old scholasticism) had no such easy way out. Eddington, in fact, made it very clear, in one of the most delightful books of this generation, that the formulas of science are merely working formulas, and must not be taken as a pictorial representation of reality, any more than the shorthand notes of a speech could be taken as a picture of Mr. Winston Churchill's face when he is expressing his views on modern art at an Academy banquet.

When Einstein wrote about religion, he revealed in a surprising and almost startling way the limitations of his mind, and its real inferiority to that of Eddington. Einstein was apparently quite unacquainted with any philosophy of religion, and when he solemnly told religious thinkers that they must get rid of their idea of a personal God, it became apparent that Einstein really thought the God of the New Testament and of St. Augustine was an old Hebrew gentleman, probably with a white beard. If he had only read a chapter of the *Confessions* which soars from height to transcendental height until it comes upon "That Which *Is*," he might have confined himself to his unquestionably more mathematical task of demonstrating that Euclid was wrong and that parallel lines may meet as soon as they cease to be parallel, i. e., at an infinite distance; for infinite in a mathematical sense meaning no end, these lines do naturally meet at no end. All kinds of complicated mathematical formulas may be drawn up which, to the unwary, may convey the strange conviction that meeting at no end (infinity) is really different from not meeting at any end. The supplanters of Euclid have even used an optical illusion (the way in which railway lines appear to converge in the distance) to support their case with the credulous layman. I am simple enough still to believe that $2 \times 2 = 4$.

When people talk of "bounded space" I am not altogether content with the old answer of Pasteur in his address to the French Academy: "What lies beyond?" I am sceptical enough to ask, first of all, what we mean by the word "space," and whether it is anything but a relationship between one thing and another. In any case, I hold to those axioms for lack of which, as it seems to me, our modern world is ceasing to be able to think honestly and clearly. I still believe that the shortest distance between two points is in a straight line. I find that not only my reason but my religion depends on the certainty that you cannot evolve plus out of minus, or Beethoven out of a cloud of hydrogen gas (the primal nebula) unless you have a very big plus working through the whole process.

Believing these things I find that I am completely sceptical about much that seems acceptable to the contemporary mind, especially when that mind has broken away from the foundations of thought. Even among men of a very high intellectual capacity there is an apparent blindness to logical fallacies which in any other age would have been possible only to the half-baked.

Sir William Crookes and Sir Oliver Lodge were quite sincere in their attempts to demonstrate the realities of the spiritual world by scientific experiment, and they were men of great distinction and great achievement in their own fields; but a personal experience that I had with Sir Oliver Lodge convinced me that the very qualities which had given him pre-eminence in the scientific search for truth had made him an easier victim of skillful manipulators of evidence. The scientist whose aim is truth does not expect the assistants in his laboratory to play tricks with his apparatus, or to fake reports. Sir Oliver Lodge was a believer in the reality of the spiritual world; his belief that its reality could be demonstrated by physical experiment was neither illogical nor entirely out of accord with the older idea that the invisible things of God may be learned through the visible world around us. The method of his physical experiment, however, was a little too like that of the atheist who took out his watch and challenged God to strike him dead within ten seconds, or else admit His non-existence. It was of course His existence and the existence of the spiritual world that Sir Oliver Lodge was anxious to demonstrate.

He was one of the great pioneers of wireless telegraphy. This, in some of its aspects, comes nearer to what may be called the physically miraculous than anything known to his scientific predecessors. Marconi, who adapted the ideas of Lodge to practical purposes, wrote as if wireless telegraphy made it easier for him to believe in profounder forms of communication. He wrote:

"Every scientist knows that there are mysteries which science will never be able to solve.

"Faith alone, faith in the Supreme Being whose rule we must obey, alone can help us to face with courage and strength the great mystery of life.

"It is a mistake to believe that faith and science can never exist together. Science cannot kill faith. The two stand side by side, for there are boundaries beyond which faith alone can sustain and comfort us.

"I am proud of saying that I am a Christian and a believer. I believe in the power of prayer. I believe in it not only as a devout Catholic but as a scientist.

"A wireless set no bigger than your hand can transmit messages across the ocean, but the human brain is something far more intricate than anything ever devised by man. The wireless set sends out vibrations to their destinations; is it not reasonable to believe that this greater miracle, this super-set, which is called the human brain, may send out vibrations in the form of prayer which, too, reach their destination?"

It should be remarked, moreover, that in this latter case there are no distances of space to be overcome, since the communication is to One in Whom we live and move and have our being.

Sir Oliver Lodge himself, in certain chapters which he wrote on the ether, illuminated in a very remarkable way not only what St. Paul said of the spiritual body, but also what was said of a certain Figure entering through a locked door into the room where the disciples were sitting. There is a great deal more in what Lodge said than has yet been discovered by men of science, or by the credulous and superficial people whose attention is concentrated on Sludge the Medium, with his box of conjuring tricks.

When Sir Oliver and Lady Lodge asked me to stay for a week-end at their house near Salisbury I felt intuitively that I was in for an experiment. He had written a very generous letter to *The Times* about my *Watchers of the Sky* not long before; but, from one or two things he said to me, I thought I detected a hint that, as poets did not usually acquire such scientific information, the ghost of Galileo or Herschel might have been talking to me. In one sense it was flattering to myself, but not altogether satisfactory that the credit of my poem should be given to those ghostly men of science. However, it was only a suspicion.

My premonition of an impending experiment was confirmed when I arrived at Sir Oliver's Wiltshire home. He may have thought poets were good instruments for psychical research, and I think he was puzzled by my adherence to strict logic. Perhaps as a concession to this he took me first of all to his very fine laboratory, a large room elaborately equipped with scientific apparatus. He showed me how the atom was "bombarded," and many other things which certainly demonstrated that Sir Oliver knew his way about the physical world as well as anyone living.

It was all the more startling, therefore, when he proceeded to show me some photographs that he said he had taken and developed himself. In these photographs some rather ghastly apparitions appeared to be standing behind a group of the Lodge family. I was not quite satisfied, however, with the provenance of the films or plates from which these pictures had been developed, and I asked him what direct personal experience of his own he had found most convincing. Sir Oliver then told me of an incident which he describes in one of his books as conclusive:

When he was living in Birmingham some of the Lodge family went to see a very efficient medium in London, through whom they hoped to have a long conversation with their brother Raymond. During their absence the rest of the family at Birmingham decided to communicate with Raymond and ask him to mention the word "Honolulu" to those in London.

A complete record of the London conversation was brought back to Birmingham and showed that the word Honolulu had been used several times.

The facts as stated were remarkable. The flaw in the "conclusive" evidence was that Raymond was very fond of a song with a refrain about Honolulu and that this refrain very frequently entered into their conversations with him. Sir Oliver did not conceal this fact. Indeed he mentions it in his book, but for some strange reason he does not mention it in connection with this story or in any way that would call attention to the flaw in the argument. I suggested that if the group in Birmingham had chosen the word "Timbuctoo" it might have been more effective, and I am afraid Sir Oliver began to regard me as an incurable sceptic.

Nevertheless the next evening, one of the most creepy I have ever experienced, he told me that when he and Lady Lodge were alone together queer things occasionally happened. It did not seem very reasonable for spiritual beings to frighten people by moving furniture about; but I understood that the sofa had once behaved very affectionately to Lady Lodge. Some of the alleged attempts seemed to be quite grotesque, but Sir Oliver had his own answers to that. "If you were a ship-wrecked sailor on a raft, you might try to attract attention in any way you could."

Then after dinner the creepy evening began. I was the only guest in the house. Sir Oliver was a man of gigantic stature; his face reminded one of Darwin, and his conversation, terse and precise, continually seemed to be hinting at some formidable occult secret of which he preferred not to speak. It was obvious that they were expecting something to happen. Whether a communication was to come from Galileo or Herschel I was not sure. In the drawing-room Lady Lodge lay on a sofa, without speaking; Sir Oliver sat in a large armchair on the other side of the room, hiding his face behind a newspaper, and I sat between them in another armchair.

From time to time Sir Oliver would steal a glance, without speaking, first at Lady Lodge and then at me, and sometimes in a sort of stealthy survey of the room, after which he would again hide his face behind the newspaper. We were obviously waiting for something, and the fact that nothing happened made the waiting and the silence all the more creepy. Conversation was completely inhibited. Lady Lodge seemed to be in a kind of breathless trance, her eyes wide open staring at the ceiling, and this, with the stealthy intensity of the glances from the giant behind the newspaper, made me feel that I had somehow strayed into a "mental home."

We sat like this for nearly two hours, then a maid brought in a large glass of milk for Sir Oliver. He put down his newspaper, looking rather disappointed, and I realized that the experiment was over. My host and hostess began to talk quite normally, and after half an hour's pleasant conversation I went to bed. But not to sleep. I had put the lights out and was just dozing off when a sudden swishing sound over my head made me leap out of bed and hurriedly switch the lights on again. I found that the long curtains in front of the open window were streaming and flapping over the bed in a gale of wind. But although the cause was now apparent and this particular ghost could be shut out by merely closing the window, the whole house itself seemed to be on the watch for something. I kept the light on all night and read a book which I found on the bedside table. Unfortunately it was a murder story by Edgar Wallace.

The next day Sir Oliver told me of the extraordinary powers which he believed were possessed by a medium in London, whom he was anxious that I should visit. I was completely sceptical about all that kind of thing, but he was so urgent in his persuasions that, as I did not want to be like the man who refused to look through the telescope, I consented. He told me he would make all the arrangements, and these were so peculiar that again I had the feeling I had somehow strayed into a crazy world. It reminded me of the romantic plan made by Tom Sawyer and Huckleberry Finn for the rescue of the Negro Jim. Apparently everything had to be done in the most roundabout way. Sir Oliver (in Wiltshire) was to communicate with a secretary whom he retained in Birmingham, the secretary then to communicate with the medium in London, telling her to expect a call from "a friend of Sir Oliver Lodge" (without mentioning my name) who would like to make an appointment. The secretary in Birmingham was then to communicate with me, giving me the telephone number of the medium in London, and I was then to ring up that number, announce that I was the nameless friend of Sir Oliver, and arrange the day and hour of the appointment. The ostensible reason for this roundabout method was that the medium should not know who I was.

When the letter from Birmingham reached me with the telephone number, there was one small point which aroused my interest. The letter was friendly even to chattiness, and although great stress was laid on the fact that the medium in London would know nothing of me, the lady in Birmingham seemed quite interested to know what I had been reading lately. I did not enlighten her; but I rang up the telephone number she had given me, and made an appointment for "a friend of Sir Oliver Lodge" on the following Saturday at five o'clock.

On Saturday morning, however, I found that five o'clock would be inconvenient, and rang up again to enquire if the hour could be changed, saying as before that it was "a friend of Sir Oliver Lodge speaking." Possibly in compensation for defective sight, I have very keen hearing, and I distinctly heard at the other end of the line a whispered aside: "It's Mr. Noyes." The concealment of my name had been so emphasized that this incident (though it did not surprise me) naturally confirmed a suspicion. Those who believe in such things, however, might suggest that a lady with unlimited access to spooks would have no difficulty in obtaining the information. Unfortunately for that theory, the next remark intended for my own ears was the sweetly innocent enquiry: "Is that Sir Oliver Lodge?" I replied merely, "No, it is a *friend* of Sir Oliver Lodge speaking, and I want to cancel the appointment for today."

I wrote to Sir Oliver, telling him what had happened, for I felt sure he was being victimized. He made no reply for several months, and when he did write he avoided the subject altogether.

And now having said all this, let me add that for years I have felt quite certain that communications from the invisible world do come unpredictably in quite a different way, subtle as the language of music or the colours of an evening sky, in aid and consolation to the lonely heart of man. On some of these personal experiences, I have dwelt in *The Last Voyage,* but it is a matter of living experience, not of detached experiment.

XXXIII

Second Marriage—Canada

IT WAS natural enough, I suppose, that when I took the decisive step of entering the Catholic Church in 1927 it should be assumed that this was directly connected with my marriage in the autumn of that year to Mary Weld-Blundell, who belonged to one of the oldest Catholic families in England. My beliefs, however, have never been formed in that way. My wife was anxious that I should not make the decision until I was absolutely certain of its rightness in my own case. One of her sisters, incidentally, was very happily married to a non-Catholic, Francis Engleheart.

My wife's first husband was Richard Shireburn Weld-Blundell, her cousin. On January 1, 1916, he was killed in the first world war when a young lieutenant in the Coldstream Guards. They had been married only a few months. There was one child of the marriage, Agnes, who was eleven years old when her mother and I were married at the Brompton Oratory. During the intervening years they had lived with my wife's parents at a house on the outskirts of Ipswich, named Grace-Dieu after the home of her maternal forebears.

Agnes was a very beautiful child. Occasionally I remind her that when she was eleven she entered into a remarkable arrangement with me. She had felt some alarm at the prospect of losing her mother during our honeymoon, and she was not easily convinced that we would soon return. Eventually I asked: "Will you let her go away for a short time if I give you two blue budgerigars?" Immediately her large dark eyes were raised, and her ecstatic acceptance of the offer sealed a life-long understanding. Now that she is an equally beautiful woman, and the wife of Paul Grey (at the moment of writing, our Minister to Moscow), the two blue budgerigars are still a bond between us, though they long ago escaped into the *ewigkeit.*

After a fortnight in Paris our wedding journey was continued in Canada and the United States. This visit to Canada was undertaken at the instance of the Duchess of Atholl. She had been approached by a Canadian organization (The National Council of Education) one of whose objects was to develop the literary relations of the two countries. The scheme was discussed with the Atholls at a luncheon in their London house. The only other guest was Philip Snowden, at whose thin pale face Mr. Balfour once pointed a minatory finger in the House of Commons, singling him out as the real danger, the future Robespierre of an English revolution. However, "the sea-green Incorruptible" had recently acquired a coronet and appeared to be on remarkably good terms with the Duke, but he looked ill and tired. If the lameness which almost crippled him had ever suggested the cynical characteristics of Long John Silver, it now, like Chatham's gout, gave him the appropriate air of an elder statesman. He told me that at a recent discussion of certain housing problems with technical experts, one of them, who had not recognised the Duke, asked Snowden who that burly chap was who really knew more about the subject than all the rest of them put together.

As a result of the discussion of the Canadian scheme it was arranged for my wife and myself to make a tour of Canada from coast to coast. I was to lecture on English literature at the Universities and in all the chief towns; and a very pleasant part of the arrangement was that no fees were to be paid to me, the National Council of Education making itself responsible for all travelling and hotel accommodations. We were to have a "drawing-room" on all the trains we took across the continent.

Neither of us will easily forget the warm-hearted hospitality which we met on this journey, from the moment when, at the Château Frontenac in Quebec, we looked out of our sitting-room window at the St. Lawrence far below.

On our way across the continent we stayed a night or two with the Willingdons (Lord Willingdon was then Governor-General) at Government House in Ottawa. Mr. Mackenzie King also gave us a hospitable welcome. At Winnipeg we stayed with the Governor of Manitoba, and when we arrived at Victoria I met an old friend. In the previous year Governor Bruce and I had received the honorary degree of LL.D. at Glasgow University, and on parting he had said to me, "We shall meet in Victoria." I had no expectation then of visiting Canada, but after that marvelous little voyage from Vancouver, between what must be the most picturesque islands on the Pacific Coast, he met us on the steps of Government House, and remarked, "I told you so."

On our return journey there was one slight misadventure. With fewer minutes to spare than we realized, before boarding the train at Saskatoon, my wife and I were walking up and down the platform to get a little exercise in preparation for the long journey to Ottawa, when to our horror the train slid out of the station, leaving us behind. It was the only train that would bring us to Ottawa in time for a big dinner party on the following evening at the Willingdons. Our suitcases and trunks (with one unfortunate exception, as I realized later) were on the train. Suddenly, as we stood planted there, a little man who looked like Puck, and certainly should have borne his other name of Robin Goodfellow, dashed up to us, exclaiming, "Follow me!" and without stopping for explanations, ran ahead of us. We obeyed blindly, dodging around trucks and by underpasses until, after what seemed to me a very long sprint, we arrived at a parking ground. He opened the door of a car: "Jump in!" he cried, and again we obeyed.

For the next few minutes, while he drove at breakneck speed, there was no question, answer or explanation. The eyes of Robin Goodfellow were grimly on the road before him, and the the only remark he made was an occasional "Don't worry,"—which might apply either to our missing the train or to the appalling speed at which we were travelling.

Eventually we drew up at a junction just as our train came in. Passengers were not taken on at that point, but, with only a few seconds to spare, we managed to attract the attention of a surprised Pullman porter, who opened a door and helped us to scramble in. We hadn't a moment even to thank Robin Goodfellow, but I hope if he ever reads this he will accept our thanks now for his most kindly act to two complete strangers.

We arrived in Ottawa just in time for the big dinner party, but, alas, one trunk was missing, and it contained my wife's evening dresses and my own evening coat. My wife's figure being of the right kind, she was easily fitted out by Lady Willingdon. For myself the problem was more difficult. Fortunately I had my evening trousers, but when the butler tried to fit me with a coat belonging to Lord Willingdon, who was exceedingly slender, I found that it would clothe no more than my right arm. Eventually a coat was produced which erred in the other direction, and billowed out like the sails of a frigate. However, there were about sixty guests at the dinner, and one could at least pass muster when one was sitting down, though in a standing position I had to do a little judicious reefing of the sails.

The romance and history of Canada with its French and Indian Wars, and those magnificent landscapes of lake, forest and mountain, from Quebec on its crags in the east to British Columbia on the Pacific, offer a field to the creative imagination which would have intoxicated the author of the *Bride of Lammermoor,* and await perhaps a still greater wizard; but the poets and painters of Canada have already flung open the gates of the mind to that new country.

Some of these men it was my privilege to know personally. To others, painters like Krieghoff, Cornelius, Coburn, Varley, and the School of Seven, I was introduced only through their work. The vivid impression it made on me is recorded in some lines* that I wrote at the time, recalling also the sights and sounds and colours I then saw in the Canadian scene itself:

> On a bank of the mighty river,
> The *Richelieu,* flowing around its hundred isles,
> Bright with their silver birches, dark with pines,
> All flooded with sun,—a voice of France arose,
> Lilting a lonely song.
>
> In that province of old Quebec,
> No exile he, nor "habitant"; only a son
> Of the great new world. But something older than France
> Woke in his mind, a *revenant,* singing aloud
> In his careless make-shift French, that lonely song.

* Not published in *Collected Poems.*

It was the Spring. Great floes of ice in thaw
Came crackling down the Cardinal's giant stream.
Legend, and history too, came glistening down
By small French villages with their narrow streets
And shacks of the old Canadian-Indian red
That Krieghoff loved; the cosy *auberges; boutiques*
Lifting a daffodil sign-board over the snow,—
Boulanger; or, like crocuses of all hues,
Emblazoning window and wall with *Alouette*
and *Tabac Naturel;* or, one blithe word
From each divided tongue,—*Sweet Caporal,*
Sweet Caporal everywhere.

By convent wall
And snow-bound shrine, great *Richelieu* flowed on,
And saw a hundred pictures on his way;
A lumber team (by Krieghoff) in a thaw
Of misty green, drawing a loaded sledge
Of fresh-cut pines along the logging road,
The red-scarfed driver in his round fur cap,
The smoking horses with their snow-muffled tread,
Cornelius painted it; while, beyond them, gleamed
Coburns and Varleys, Gagnons and Paul Kanes,
Or some lone splendour from the School of Seven,
Those new-old masters of the great new world.
But, through them all, the old life-stream went its way.
The farmers riding in their bear-skin coats
On jingling sleighs, a memory in each bell
That broke the tingling air; the dark red barns;
The small white wooden churches with slim spires;
The cassocked curés with their flat black hats
And well-lined overshoes, like kindly crows
Walking to Benediction. France was there.

Then solitude, once again; the immense white world,
Darkened with pines; and *Richelieu,* flowing on,
The wide flood smoking in the sun of Spring
And rolling down with all its blocks of ice
To join the great Saint Lawrence.

The plump snow
Fell. The green fir-boughs glistened in the sun.
The maple buds were swelling. Everywhere

Spring brewed her magic. Then that lonely voice
Rose and re-echoed through the echoing hills.
Not "habitant"; nor French; Canadian born;
But welling up from some unconscious life—
Autrefois, when his grandad's echoing axe
Rang through a new-found forest, by a lake
Among the high Laurentians; and the moose,
Wading to feed on water-lily leaves
In high mid-summer, lifted up his head
And stood, haunch-deep, to hear.

Among the pines,
The squirrel and chickadee forgot their war;
The wild duck squattering in the thin wild rice
Grew stiller than the heron.

Far away,
On her proud rock, Quebec remembered France
But that one golden hour was given to peace.

When the woods of Canada come into my mind, they invariably bring with them the words of Bliss Carman, whom I met several times:

The scarlet of the maples can shake me like a cry
Of bugles going by.

Among the guests that we met at the Willingdons was my friend Duncan Campbell Scott, the Dean of Canadian poets, whose beautiful work will remain a permanent contribution to the literature of the English-speaking world.

On subsequent visits to Ottawa we spent many pleasant days as the guests of Duncan and his wife Elise, who is herself a poet, and his friendship was one of the great treasures that Canada bestowed upon me. They stayed with us later in the Isle of Wight, and we had long ambrosial evenings talking of poetry.

Duncan was a great lover of music, and himself an accomplished musician. One of his most exquisite poems, "Compline," tells, with a touch entirely his own, how the birds, settling on some telegraph wires, looked like notes in the musical score of a mediaeval hymn. It has all the beauty of that hour described by Wordsworth:

> The holy time is quiet as a nun
> Breathless with adoration. . . .

The primal stillness of the majestic Canadian landscape, behind those thin dark wires of modernity, and a few musical phrases of the old Latin hymn accidentally imprinted on the glowing sky by the birds, bring all the ages together:

> I see the wires as the old music-staff,
> Four lines and three spaces,
> The swallows clinging there, . . .

The sunset sky looks like the vellum page of a Mass book, coloured like old ivory under the fading gems of a rose window, while the great pine forests give up their incense. In imagination he hears the words that accompany the music, arising out of the old French-Canadian history, where they had been so often repeated, a voice imploring out of the past in a vault of shadow:

> *Sancta Maria—Mater Dei,*
> *Ora pro nobis peccatoribus*
> *Nunc et in hora*
> *Mortis nostrae.*

On the surface it all comes about by accident, but I know of no modern poem which more subtly conveys the profound truth so often expressed by the great mystics and adumbrated in all great art, that the universe itself is one vast symphony in which every apparently accidental detail has its own place and significance like a note in music. Duncan Campbell Scott was not a Catholic, but when he looked at nature, under the eternal aspect he heard that voice "out of the past, imploring in a world of shadows."

Like some of our English poets, Duncan had held various official posts, but in a more romantic capacity, and he was now head of the department which superintended the affairs of the Red Man. He was also President of the Royal Society of Canada. But his life was in poetry and music. He had something of the austerity of Wordsworth, but a far keener sense of humour, all the keener, perhaps, because it was expressed with extreme reticence, sometimes by a mere twinkle of the eye, or, as on one occasion which I remember very vividly, by opening his mouth slightly and staring at you to see whether you had observed the fun of it yourself.

It was with just that interrogative expression that he indicated a passage in the letters of W. B. Yeats, in which he tells how his romantic life is to be prolonged by the use of monkey glands. Duncan's only spoken comment was, "What do you think of that?" His finger indicated the passage in which Yeats condemns A. E. for "preferring to die." Duncan's humorous stare and slightly open mouth were quite unforgettable.

On our way home from the 1927 visit to Canada, we stayed for a few days at Niagara, then went over to Buffalo to see my old friends the Albrights. Mr. Albright had lost a large fortune which he had made by harnessing Niagara to supply light and power to some scores of America cities, and he was now living, with the simplicity of a Thoreau, in a small frame house.

The splendid art gallery which he had given to the city of Buffalo had passed out of his control, and he was humorously indignant about some of its modern acquisitions. He said they had given the most important place in the exhibition to what he called "a brass egg." He insisted that we should go with him to see it.

The Albright Gallery contained much that was beautiful—but there it was, solemnly pedestalled in the centre of all that fine craftsmanship, a great brass egg slightly tilted to one side, and (if I remember rightly) somewhere about the middle the faintest suggestion of an embryo human nose. (In this respect it was not so highly developed as Tenniel's Humpty Dumpty.) The disconsolate founder of the gallery led us up to it. We were accompanied by the Curator, whom Mr. Albright with great solemnity had asked to explain the work to us. The Curator took the request quite seriously, and, tilting his head to the exact angle of the egg, placed one finger on his forehead, and in a deep earnest voice remarked, "Well, to begin with, it is an Abstraction." At this, to the obvious surprise of the Curator, Mr. Albright went into another room. When he returned he was still wiping the tears from his eyes.

I think he must have been the happiest millionaire who ever lost his millions, for now he was able to see the fun of what the "new age" would do to his art gallery.

It will probably increase the gaiety of posterity when it writes the comedy of our times, that in the conventional patter the word "Abstraction" has been applied even to things as concrete as a brass egg. A follower of this fashion, completely innocent of precise meanings, once asked me if Robert Browning did not write abstract poetry. All that he meant, of course, was that Browning (one of the truest poets that ever lived) was to him more or less incomprehensible. Lewis Carroll would have enjoyed the reasoning: All abstractions are incomprehensible, Sordello is incomprehensible, therefore Sordello is an Abstraction.

We sailed from New York, where this time we could spend only a few days, as even two blue budgerigars would not appease Agnes if we were not at home for Christmas. But these few days were made memorable by a dinner given for us by Mrs. Douglas Robinson, at which there was a great gathering of the Roosevelts, and among them—not yet world-famous—a lame man who walked with a stick and who was about to become Governor of New York.

On our return we had taken a house at No. 13 Hanover Terrace, Regent's Park. The former owner had superstitiously numbered it 12-A, but my wife and I, strong in the faith of the Dark Ages, decided to call it 13, even though we entered it on a Friday. Gosse, who lived at No. 17, sent me a pleasant little note approving what he called "the manliness of the change"; and almost by the same post I received a letter from Barry Pain displaying a certain nervousness about the proximity of Gosse:

"Your house seems to be perfectly delightful. It is the kind that one sees but never gets. Still, you must take one consideration with another. You have the ornamental water, but is not our dear Mr. Gosse also of Regent's Park? Eau et Gosse à tous les étages, as they say in the advertisement. Be careful.

"I am bitter because, as you know, I had tried to find a hut by the sea wherein to die. I could imagine my obituarist beginning his notice 'Barry Pain went out with the tide.' And jolly good too. But the sea had nothing for me. So I remain in my sordid dog-kennel. I have re-decorated it, which I should hate less if I had not also paid for it.

"I am not particularly well, but my age is advanced. I must expect little. I am especially glad to hear the good news that comes to you this year. The best of good wishes from me to all of you."

His death occurred not long after this letter was written, at Bushey, where the early days of his married life were spent. But it was a very different Bushey at that time, when W. S. Gilbert and Herkomer were among their neighbours. Though Barry Pain's tiny garden with its damson and pear trees made a brave fight against the legions of red brick, it was a losing battle. Once a week he went to play bridge at the Arts Club in Dover Street, and lunched with three friends at a table which was always reserved for them and known as The Rogues' Table. He had more friends among the painters than among the writers, and the Arts Club was his favourite port of call. A very fine portrait of him by his father-in-law, Rudolph Lehmann, now occupies a place of honour in the Club.

XXXIV

Hanover Terrace

FOR THE first year or two after our marriage we lived almost continuously in London. They were years of many friendships and many delightful occasions; afternoons in the studio of Bernard Partridge; dinner with the editor of *Punch* (Owen Seaman), with Mr. and Mrs. A. P. Herbert and Dorothy Margaret Stuart as fellow-guests; a weird luncheon party given by Evan Morgan (Lord Tredegar), during which Augustus John became involved in an argument; these are among the memories of those days.

The Augustus John episode was a little comedy for the hand of a modern Molière, if there had been one to write it. His interlocutrix was a lady of great wealth who a year or so earlier had been advised by him to employ a young painter of genius to adorn with frescoes the spacious hall of her London house. While the work was in progress she had gone to the Riviera, and on her return found the paintings completed in so Pompeian a style that, in her own words, she was obliged to put up an umbrella when she entered her hall. She said that she could not possibly ask her guests to pass through those orgiastic revels, "and think of the effect upon the servants!"

But Augustus John was undisturbed by that moving appeal. He replied firmly, "You can't possibly remove them; they are works of genius."

"Then," exclaimed the distressed lady, "I shall have to have another entrance made to the house!"

The portrait which Augustus John painted of Evan Morgan gave a sardonically critical background to the scene of this delectable conversation. One could not help wondering whether the sitter had been conscious that the brilliantly executed portrait was also a keenly satirical criticism.

Evan Morgan himself was a somewhat extraordinary character. I first met him at Admiral Beatty's house, and afterwards went to one or two of his amazing parties in London. At one of these he had an almost fantastic admixture of guests. They included Gilbert Chesterton, Tallulah Bankhead, and the Princess Royal. At another representatives of "the World, the Flesh and the Devil," were invited to meet Cardinal Bourne—and the Cardinal had the time of his life.

I obtained only a fleeting impression of Augustus John, so fleeting that it might be quite untrue. There was something big and powerful there, but it was not an altogether facetious criticism that described him as a fine animal painter for those who didn't like animals; for he almost invariably animalizes the human countenance in a way that a good animal might find cynical.

There was certainly a modicum of truth in the implications of Barry Pain's remark: "We all know John is a genius. Now we would like to see some of his work."

Among our guests of those days was Guy Pollock, managing editor of the *Morning Post,* and at one time on the editorial staff of a Beaverbrook paper. He told me of an agitating day when Lord Beaverbrook asked him to write an article for the *Sunday Express* on his belief in God. Pollock hesitated, for though he had very deep religious convictions, he did not like wearing them on his sleeve.

Beaverbrook looked at him suspiciously, and asked sharply, "Look here, Pollock, you do believe in God, don't you?"

"Yes," replied Pollock, "but I am not sure that He is quite the same God that *you* believe in."

"What do you mean by that?" asked Beaverbrook, with some asperity.

"Well," said Pollock, "I—I—I—don't believe in a God who shaves every morning."

"Pollock," said Beaverbrook, almost choking with righteous indignation, "you're fired!"

Pollock retired with dignity.

Late that night, after he had gone to bed, his telephone rang, and on taking up the receiver he heard the voice of Lord Beaverbrook coming faintly over the wire: "Pollock, I think I'm dying, and it's *you* that have killed me!"

This, of course, was not really an obituary notice, but an overture to the reconciliation.

Another guest of that time was Lord Darling. He was not perhaps the inventor, but certainly the perfecter, of a peculiar kind of judicial question, sometimes amusing in its effect and probably useful in reminding the witness that nothing is to be taken for granted. A London witness, for instance, eloquently pouring forth his evidence about something he had seen in an underground railway station, might be gently asked by the Judge to inform the Court what he meant by the twopenny tube. Sometimes, however, Lord Darling's question acted like a boomerang. When a barrister had mentioned the name of a well-known comedian, George Robey, Lord Darling, with an air of ineffable innocence, enquired:

"And who, may I ask, is George Robey?"

The retort was instantaneous:

"He is the darling of the music-halls, me Lud."

Lord Darling had presided over many famous trials, and it was difficult to realize that this vivacious and delightful guest, with his delicately chiselled face and frail body, had sentenced so many criminals to be hanged. He told us that once, while he and his wife had been awaiting the departure of their train from Liverpool Street, they noticed a massively built man lurching up and down the platform, and glancing into their compartment with a sinister expression.

"I'm afraid that man wants to speak to me," said Lord Darling to his wife. A moment or two later the sinister one, looking horribly like a gorilla, peered through the open window.

"Mr. Justice Darling, I believe," he said.

"Oh, dear me, no," said Lord Darling.

The gorilla was unshaken by perjury. "I wonder if your Lordship remembers hanging a man by the name of Brown, some years ago?"

"Well, you know," said Lord Darling, "I hang so many people . . ."

"Ah," said the gorilla, leaning both arms on the window-frame, and sinking his voice to a confidential whisper, "but Brown happens to have been my father."

"Very painful; very painful indeed," said Lord Darling, "but you know we can't discuss that sort of thing here."

"Oh, but I don't want your Lordship to feel awkward about it," said the gorilla, disclosing a row of white teeth in an unexpectedly amiable smile. "I've been seeing some of my relations off by this train. We all of us reckernised your Lordship. My aunt she says, 'There's Lord Darling now. You reely ought to tell 'im 'ow grateful we all are.' "

One of the men whom he had sentenced to death was the provincial lawyer Armstrong who, after poisoning his wife without being discovered, made the mistake of trying to remove a rival solicitor by the same method. He put arsenic in a sandwich and invited this gentleman to tea. To make sure that the guest took the right sandwich Armstrong picked it out of the plate and handed it to him, saying politely, "Excuse fingers." The guest had a good appetite and, fortunately for himself, was very sick when he reached home. Accustomed as he was to weighing evidence, he naturally remembered the "Excuse fingers." Analytical investigation and an exhumation of the dead wife followed. Armstrong tried to persuade the jury that the arsenic found in his possession had been procured for innocent garden purposes; but, even more innocently, "What happened to the dandelions?" asked Lord Darling.

In summing up, Lord Darling asked the jury to remember that a clever and well-educated man may be able to persuade himself that he is right in doing anything that serves his end.

Armstrong was a well-educated man and a member of a famous London Club. Not long after the verdict Barry Pain and I were walking by the stately portals of this institution. He chuckled to himself as we passed, and gesturing with his thumb towards a window through which dignified and intellectual heads could be seen over the backs of comfortable armchairs, he said cheerfully, "They hanged one of *them* the other day."

Occasionally, in his judicial capacity, Lord Darling had to make decisions that affected the modern literary world. It was in his court that the notorious *Ulysses* of James Joyce was condemned, on the initiative of the public prosecutor. Instructions were given to the police, and it became illegal for bookshops to sell it. At once, of course, the familiar racket began. It had received an advertisement which it could not have gained in any other way. It was sold surreptitiously at greatly enhanced prices, and began to be described by a certain section of the public as a work of genius. The objection to it, of course, was not concerned with that, but merely with the admitted fact that it was filthy. Edmund Gosse in two words exactly described it as a "foul chaos." The best critics, in fact, treated it with contempt—and there was far more silent contempt than its vocal defenders ever realized.

Censorship and suppression are almost always a mistake, though there is something in the argument that a label is necessary for poisons. This label, as a rule, can be supplied only by critical reference to "the best that is known and thought in the world." In the case of Joyce the other course was followed, with the usual consequences and, very much against my own inclination, I was drawn into the conflict—but of this I will speak later.

In the meantime, the affair led to some almost farcical situations. The general confusion was illustrated in England by a writer in a leading newspaper, who remarked, taking advantage of the fact that editors cannot always know the contents of the books reviewed in their columns: "Its very obscenity is somehow beautiful, and if that is not high art, what is?" Some of us could have given him the answer, but he did not wait for a reply. A very good critic told me that he had brought the statement to the attention of the editor, who at first gave the usual evasion of the responsible, saying that he had not read the book himself. A copy was sent to him, and he wrote privately, "I have now read *Ulysses.* It is unspeakable," but no public correction was made, and it became a kind of cliché to describe Joyce as one of our masters.

One of the most farcical incidents of this confusion was that it brought disaster upon the editor of the *Sporting Times,* commonly known as the "Pink 'Un." He was apparently smarting under the charge that his journal lacked the refinement of the *Manchester Guardian* and, having read that the obscenity of *Ulysses* was "somehow beautiful," he procured a copy of the work for the education of his staff. On reading it, however, he felt as Miss Mitford might if she had fallen into a cess-pool. He rose spluttering and gasping, and in a burst of moral indignation wrote an article (the first of its kind ever to be seen in the Pink 'Un) to the effect that while the Pink 'Un had sometimes been criticized for its laxity of tone, here was a specimen of what the high-brows admired. He proceeded to quote a single paragraph from *Ulysses,* and was promptly haled before a magistrate. Vainly he protested that what he had quoted had been described in the public Press (without quotation of the operative pages) as beautiful, and extolled by echo after echo. Vainly he explained that he was protesting against this nasty mess. "The others didn't make the mistake of quoting it," said the magistrate. And, for one of the most genuinely moral acts in the life of the Pink 'Un, its unfortunate editor was given a severe sentence.

But there were more serious repercussions. One morning the editor of *Blackwood's Magazine,* who was then the President of the Publishers' Association, telephoned to me saying that he thought we ought to do something about an announcement that had just been made by the B.B.C. Apparently Mr. —— was to give an address the following week recommending the wretched stuff as a masterpiece. In Blackwood's opinion this was making use of a government organization to over-ride the decision of the law-courts and induce booksellers to break the law. It might be answered that "freedom of speech" was also involved; but in actual fact Blackwood appeared to be right.

One of his own editorial staff, J. H. Lobban (a brother-in-law of Quiller-Couch), was a lecturer at Birkbeck College and had been greatly disturbed by the fact that the book, which the editor of the Pink 'Un had been sentenced for merely quoting, was being recommended to young students, in a syllabus issued without the approval of the authorities, by a more "advanced" lecturer in the University of London. The students had naturally enquired at the bookshops, and in one case a young girl student, who had asked for it quite ingenuously, had met with a very ignominious reprimand from the bookseller. She had protested bitterly about it to Blackwood's friend.

In the meantime I thought the best thing to do was to discuss the B.B.C. announcement with those responsible. Accordingly I gave a little luncheon at 13 Hanover Terrace, to which there came, among others, the Director of the B.B.C., Sir John Reith as he was then, Miss Elizabeth Haldane, who was on the programme committee, Lord Charnwood (who had just published his *Life of Lincoln*), and James Blackwood who, as President of the Publishers' Association and head of a firm with more than one hundred years' experience, might certainly represent the best of his profession. Curiously enough, all the men were in agreement (they had now read the book, and thought, as Gosse did, that it was a "foul chaos"). Miss Elizabeth Haldane, who had something of the philosophic impartiality of her more famous brother, Lord Haldane, was not so much concerned about the diffusion of the poison. To stop it, she thought, would be an interference with freedom. Her argument, identifying freedom with the right to diffuse poison, suddenly collapsed when Blackwood asked her if she had read the book. She had not read a line of it.

"If I were to read one of its pages to you here," said Blackwood, "you would certainly never speak to me again. I suppose that, in a sense, is a limitation of my freedom." Miss Haldane afterwards read a page or two, was extremely nauseated, and agreed.

Reith told us that one of his difficulties in the B.B.C. was that while the "advanced" importers of decay were persistently vocal and clamouring to be heard, those who really represented the mind and character of the country remained silent. It reminded one of the saying of Burke that while the grasshoppers kept up a constant chatter, there were many great beasts of a far more solid character quietly ruminating in the shade of the trees. Many of the critics, in fact, were simply afraid of being "behind the times." Chesterton once remarked, "I am quite content to be behind the times when I see the ghastly people who are abreast of the times, and the still more ghastly people who are ahead of the times."

Mr. St. John Ervine, a critic of very wide experience, not at all afraid of calling a spade a bloody shovel, used exactly the same terms that Gosse had used about the book. He said: "Art requires selection. This is a dirty chaos." It had been sent for review to him, he said in his rich Irish brogue, and "I locked it up in the safe for fear it would go crawling about the house at night."

Reith suggested that his hands would be strengthened if some of us would give him public support. After discussion it was decided that I should write a letter to *The Times* calling attention to the fact that a government organization was being used to over-ride the decision of the law-courts. *The Times* printed it in large type on the leading article page.

The reaction was immediate. A rather long letter appeared in answer a day or two later, protesting against this attempt to support the law by limiting the diffusion of poison. The signatories naturally included Bernard Shaw and Hugh Walpole. It was a little odd, however, to find among their meekly acquiescent followers the Headmaster of Eton and the Bishop of Chichester, but immediately beneath this letter there appeared in large type a letter from the President of the Publishers' Association affirming that most people would be grateful to me for the line I had taken; and that it could only be supposed that the bearers of some respected names appended to the protest had not read a book "which would make a Hottentot sick."

The ludicrous situation that now presented itself is worth recording, because it illustrates the dilemma which the contemporary mind (if it can be called a mind) had now prepared for itself. Here was a book of which one of the most experienced criminal judges in England had said that he disliked turning the pages because it stained the mind to look at them. It had been rapturously acclaimed in reviews which, wisely, did not quote what they admired. The one man who did quote the relevant pages, and supported the decision of the law-courts, was severely sentenced while the Bishop of Chichester and the Headmaster of Eton, in their anxiety to be broad-minded and associated with what they believed (without the slightest investigation) to be "liberal thought," were signing a public manifesto supporting the widest official glorification of obscenities which, in the first chapter of the Epistle to the Romans, are described as worthy of death.

It should be noted that it was not then a question of censorship or suppression. This, rightly or wrongly, had been settled and the police had been ordered to take action. It was now simply a question whether a national instrument should be used to glorify and disseminate to listening millions stuff which, if they realized what they had signed, would have turned the Bishop into a Holy Roller, and sent the Headmaster of Eton staggering down to Borstal.

It may be remarked that there is no novelty about the representation of "a stream of subconscious ideas." The opening pages of *Edwin Drood,* about the opium den, are a superb example of how a true artist can do it, but Dickens knew that if all the occupants of a ship are asleep it cannot be steered by their nightmares to either a geographic or an artistic goal. After achieving his effect (not by pouring in everything, including the entire contents of the garbage can and the sewer, but by selection) he allows us to recover consciousness and sanity. The other method is merely another way of making art easy—the kind of automatic writing in which you merely scribble every disgusting idea that comes into your head, and try to attract attention by their lubricity.

The question was not whether Joyce was a genius, but whether any man had a right to scatter filth through the bookshops. Moreover, if a "genius" wheels a dung-heap into the dining-room, it is the stink to which we object, not the flashing eye of the artist. However, to those who like such fodder, I can only say, *"Bon appétit!"* Personally, I dine elsewhere.

A dinner party had been arranged in Paris for the author of the book, at which the gleeful guests expected to hear the promised broadcast discomfiting the British law-courts and prophesying immortality for what an American Judge called an emetic. All that they heard, however, was the curt announcement that the address of recommendation had been cancelled. After the pronouncement of a Judge in Chicago, tactfully condemning the book as emetic rather than pornographic (for he did not wish to increase its sales), an enterprising publisher announced that it had been absolved and must now be regarded as a classic. It is true that the three words applied to it all end in "ic"!

A final touch of comedy to the whole episode occurred after the death of Lord Birkenhead, when his library came up for sale. I went to look at the books, some of which I thought I might buy for my own library. One of the first that caught my eye was a sumptuously bound edition of the nasty mess. Here indeed was a comic anomaly, typical of the confusions of our time: While little booksellers were being prosecuted for selling or displaying the book, and the editor of the *Sporting Times* was being punished for quoting it, a finely bound copy was about to be sold at a Mayfair auction for the estate of the Lord Chancellor!

Lord Darling happened to telephone to me that evening accepting an invitation for the following week. I told him of what I called the auctioneer's comedy, and he startled me by saying, rather sharply, "I shall ring up Scotland Yard." I thought at first he was joking, but he said the sale would have undesirable repercussions and must be stopped. In a very short time two representatives of the Yard called at 13 Hanover Terrace. Lord Darling had apparently told them that I could give any information they might require. They were greatly interested in the fact that the Lord Chancellor had provided that kind of book with so sumptuous a binding. They also told me that while

Scotland Yard had many "funny" books in its collection, they didn't think it had anything quite so "funny" as that one. They seemed anxious to acquire it. Whether they seized it or not I do not know. It did not appear at the sale.

I have never ceased to find satisfaction in the memory of those two solemn faces from Scotland Yard which I had the pleasure of setting upon the track of the deceased Lord Chancellor. How delighted Belloc would have been if he had had the opportunity of putting Scotland Yard on the track of Lord Reading. "But *Soft! We Are Observed!*"

XXXV

The Wards, Hilaire Belloc and Others

AMONG THE friends of whom we saw a good deal from 1928 onwards was Mrs. Wilfrid Ward, who sent me, as a wedding present, her husband's noble biography of Newman, a treasure-house of thought and wisdom, illuminating the religious history of the nineteenth century.

To Mrs. Ward's house in Pelham Place came some of the most interesting figures in the London of that day. Among them was the Anglican Bishop Gore, whom I met at luncheon there. I was amused to hear that he had asked Mrs. Ward if she knew why I had become a Catholic, and that she had replied: "I believe very largely through reading your books."

Hilaire Belloc too I met there at luncheon. On our first meeting I was a little disconcerted (as others have been) by a brusquerie of manner which was almost habitual with him, though it alternated with an old-fashioned courtesy worthy of Sir Roger de Coverley. I had a great admiration for some of Chesterton's poems, particularly his *Lepanto.* Belloc asked me if I did not think it one of the finest of contemporary poems, and before I could express my cordial agreement, he added, "Oh, but of course you wouldn't. All poets are jealous." My only possible reply was, "In that case I'm not a poet," after which he became quite charming and conciliatory, and later added to the treasures of my library by sending me a pleasantly inscribed copy of that brilliant tour-de-force *Belinda.*

Herbert Ward (the elder son of Wilfrid Ward) told me of a journey he had once made with Belloc, from Rome to England. The cross-channel boat was crowded, and when they went into the dining-room they could find seats only at a table for four. The other two seats were occupied by a miserable-looking stock broker and his wife, a sour-faced woman who was severely nagging her husband. After a few minutes Belloc could stand it no longer. He nudged Ward in the ribs and led him out of the dining-room to a place on the deck where there was a small window overlooking the table they had just left. Here Belloc took his stand, and in a stentorian voice bellowed: "Ward, did you notice how that unfortunate man was being hen-pecked by his wife?" Silence fell upon the table below, but Belloc was nothing if not impartial. "I have no doubt," he continued in the same stentorian tones, "that it was due to something evil in his past life. Possibly he has lent money at usurious interest." The excitement was continued on the boat train when Belloc and Ward entered the restaurant car. Lord Reading had just become an Imperial Viceroy, and the event had revived Belloc's wrath about the Marconi scandal. Accordingly, during an appropriate silence, Belloc's voice rang out like a trumpet-call: "Ward, did I ever tell you why Reading went to hide his head in India?" There followed an impressive detailed account, also in the best vein of *Soft! We Are Observed!* They were.

One evening I went as Mrs. Wilfrid Ward's guest to a meeting at Chatham House where Algernon Cecil was to read a paper on the relations between the Vatican and the Italian Government. He had a large and distinguished audience. When he had finished, Mr. Wickham Steed, formerly Foreign Editor of *The Times,* rose to speak. Steed, with his neatly pointed beard, looked very like the romantic diplomat of fiction, who lives in a world of champagne, glittering candelabra and beautiful spies. Completely unaware of the presence of Mrs. Wilfrid Ward, he told an enthralled audience of an occasion when Wilfrid Ward had been secretly commissioned by the Duke of Norfolk to conduct certain negotiations with the Pope. Steed said that he had acted as interpreter in that interesting conversation, as Wilfrid Ward could not speak Italian. When he sat down Mrs. Wilfrid Ward rose, and very quietly, with a mixture of amusement and gentle indignation, told an even more interested audience that there was not a word of truth in what the romantic Mr. Steed had been saying; her husband, Wilfrid Ward, spoke Italian fluently and had no possible need of an interpreter, nor had he ever gone to the Vatican on behalf of the Duke of Norfolk in any such way.

While the enraptured audience was listening to her, completely spellbound, I turned my head to see what was happening to Mr. Steed; and out of the corner of my eye, to my intense delight I saw him tiptoeing out of the room with long stealthy cat-like strides.

Leo Ward, Mrs. Ward's younger son, who had recently entered the priesthood, often visited us at Hanover Terrace. He had a wide range of friends, among whom was Aldous Huxley. Leo thought that Aldous Huxley would one day become a Catholic. I did not think it likely, but in view of Aldous Huxley's later books, *Gray Eminence* and what he called *The Perennial Philosophy* (though it had little to do with the *philosophia perennis*) I have to admit that Leo caught glimpses of something that I had missed. Aldous Huxley, on the other hand, perpetrated a somewhat tantalizing limerick on Leo Ward and his admiration of Newman's essay, *The Development of Christian Doctrine:*

There once was a terrible Neo-
Scholastical bigot called Leo,
Who set out to prove
That though Rome doesn't move,
She develops *scherzando con brio.*

Leo Ward was one of the happiest, gentlest and kindest of men. He never lost the young enthusiasm of his Oxford days. He read widely and thought deeply. He went to Japan as a missionary shortly before the war and later was imprisoned in a Japanese concentration camp. A correspondent who had known him there wrote:

"It was quite obvious that the humiliations, both actual and attempted, of the prison regime had made no impression whatever upon his inherent dignity. He remained, as a priest should, completely undefiled and undefeated by his environment."

He died shortly after his release, as a result of the treatment he received there. In a letter to his sister, Maisie Ward, written shortly before his death, he tried to minimize what he had endured, saying that it amounted to "little more than a few kicks," but for those who knew that fine and radiant spirit, the thought of such things is almost intolerable.

What Mrs. Wilfrid Ward said of my conversion, in the open letter with which she prefaced her *Tudor Sunset,* may be recorded here as an addition to my apologia—a too generous addition, but nevertheless a part of it. (The reference to Abbotsford recalls the fact that Mrs. Ward was a kinswoman of Sir Walter.)

"MY DEAR ALFRED:

"You have now, for three years at least, shown a very patient sympathy with me as to the making of this book. Therefore, feeling that I must at last make an end of my task, and being willing to justify myself, I am writing this letter to you.

"Shades of Sir Walter! When I played as a child amidst the coats of mail in the Hall of Abbotsford and passed between them shivering with terror on my lonely way to bed, how little I thought that I should ever attempt to write an historical novel!

"Without pretending to the role of historian, I have studied to my utmost to make *Tudor Sunset* fiction that is true to character and atmosphere. . . .

"It is not only because I seek the shadow of your name to shelter my work that I am writing to you. It is because yours is a genius which blends, harmoniously and naturally, loyalty to your country and loyalty to the City of God. With you there has been no reaction, as you went forward, against what you had held rightly from the first. The spirit of the *Torch-Bearers* is so essentially an English spirit that no friend of your earlier poems need feel that you are now less with them because linked with a more ancient and no less English tradition.

"Is there not in English history a peculiar fascination in the pathos of conflicting loyalties . . . whether in the patriotism that seeks peace rather than aggrandisement or in the faith by which men serve their country in spite of herself. Each according to his lights will be truer to the lesser claims when he seems to sacrifice them to the greater."

XXXVI

The Luttrell Psalter

IT MADE me feel that I had a personal acquaintance with Beaumont and Fletcher to find on the title page of their works a little engraving of Grace-Dieu, the home of the de Lisles, my wife's grandparents on the maternal side. Sir John Beaumont, the father of Francis Beaumont, had occupied it in the reign of Henry VIII, on the dissolution of the monasteries, and in circumstances which are described in amusingly different ways by the biographer of Francis Beaumont and by Ambrose Phillipps de Lisle, as quoted by his biographer.

The former says:

"Beaumont and Fletcher were both born in the aristocratical purple. . . . Beaumont's family, however, the older and more honourable, long had its seat at Grace-Dieu, in Leicestershire. . . . Our British Parnassus numbers no less than five relatives of Beaumont, along with himself."

On the other hand, Ambrose Phillipps de Lisle says:

"Grace-Dieu was originally a priory of nuns of the order of Saint Augustine. . . . At the dissolution of the monasteries by Henry VIII the priory was suppressed and, in reward of his servility to the King, passed into the hands of John Beaumont of the adjoining Parish of Thringstone, one of the Royal Commissioners. The manor of Grace-Dieu remained in the unholy possession of the robber—I beg pardon —the Royal Commissioner of the robber King. In 1683 Grace-Dieu was released from its bondage, for it was purchased by Sir Ambrose

Phillipps of Garendon. The old priory church was in ruins, a few traces of which still remain."

These old English Catholic families form a closely interwoven clan; and those who had lived through the persecution times might well look upon a newcomer as one who had not borne the heat and burden of the day; but on my marriage I received what St. Paul calls "the adoption of a son" and my wife's mother, giving me the biography of her own grandfather, inscribed it "For Alfred. The life of his great-grandfather."

In 1811 Wordsworth commemorated the associations of Grace-Dieu with English poetry:

> Beneath yon eastern ridge, the craggy bound,
> Rugged and high, of Charnwood's forest ground,
> Stand yet, but, stranger, hidden from thy view,
> The ivied ruins of forlorn Grace-Dieu;
> Erst a religious house, which day and night
> With hymns resounded, and the chanted rite;
> And when those rites had ceased, the spot gave birth
> To honourable men of various worth;
> There, on the margin of a streamlet wild,
> Did Francis Beaumont sport, an eager child;
> There, under shadow of the neighbouring rocks,
> Sang youthful tales of shepherds and their flocks;
> Unconscious prelude to heroic themes,
> Heart-breaking tears, and melancholy dreams
> Of slighted love, and scorn, and jealous rage,
> With which his genius shook the buskined stage.

There was a more indirect connection with English poetry when Augusta Jane Lisle married in 1832 John Purcell Fitzgerald of Boulge Hall, Suffolk, a brother of Edward Fitzgerald.

There were other associations of the kind. Dryden had written part of *The Hind and the Panther,* and finished his translation of Virgil, at Ugbrook, the home of my wife's sister Clare (Lady Clifford of Chudleigh). The place where he used to sit and meditate is still traditionally known as Dryden's seat. One of Wordsworth's most beautiful poems, "Song at the Feast of Brougham Castle," tells of an old family legend of the Cliffords, and contains some of his finest lines:

> The silence that is in the starry sky,
> The sleep that is among the lonely hills.

The historian who one day will give the full history of these old Catholic families will have an enviable subject, but it will need the combined genius of an Acton, a Newman and a Walter Scott to do it rightly. The de Lisle who played his part in Newman's movement at Oxford could look back to Sir John Lisle, who in 1520 accompanied Henry VII to France where he entered the lists of the celebrated tournaments of the Field of the Cloth of Gold as one of twenty-one knights chosen to represent the chivalry of England.

On the Weld side of my wife's family there are further associations with history and poetry. Her grandfather, Sir Frederick Weld, was a friend of Tennyson, and when he was Premier of New Zealand (in the days when Premiers were appointed from the mother country) he named a lake there after the poet, as Hallam Tennyson records in his biography. A water-colour drawing of this lake by Sir Frederick Weld hung at Farringford for many years, with a note attached by the poet, "Given to me by Governor Weld. A. T." It is now at our own house in the Isle of Wight.

Shortly after we were married there was a curious episode. Richard Weld-Blundell had been heir to Lulworth, and on his death in 1916 (leaving no male heir) and that of his father in 1927, Lulworth passed in 1927 to an elderly uncle, Herbert Weld.

My wife and I were in Wiesbaden, where we had taken Agnes to see an oculist, when a letter arrived from Herbert Weld saying that in order to pay his death duties he had decided to sell the Luttrell Psalter (a Weld heirloom which had been for more than thirty years on loan to the British Museum). A complication had arisen, however, through the wording of the documents relating to the entail, and by the will of Richard Weld-Blundell it appeared that all his personal property had been left to his wife, so that there was some doubt as to the legal ownership of the Luttrell Psalter. Herbert Weld suggested, therefore, that they come to some arrangement, and that the proceeds from the sale of the book should be shared between my wife and himself.

My wife immediately wrote to say that he was perfectly free to sell the book, so far as she was concerned, and she certainly would not wish to avail herself of the ambiguity he had mentioned. A few weeks later, after our return to England, a further letter, this time from Herbert Weld's lawyers, reached her, thanking her for her wish to release him from any obligation, but saying that the matter was more serious than had been indicated in his letter, and that the Lulworth Trustees had decided to ask the courts for a legal decision. This would involve not only the ownership of the Luttrell Psalter, but the entire contents of Lulworth Castle. A test case was therefore submitted and a curious little drama ensued.

Herbert Weld had the Luttrell Psalter removed from the British Museum, much to the annoyance of that institution, and sent to Sotheby's, together with the Bedford Book of Hours. The date of the sale had been fixed, and famous book dealers from all over the world were already arriving in London. It was known that Mr. J. Pierpont Morgan particularly wished to acquire both books for his library, and English newspapers were beginning to protest against these "national monuments" going out of the country. The Luttrell Psalter was known to the general public through illustrations taken from it in books like Green's *History of the English People.*

Only three days before the sale was due to begin, the Court gave its decision that the two books, together with the contents of Lulworth Castle, were the property of my wife.

Incidentally, though this had nothing to do with the decision, my wife, through her grandfather Sir Frederick Weld, had a more direct connection with Lulworth than had the uncle who now occupied it; and she was certainly more anxious that the Luttrell Psalter should be retained in the British Museum.

As soon as the decision of the Court became known, Sir Frederick Kenyon, the Principal Librarian of the British Museum, arrived at 13 Hanover Terrace to plead that the book should be withdrawn from the sale and the British Museum allowed to have it for a fixed sum.

A few minutes later one of the Directors of Sotheby's arrived, and in another room begged me to persuade my wife not to withdraw it. "You can fix almost any reserve you like on it," he said. But I told him that my wife very much wanted the book to go to the British Museum. She had in fact promised Sir Frederick Kenyon to let him know the same evening the figure at which it could be withdrawn. Sir Frederick was going down to Winchester that evening, and asked that we telephone to him there.

Accordingly I rang him up at an appointed hour, and completed arrangements in what must have been record time for a transaction of that kind. I told him that my wife would withdraw the book at thirty thousand guineas, and before I had completed the sentence Sir Frederick said: "I accept that." This was actually £20,000 less than we had been led to understand it would have fetched in the sale room, where certain French and American bidders would have been competing with Mr. J. Pierpont Morgan.

Sir Frederick, however, continued the conversation. "We want very much to have the Bedford Book of Hours as well," he said. "Of course it is not quite so outstanding as the Luttrell Psalter, so perhaps Mrs. Noyes would let us have it for an additional £10,000?"

The Bedford Book of Hours is perhaps a more beautiful work than the Luttrell Psalter, and many of its illustrations have a unique historical value. As my wife had withdrawn the Luttrell Psalter from the sale, she thought it only fair that the Bedford Book of Hours should try its fortune at Sotheby's, where it had been deposited by Herbert Weld.

Sir Frederick then said, "In that case will you let us know the reserve you place upon it?" I told him that the reserve would be thirty thousand guineas, the figure at which the Luttrell Psalter was to be withdrawn. Sir Frederick then remarked, "That won't prevent it going to America."

I mention this because there is a slight mistake in the Introduction to the British Museum's beautiful reproduction of the Luttrell Psalter, in which it is said that the Bedford Book of Hours went for an unexpectedly high sum.

The scene at Sotheby's was a remarkable one. Buyers from Europe as well as from America were there, all ready to compete for the Psalter, jostling shoulders with art, literature and the social world. There was no room for my wife and myself, so we were ensconced in a corner behind the auctioneer's rostrum. The proceedings were almost as brief as my conversation with Sir Frederick Kenyon over the telephone. The auctioneer began by announcing that the Luttrell Psalter had been withdrawn from the sale by the owner, on behalf of the British Museum, for the sum of thirty thousand guineas. At this there was a burst of applause.

Then came the Bedford Book of Hours, which had not been withdrawn. The bidding lasted about one minute. It began at about fifteen thousand guineas, and the book was knocked down to the British Museum at £33,000.

In the history of the Luttrell Psalter, forming part of the Introduction to the British Museum's reproduction of the book, the ownership of the manuscript is described as passing from Sir Geoffrey Luttrell to the Earl of Arundel, and through marriage to Sir Nicholas Shireburn of Stonyhurst. The Introduction continues: "His property was inherited by his only daughter, Mary, Duchess of Norfolk, and in 1754 passed by her bequest to the Weld family of Lulworth Castle, Dorset, in consequence of the marriage of Elizabeth, sister of Sir Nicholas Shireburn, to William Weld, in 1672. . . . Thomas Weld (great-grandson of William Weld) in 1794 placed the mansion of Stonyhurst at the disposal of the English Jesuit College, the members of which had been driven from the Continent by the French Revolution, and thereby brought the present Stonyhurst College into existence. The manuscript . . . was preserved at Lulworth until 1896, in which year it was deposited in the British Museum by the Weld Trustees. . . . In September, 1928, however, Mr. Herbert Weld, who had succeeded to Lulworth Castle . . . announced his intention of selling the Psalter, and on January 8, 1929, the manuscript was removed from the Museum by Messrs. Sotheby, on the authority of a letter from Mr. Weld. . . . The loss of this great national monument to the country seemed a certainty, as the Museum could not hope, under ordinary conditions, to compete for such a book in the open market. . . . Three days before the sale an unexpected development occurred in the chance discovery by the Museum of the existence of legal proceedings whereby the Luttrell and Bedford Psalters, with other Lulworth heirlooms, had been adjudged the property of Mrs. Alfred Noyes."

"Mrs. Noyes, a granddaughter of Sir Frederick Aloysius Weld, derived her title to the heirlooms by virtue of the will of her late husband and cousin, Richard Shireburn Weld-Blundell, who was killed in the first world war."

The appeal for contributions to the purchase fund was issued over the signatures of the Archbishop of Canterbury and the Trustees of the British Museum. It said:

"British Museum, London W. C. 1.
March 1930.

"The following letter has been addressed to the Press by the Trustees of the British Museum:

"Sir,— . . .

"Through the public spirit of the owner, Mrs. Alfred Noyes, the Luttrell book was withdrawn from public competition, and was sold direct to the British Museum for £31,500; the Bedford book was put up to auction on July 29th, and was bought for £33,000, a figure which goes far to prove that the price paid for the Luttrell book was eminently reasonable. The money for both purchases was advanced to the Museum by Mr. J. Pierpont Morgan—an act of quite remarkable generosity on the part of an American collector who would have dearly liked to see both volumes in his own famous library in New York, but who recognised the paramount claims of England to the possession of these National Heirlooms. The money is lent for a year, without interest, on the terms that if the purchase money for either book is not repaid at the end of that time that book shall become Mr. Morgan's property.

. . . . . .

"His Majesty's Government have agreed to ask Parliament to make a special grant of £7,500. . . .

"The National importance of both books is unquestionable. Both are representative examples of English pictorial art, the one belonging to the great school that flourished in the Eastern counties in the first half of the fourteenth century, the other to the new style which made its appearance in the last quarter of that century and is the last great period in English illuminated art. Both are likewise historical monuments. The Luttrell Psalter has long been famous for its unrivalled series of pictures of English country life—its agriculture, its domestic customs, its games, its occupations, its beggars and pedlars, its tinkers and publicans. The Bedford Book of Hours, in addition to its interest as having been prepared for the brother of Henry V, and having belonged subsequently to William Catesby, the ill-famed Minister of Richard III, is unique in respect of its series of nearly 300 small portrait heads, representing various classes of society, from kings and nobles (including notably a portrait of Henry IV) to monks and laymen. It forms a portrait gallery of England at the time of Agincourt, which will be invaluable for purposes of comparison, or in deciding questions as to the nationality of pictures, such as recently arose in connection with the Wilton Diptych."

By what the British Museum called "a tragic coincidence," about a month later Lulworth Castle was destroyed by fire. My wife and I, by a further coincidence, were staying with the Weld-Blundells at Ince-Blundell Hall in Lancashire, when *The Times* at breakfast gave us the news by a large picture of Lulworth Castle in flames. Fortunately a tank corps which had been encamped in the neighborhood succeeded in saving practically all the contents of the Castle. Pictures by Gainsborough, Reynolds, Lawrence, Breughel, Lely, Janssen, Gerard David, and others, were dragged out of the building at considerable risk but without the slightest damage. Thousands of books from the fine old library were strewn all over the lawn (and as far as I could discover not one of them was injured), together with a chaos of beautiful old Chippendale furniture, all completely unscathed.

XXXVII

Bishop Barnes

IN 1928 Bishop Barnes of Birmingham perturbed the Anglican Church, to which he belonged, by a series of statements directly contradicting almost every article of the Creed he professed. He did it in a way that vitally concerned many millions outside the Anglican communion, for he frequently attacked their most sacred beliefs with a curiously insensitive crudity, and at times an almost incredible ignorance of the beliefs he was attacking. His abuse of the Church to which I belong was intellectually on a level with a quaint little catechism which once appeared in a Kensitite paper:

Q. What is the religion of the Italians?
A. They are Roman Catholics.
Q. What do Roman Catholics worship?
A. They worship idols and bits of bread.
Q. If God knew this would He not be very angry with the Italians?
A. God *is* very angry with the Italians.

Bishop Barnes, indeed, wished to make a chemical analysis of the bread and wine used in the Eucharist, thereby revealing his ignorance of the doctrine he was attacking, and of the distinction it makes (in common with the profoundest of modern secular philosophies) between the phenomenal world and the world of ultimate reality, which is the origin, end and "substantial" sustainment of all things. He would probably have agreed with the English peer who told me that to accept the Latin meaning of substance for philosophical purposes was "most un-English."

In a speech at the Birmingham Midland Institute on January 22, 1930, Bishop Barnes, again equally ignorant of the nature of the belief embodied in his own Creed, used disgusting language about the doctrine of the Virgin birth as it is set forth in that Creed. The only excuse that can be made for him is that he obviously neither understood the doctrine nor had any feeling at all for its hallowed associations. He said:

"The insects are remotely akin to ourselves. Among them virgin births are common. Yet none would pretend that such births imply divinity."

Bishop Barnes was apparently able to believe in the virgin birth of the entire universe, including himself, from a cloud of hydrogen gas, the primal nebula, but he was unable to believe that in the unique event of the Incarnation there was anything in the least exceptional, though in the tremendous assertion of Christianity it was the moment when, for men and their salvation, the Creator of the whole universe initiated a new life into which men must be born again. This, not its physical corollary, is the basis of the doctrine.

Bishop Barnes was reputed to be a good mathematician, but his reliance upon the outworn materialism of the Haeckel period had completely muddled his views on anything that transcends popular Victorian science.

On April 28, 1928, I wrote an article in the *Spectator,* entitled "The Diminishing Road," dealing with some of the questions which had thus been raised. I give a short extract:

"Even the most 'scientific' of the Bishops would hardly repudiate the idea of a Real Presence behind the 'accidents' of the smallest particle of the material universe, which was affirmed by the 'atheist' Shelley no less than by Blake and Wordsworth:

> Of Something far more deeply interfused,
> Whose dwelling is the light of setting suns, . . .
> A motion and a Spirit that impels
> All thinking things, all objects of all thought . . .

"Seen rightly, the very existence of the smallest grain of dust is an inconceivable miracle, an impossibility that has somehow happened, where, logically, there should be nothing at all. It seems more than a little odd, therefore (if they believe what they say they believe) that, in the special circumstances of the Eucharist, religious leaders should condemn as a necessarily foolish superstition the one public recognition of this ultimate and miraculous fact; a little strange that they should loosely brand as 'a magical process' the one common approach, 'not vaguely and in the void, but here and now,' through definite, concrete, localized instances, to the Spiritual Reality behind the veil; and that, while they are ready to follow all the interwoven spells of the late Professor Bradley (for that is a matter of intellectual pride) they should particularly repudiate the profoundly vital and triumphant analysis of Appearance and Reality, 'wherever the Sacrament of the Body broken, the Blood shed, is offered, received and pleaded,' in what even Carlyle* called 'the most genuine relic of religious belief now left to us.' "

Later Bishop Barnes used language so offensive about the faith held by the Catholic Church throughout the world that I decided to answer him. Accordingly I wrote a letter which appeared in *The Times* of Dec. 28, 1929.

There were many answers from correspondents, some of whom persisted in forgetting my own enthusiasm for the achievements of modern science. Bishop Barnes himself talked as if belief in the Nicene Creed necessarily meant the rejection of modern science. To all this I gave a reply which *The Times* printed on January 8th:

"*To the Editor of* The Times,

"SIR,— Unless my facts were unassailable, my criticism of Dr. Barnes would have been a grave injustice. One of your correspondents has denied those facts; and, since he is quite honestly indignant, silence on my part might be misunderstood.

"Dr. Barnes affirmed (page 152 of *Should Such a Faith Offend?*) that 'the Christian Church has never made the unguarded statement that Jesus was God.'

"I replied that, whether this historical Christian belief were true or false, it was the corner-stone of the whole fabric. In order to close what would seem the easiest door of escape to an evasive mind, I expressly dwelt upon the explicit language of the Nicene Creed concerning *both* the Godhead *and* the manhood. [God of God, Light of Light, very God of very God.]

"Your correspondent, ignoring this, says that Dr. Barnes meant

* *Thomas Carlyle, Life in London,* by Froude, Vol. II, p. 455.

only that the Church had always insisted that Jesus was *also* really and truly man. Dr. Barnes is so convinced of the Godhead of Jesus and finds the world so convinced of it at the present day, that he must really try to prove to us that Jesus was *also* really and truly man. This was for a modern audience to whom, as your correspondent suggests, *the Godhead was the chief difficulty;* and it only means that 'the human conditions under which the earthly life was passed involved a temporary and voluntary surrender of some of the functions of Godhead, such as omnipotence or omniscience.'

"Incredible as it must seem, not a single word of this explanation is true. There is not a single word in Dr. Barnes' discourse on the Deity of Christ about that temporary and voluntary surrender. He merely says that 'plainly, he was not omnipotent.' He has already made the statement that there may be many interpretations of the doctrine of the Incarnation; and that it is a misunderstanding to suppose it means that Jesus was God; for this would imply his omnipotence. This is followed by my original quotation. Then comes the flat statement that Jesus was really and truly man. The little word 'also' which your correspondent inserts, would have made a vast difference. But Dr. Barnes does not use it. There is not a word here with which Unitarians would disagree. He does not use the word 'also'; for that would have contradicted by implication what he had already said. *Nor, of course, does he say that the Church has never made the unguarded statement that Jesus was Man.* If not, why not? Your correspondent's appeal to the Nicene Creed surely makes this even more important in modern circumstances. The Church was not guarding itself against the fullest belief in both of those two propositions. It was guarding itself against the denial of either, a very different matter.

"Moreover, all this vague talk about 'a divine life passed among men' might occur in Plato. It has nothing in common with the tremendous affirmation of the Manhood *and also* the Godhead of the Incarnate Son, 'begotten of His Father before all worlds; God of God; Light of Light; very God of very God.' . . .

"I am not here contending for the truth of that supreme claim; but certainly this faith is not the 'truth' of Dr. Barnes. He quotes St.

Paul, in a text which is capable of many interpretations (and what he thinks of St. Paul when he disagrees with him may be discovered elsewhere), but he precedes the quotation by saying that the life which we ought to live 'was shown *finely* in Jesus of Nazareth.' Elsewhere he writes of 'His natural ability.' He makes it clear that he regards the Founder of Christianity as the culmination of man's evolution towards the divine, not as the God who, begotten before all worlds, has voluntarily descended to man, '*Et homo factus est.*' [the Son, of one substance with the Father], meeting man half-way on the road from earth to heaven, and becoming man that man might rise to God. Dr. Barnes believes in evolution; but not in this tremendous complement of the theory. He even discusses whether Jesus may, in the future, be surpassed by other men; and, though he concludes in the negative, it is clear that the Christian doctrine of the Incarnation is ruled out for him by Victorian science. But the central authority of Reason, before which the old decentralized Copernican universe begins already to fade into insignificance . . . is bringing about a new conception of the cosmos, and discovering new depths of majesty in the unique Event from which the sacramental system of Christianity has developed. Space, Time, and 'Matter' itself, no longer surround us with impenetrable walls.

"It is because Dr. Barnes rejects that unique Event, wherein earth and heaven meet, that he objects to the Sacraments. But let none think that . . . he will allow the Eucharist to be regarded as even a 'commemoration' in the sacred sense that has so long been cherished. The most solemn words that the Bishop has ever repeated, in the most august and moving rite of his own Church, 'Do this, as oft as ye shall drink it, in remembrance of Me,' he declares to be a fictitious interpolation by a later scribe, in the Gospel. On other occasions he holds up the authority of St. Paul; but St. Paul is no authority for him here; for Dr. Barnes dislikes what he says, and that destroys the value of St. Paul's testimony.

"Yet Dr. Barnes repeats those fictitious words, solemnly, at that ineffable moment; and, presumably, he intends them to be accepted by his hearers, as the solemn tones of his voice would suggest. He dismisses those heart-cleaving words on the shallowest of literary pretences, and on the authority of two small pedants. A liberal Protestant thinker, with a hundred recent authorities to support him, describes that dismissal as one of the most foolish in Biblical criticism. But I will not contend against it. I merely wonder how the Bishop of Birmingham can bring himself to repeat words that he believes to be fictitious, at the most solemn moment of his own communion service. I do not see how he can utter them over those bowed heads, knowing, as he must know, how deeply his fictitious words pierce into some hearts. This, sir, does move me profoundly, when I think of his invocation of ecclesiastical law against others, and the way in which he has spoken of what I, in common with the greater part of Christendom, truly believe.

"Your correspondent says it is 'bad taste' to criticize the Bishop of Birmingham thus. Yet, sir, not once, but hundreds of times in recent years, Dr. Barnes has trampled on the most sacred feelings of others. He has talked of 'reversions to savagery,' 'primitive magic,' 'crude superstition' in men whose intellectual shoes he cannot be allowed to unloose. He has dismissed great nations (including Italy) with progressive Christian contempt. And, frankly, I see no 'magic' in lawn-sleeves that should forbid a direct reply, couched, as it is, in far more courteous language. Lawn-sleeves, after all, are external. The things on which Dr. Barnes has set his heel are not. In many they are alive and sensitive, and they beat on the left side of the body.

"If he spoke as a Unitarian, or an agnostic, there would be nothing to say about his views. He would be entitled to them. But when he speaks as a Bishop, pledged to one thing, and following another; visiting the law on the sincere beliefs of others, and smashing the very foundations of that law himself; then, in the interests of our national integrity, the matter does most urgently require investigation.

"Yours etc.

ALFRED NOYES"

An article in *The Modern Churchman,* which looked as if it had been written by a rather illiterate and starry-eyed young man who had once read something about relativity in a newspaper, maintained the curious position that I, as a Catholic, had no right to defend the

Nicene Creed against a Protestant Bishop. The Protestant Bishop, on the other hand, had a perfect right to smash the Catholic Church because he was also attacking his own. However, the following letter from E. G. Selwyn, Dean of Winchester, one of the finest minds in the Anglican Church, more than absolved me:

"Jan. 17, 1930

"DEAR SIR,

"Will you allow me, although a stranger, to thank you for your two letters in *The Times* under the title of 'Christian Tenets.' You have, I am sure, rendered a public service in drawing attention to the inconsistencies of the Bishop of Birmingham's position; and I can imagine nothing more needful for the cause of Christianity in England today than insistence upon its distinction from Unitarianism. Further than that, there is the good faith of the Church and its ministers to be protected. Once let it be thought as Dr. Barnes' Westminster sermon last June aimed at making it thought, that the Church's formularies mean nothing in particular and can be subscribed to without further ado by any man of good-will, and the Church's distinctive task of witnessing to the Gospel is at an end.

"You have probably had many expressions of appreciation and support—as well perhaps as letters of another kind: but the issue is one where all like-minded Churchmen must stand together and discover themselves to one another.

"Believe me, dear sir,

"Yours faithfully,
E. G. SELWYN"

It may be added that Dean Inge in his diary attributes to Dr. Barnes "invincible ignorance" of Christian doctrine.

Perhaps this chapter may end with a little incident which I think is beautifully symbolical:

Bishop Barnes, at one stage in his career, constantly referred to the ritual of the Eucharist as "primitive magic"—but it is only fair to the Bishop of Birmingham to say that when the Anglican authorities tackled him about this he promised not to use that insensitive phrase again, and that he has kept his promise. One day before this concession he is said to have lost his way in the streets of Birmingham during a thick fog. Suddenly a Catholic priest emerged from the fog and asked if he might have the privilege of escorting the Bishop to his door. On arriving there Bishop Barnes asked the priest if he might know to whom he was indebted for this kindness. "Oh, merely the local magician," said the little brother of Father Brown, and disappeared.

XXXVIII

Dean Inge and Others

AT THE house of Lady Burghclere in Green Street there were frequent luncheon parties, seldom for more than six or eight, at which one met many of the most interesting figures of the day. Among these I particularly remember General Allenby, shortly after his return from Jerusalem; G. P. Gooch, the historian and editor of the *Contemporary Review;* Lady Bryce, whom I had met in Washington many years before when her husband was Ambassador there; Evelyn Underhill, a lean, brown, ascetic wisp of a woman, with an astringent face, who looked as if she might have ridden a bucking bronco, but whose books on Christian mysticism were found by Dean Inge "good, but too saccharine." There were also Stephen Gwynn, whom I had the fun of hearing discuss with great gusto an article I had written anonymously for the *Sunday Times;* and Lord Buxton, who had not long returned from his Governorship of South Africa.

My wife and I stayed with the Buxtons at New Timber, a paradisal place in Sussex which had the remarkable quality of being contemporary and at the same time melting into the landscape as if it had grown there and remembered the Middle Ages. There was a half circle of water that suggested a moat, and to fish in it would have rejoiced the heart of any monk on Friday morning. Lord Buxton was something of a naturalist and South Africa had given him a particular interest in ants. One day he received word at his London house that some remarkable ant-hills had been found at New Timber, and he decided to run down and investigate. After a happy day among the ant-hills he caught an afternoon train back to London. Very soon he began to feel uneasy. Quite a number of ants had apparently invaded his trousers and were unpleasantly active. He was alone in a first-class carriage; there was no corridor and it was a non-stop train to Victoria. He decided therefore to take off his trousers and shake them out of the window. He was doing this quite successfully when the train plunged into a tunnel, and in the sudden gust of compressed air the ballooning trousers escaped from his hands and disappeared! His first impulse was to pull the cord and stop the train, but he thought better of it. When the train reached Victoria he made the mistake of standing on his dignity, a thing not easily done, even by a peer, with his shirt-tails flapping about his bare legs. To the startled porter who looked into the compartment he announced majestically:

"I am Lord Buxton," on which the porter immediately shouted to another: "Hey, Bill, come quick! 'Ere's a bloke gone balmy!"

Ants as an explanation only confirmed the "balmyness," but eventually parliamentary experience prevailed, a taxi was brought as near as possible to the carriage, Lord Buxton leaped into it and was driven to Eaton Square, where again he made a further leap past an astounded butler, and upstairs to his bedroom.

One of the most remarkable characters I have known was Dean Inge. My wife and I first met him in July, 1926, at the house of Mr. and Mrs. Henry Dashwood in Hertfordshire. It was a very pleasant dinner party, and the Dean accompanied us back to London. In the train on our homeward journey he talked with prophetic emphasis about the black days that were to come upon England, expressing the hope that he would not live to see them. The resonance of his voice and the pungency of his remarks, however, suggested that this hope was likely to be unfulfilled. There were two elderly ladies in the compartment who looked as if they had strayed out of *Barchester Towers,* and as the Dean's prophecies of doom grew darker, they glanced anxiously from his gaiters to his face and then at one another with alarm.

They obviously felt that the atmosphere was Mephistophelian, and at the next stop they hurriedly changed compartments.

I did not meet the Dean again until after I had become a Catholic. This time we met at Lady Burghclere's house, and became great friends, though Lady Burghclere confided to me that she had wondered a little how the meeting would go off, for Dean Inge had spoken of my conversion to Catholicism as my "downfall." What he may have regarded as the political system of the Roman Church was something quite alien to his temperament and way of thought, but his understanding of the Catholic mystics was profound, and in his expositions of Christian platonism and the mystical element in religion there was a ground upon which all followers of the *philosophia perennis* could meet. Among other things, in his *Diary of a Dean* he mentions several Catholic friends, of whom I was privileged to be one, together with Christopher Dawson and von Hugel.

Incidentally, in the diary of his later years, he comments upon the crudity of the Bishop of Birmingham, and remarks, "I don't think Barnes realized how easily the Catholics could answer him." (*Diary of a Dean,* p. 161.)

The Dean and Mrs. Inge made several visits to us in the Isle of Wight, and his conversation was certainly not that of the "gloomy Dean" pictured by contemporary journalists, though there were elements in his character which might superficially have lent colour to the cliché. Sentences which looked saturnine or cutting in print had an ironical humour in real life, and came from his lips with an almost debonair gaiety. Moreover, he could tell stories at his own expense with great gusto.

The Dean took pleasure in informing his friends of an angry letter which he had received from a lady who disagreed with one of his articles.

"I am praying nightly for your death," she wrote. "It may interest you to know that in two other cases I have had great success."

When, after his retirement from the Deanery, he became a regular contributor to a London journal, he told us, with a chuckle, of the critical comment that he had ceased to be a pillar of the Church, and was now two columns of the *Evening Standard.*

Occasionally Dean Inge would let fall a startling remark with the calm of an *enfant terrible.* One such incident had implications of a serious nature. It was when Hitler was in full career. Inge had acquired a very charming house in the country, not far from Oxford. One evening, when he and Mrs. Inge were staying with us in the Isle of Wight for a week-end, he suddenly remarked at dinner: "I could have had my house in Oxfordshire for nothing if I had devoted one or two of my articles to the praise of Hitler." There was of course no question of war at the time. Having dropped his bombshell, Dean Inge relapsed into one of those trances in which his deafness was a useful defence against too curious questioning. It would have been a triumph for Nazi propaganda to have secured Inge, but that was about as likely as an exchange of pulpits between St. Paul's and Berchtesgaden.

There was a remarkable kinship between his mind and that of another famous Dean of St. Paul's, John Donne, and I could well imagine Dean Inge, if he had taken to verse instead of to prose, writing some of Donne's mystical sonnets. Curiously enough, from time to time he also reminded one of Dr. Johnson, and could make unexpected remarks almost as devastating about people with whom he disagreed. Moreover, he was almost comically unconscious of their effect upon his hearers. The eighteenth-century look was heightened by the knee-breeches, and the buckled shoes which he wore in the evening. According to his diary, however, he was greatly delighted when in his retirement he got "back to trousers"!

I sat next to him once at one of the big City companies' dinners, at the conclusion of which a very fine quartette prepared to give us some Mozart. The Dean was quite unconscious of the hush which awaited their first notes, and turning to me remarked in a high clear voice which rang through the entire hall: "There is nothing I detest more than music after dinner."

The Editor of the *Sunday Times,* Leonard Rees, who often visited us, told me that after a somewhat disastrous experience he always scrutinized with a very cautious eye the Dean's future contributions to his journal. He had sent one of these articles to the press unread, taking it for granted that he could trust so eminent a dignitary of the

Church to say nothing particularly naughty. To his horror, he was roused from his late slumbers on Sunday morning by the ringing of the telephone; the proprietor of the *Sunday Times* was on the line, acidly inviting him to read a certain paragraph in Dean Inge's article. Afterwards there followed a wild succession of telephone calls, some from Hibernian gentlemen expressing desires to take the editor of the *Sunday Times* to pieces. When at last he secured a copy of his own paper, he turned to Dean Inge's article, and there, in large type on the front page, he discovered a sentence which gaily referred to "that bloody and treacherous corporation, the Roman Catholic Church!" It was a very pale and subdued editor who later in the afternoon requested the telephone company to put through no more calls that day.

There was of course no possible excuse for the phrase, but St. Augustine might have exclaimed, *"Felix culpa!"* for it inspired some of the most superb pages in the English language, Belloc's open letter to Dean Inge. But the Dean simply did not mean it. In one of his pessimistic moods he might startle his readers by prophesying the catastrophic downfall of England, and yet in time of real crisis affirm his belief in her greatness. If he had been reading a book on the cruelties of Alva he might let fly a phrase which he would completely contradict in speaking of St. Augustine or some of the twentieth-century Neo-Thomists, and especially perhaps when in St. Paul's Cathedral he was reciting, as a part of the Creed, his belief in one holy Catholic and Apostolic Church.

Christian mystics, with whom so much of his best writing is concerned, were nearly all of course Catholics. I think that his occasional ejaculations against Rome were, more often than not, caused by the irritations of personal controversy. They were political, rather than religious.

One of the first letters I received from Dean Inge was evidently written when he was smarting under some uncomprehending attacks. I had sent him the third volume of my *Torch-Bearers,* in which the conclusion of a poem about the significant moments in scientific discovery was their consummation in the perennial philosophy of the *Civitas Dei.* He replied:

"Thank you for sending me the last volume of *The Torch-Bearers.*

It seems to me worthy of the other two, than which I can think of no higher praise.

"I am told that you excused yourself from vilifying me in the *Dublin Review;* and since I believe that every proselyte to your religion is expected to show his zeal by insulting me, I thank you sincerely, and hope you will not be made to suffer for it. I have had the honour and privilege of talking to Mrs. Noyes, and can well understand that you wish to worship at the same altar with her, though there may have been other reasons less intelligible to me!"

I was ill at the time, but in a letter which my wife was writing to Mrs. Inge I sent him a message giving him reasons which I hoped he might find intelligible; and Mrs. Inge wrote to my wife in reply:

"My husband was so grateful to you for giving him your husband's kind message. He was so anxious lest he might have hurt him, and you know his great admiration and affection for Mr. Noyes: you have made him very happy."

Developing the "intelligible reasons" still further, I ventured to send him my book *The Unknown God,* and he answered:

"Thank you very much for *The Unknown God.* I have read it, I hope with profit; and certainly with great admiration. The deep religious conviction impresses me even more than the beauty of the style. *Utinam noster esses!"*

Shortly after this the Inges came to us for a week-end. The Dean displayed great interest in a portrait (one of the Lulworth collection) of Cardinal Pole, by Sir Anthony More. The mother of the Cardinal, Margaret Pole, who at the age of eighty was executed by Henry VIII, was a forbear of the Welds. I noticed no shudderings over the Babylonian woe as Dean Inge examined another portrait, that of Cardinal Weld, the first English Cardinal since the Reformation (with the peculiar exception of Cardinal York).

The eagle-beaked portrait of Thomas Weld of Lulworth, by Beach, which faced the Dean at dinner, shows him clasping a plan of the first Catholic chapel built in England since the Reformation. George III gave him permission to build it, "but make it look like a Greek temple," he said, "or my idiotic subjects will burn it down."

"Very sensible of him," said the Dean.

Mrs. Inge, an angel in the house, with the delicate colouring of a Kate Greenaway picture, watched over the Dean and guarded him with her affection; while there were occasions when, wrapped in his own thoughts, he might have sat for a portrait of St. John of the Cross meditating on the dark night of the soul.

On May 14, 1932, my wife gave a coming-out dance for my step-daughter Agnes Weld-Blundell (afterwards Mrs. Paul Grey), and Mrs. Inge brought her young son and daughter to it. At the dance, owing to the burning out of a fuse, all the lights in the house went out for a minute or two just as the Mottistones were bringing a party of young people up the stairs to the ballroom. Lord Mottistone professed to be grateful for the incident as it had given him an opportunity to kiss the prettiest girl in his party. However, the next day Lady Mottistone told us that unfortunately the recipient of the embrace had broken out in measles, and the whole family was anxiously watching Papa for symptoms.

Behind all Dean Inge's wit there was a breadth of scholarship and a depth of thought which made his *Plotinus* one of the memorable books of our time, and established him as the leading exponent of Christian platonism in his generation. I think he came to understand Catholics better as time went on. He once told me that he had found more intellectual sustenance in the writings of the Neo-Thomists and other Catholics than in any other writings of our time. His only criticism of the Neo-Thomists was that they were not interested enough in the mystical elements in Catholicism.

The intellectual ground upon which he could meet Catholics is indicated in the following letter:

"I shall be seventy-seven in June, and sometimes think I have lived too long. I wish I had belonged to my grandparents' generation, and had gone out before the end of the century. The cruelty and callousness of our age appal me. It is the one thing that I had never expected. But I suppose things will right themselves in time. . . . The only book by Gilson that I have read is the Gifford Lectures, a fine book. But the Neo-Thomists are more Aristotelian and less Platonist than I realized—not really favourable to mysticism, and distrustful of Augustine. There is very good stuff in Berdyaeff; I still hope that Russia will revive what is good in Eastern Christianity."

It is a little surprising that he had not realized the Aristotelian basis of the Thomists, since the *Summa* of St. Thomas himself might be regarded as a baptizing of the *Stagirite*.

Dean Inge did not understand Chesterton or Belloc and I don't think they understood him. Once in accepting an invitation to lunch, he expressed a hope that he was not going to meet them. Belloc's open letter to Dean Inge is a masterpiece of English prose, but it is written to an imaginary character, who bore no resemblance to the author of the books on the Christian mystics, and of the remark which I quoted before about the Neo-Thomists. Belloc was merciless to the imaginary character, whom of course he left absolutely defeated.

Chesterton, if he had known Inge well, would certainly have revised his ideas about him, but he clung to the gloomy picture, and, amusingly enough, observed in one of his essays that while Father Christmas was a figure created by the normal joyousness of Christian people, he could hardly imagine anything less suitable for a Christmas card than a portrait of Dean Inge. Chesterton's wit, however, often made its point by excluding other considerations. Joan of Arc in flames and a plum pudding bathed in the blue fire of brandy cannot very well be brought into the same picture. Chesterton had never seen the twinkle in Dean Inge's eyes which made his outwardly sardonic remarks as amusing as Chesterton's brilliant explosions of Alice-in-Wonderland paradox.

It must be admitted that some of Dean Inge's remarks appeared outwardly to confirm a wicked little limerick on a Lambeth Conference:

> O God, forasmuch as without Thee,
> Our Bishops and Deans cannot doubt Thee,
> Give us grace in Thy name
> With one voice to proclaim
> We know nothing whatever about Thee.

On one occasion the Dean's son Craufurd asked his mother to explain the doctrine of the Trinity. Mrs. Inge, thinking this was really a matter for the theological learning of the Dean, suggested that he should see his father about it. Craufurd accordingly visited the Dean in his sanctum. To his mother's surprise he reappeared in exactly half a minute, with the reply, "Daddy says he knows no more about it than you do."

Perhaps this rather ludicrous incident masked a certain humility, but more probably the Dean was preparing his next sermon.

On one of the Dean's week-end visits we had a number of Catholic guests to meet him, among them Mr. and Mrs. Frank Sheed (Maisie Ward), Mr. and Mrs. Herbert Ward and Father MacDonald. The letter which Mrs. Inge wrote to my wife afterwards about this visit hardly suggests that the Dean felt himself in the midst of a "bloody and treacherous corporation."

"After such a superlatively happy visit, and such wonderful kindness shown to us both by you and the Poet, I hardly know how to begin my thanks.

"Our visit to you was not just a 'week-end,' it was something much bigger and deeper. To me the happiness was something I rarely enjoy, which was to know that my Ralph was supremely happy. . . . It was also a great pleasure to have met Mr. and Mrs. Sheed—they and the children all seem to have added to the wonderful hours we spent with you. . . ."

There were many pleasant references in letters from the Dean and his wife to our "happy island" and the Undercliff, where before the roses finish blooming the primroses appear in great clusters along our little falling brook. There was mention too of raspberries, and cream from the Guernsey herd.

I sent the Dean my book *Orchard's Bay,* in which each chapter, beginning with some feature of the garden or the Undercliff as a text, branches out into such subjects as the garden of St. Clare at Assisi, and the illustration of the perennial philosophy which St. Augustine drew from the reflection of a tree in a pool: "The reflection is caused by the tree, yet is coeval with it."

The war-clouds were thickening at this time, and the Dean profoundly distrusted the political manoeuvres of the day; he thought that a kind of madness had come upon the politicians. One sentence in his reply was prophetic:

"We have both been enjoying immensely your charming account of your earthly paradise. I have never seen a house and grounds which so completely realize my ideal of a country house. Do you know that I once thought of buying Southview at Blackgang? It never came to anything, but I did look at it. There is no place like the Island. Like other men of my age I feel that I have lived too long, and shall be glad to be spared what is coming for us all. *Stultum facit Fortuna quem vult perdere.*"

During the early months of the war, although Southampton and Portsmouth were targets for bombers, the Inges visited us at Lisle Combe more than once. The Dean had a far more prophetic insight into the evil days that were coming than any of the political leaders, and he could not bear to hear the news broadcasts. One of the friends whose historical views he shared died in April, 1940, and both he and Mrs. Inge felt the loss keenly. She wrote to my wife:

"I have just seen *The Times,* 8 o'clock. We have lost one of our best and most honoured friends in H. A. L. Fisher. Like Saul, his strength of intellect, mind and wit was not abated. I hoped for much still from his pen."

Shortly after this, Mrs. Inge wrote again to my wife:

"Ralph has been deeply stirred by a book sent him by the *Evening Standard, The Diary of a Country Priest* by Georges Bernanos. He predicts that it will be a classic. He wrote an article last week on it, called "The Soul of a Priest." The language is beautiful in its great simplicity, and the author lays bare the soul of his hero."

During the war the Dean and Mrs. Inge stayed for some weeks with my sister-in-law, Mrs. Walmesley, at Culmhead, near Taunton in Somerset. Colonel Walmesley, her husband, came of one of the old English Catholic families, and they had their private chapel in the house. Dean Inge did not attend the services, but he spent hours alone in the chapel, where the altar lamp burned before the Blessed Sacrament.

A letter from Mrs. Inge to my wife, when we were in America, indicates what they had found in this Catholic house:

"I feel it is through your dear friendship and that of the Poet that we have had one of the happiest week-ends we have ever spent together. I could not feel strange or shy here—for your dear sister talks so exactly like you that if I shut my eyes I could almost believe I was listening to you. This whole house radiates kindness and happiness—just because they live by their high traditions. . . . I have been thinking so much of you lately. If you have a moment, do go 'down town' and look at old Holy Trinity Church [New York], the great bronze doors at the west end, finely sculptured, were given by my great uncles, Gouverneur Morris of Morrisania, and his younger brother."

A son of the Inges died heroically during the second world war, in which the Dean thought we had made some dire mistakes, a reflection which gave a touch of Greek tragedy to a noble death. There is a reference to this in a letter from Mrs. Inge to my wife, speaking of the brutal way in which it was announced: "Your son was killed this morning and we should like to know where you wish him to be buried."

She also wrote of a visit to Downside:

"I have for the moment a little lost touch with my loved Walmesley family. . . . I took WRI up for a week at the Cumberland Hotel and arranged he should see most of his old friends. We lunched with his faithful friend Beaverbrook, Lord Privy Seal, who had just brought the P. M. safely home from Morocco. The P. M. should have an illness once a year like this one, that is the *only* way to make him rest! On the whole we felt Beaverbrook was in good spirits about the war and in extremely good health himself. . . . Do you know we actually spent a long and *most* happy day at Downside with Mme. de Lagarenne and Mr. Algernon Cecil, and were entertained to tea by the Lord Abbot. It was amusing to see the two men (WRI and the Abbot) finding more and more in common with each other and drawing their chairs closer and closer together!

"WRI has set all the Press of the country by the ears over his tiny speech of 8" at the Ruskin Lunch in London. There were seven other speakers drearily long who talked in honour of my old friend John

Ruskin. His was the only one which *The Times* reported and it has been copied throughout the length of the kingdom, generally with angry comments and once more his epithet 'Gloomy' is in full swing! —Angry articles and some brilliant cartoons because he said he foresaw an England . . . of 20 million agriculturists, craftsmen and others, and that a nation who had higher wages than any other and who lived by imports could not possibly compete. He warned the country 30 years ago, not so drastically, and was dubbed *Gloomy* then and is now *Gloomier*. The *Daily Express* had an article headed *Ingeland*."

Just before the Dean's ninety-first birthday I wrote to thank him for a very kind letter about my seventieth birthday, and in his reply he quoted a phrase from the great Catholic poem by Bernard of Cluny, *"Hora novissima, tempora pessima sunt. Vigilemus,"* which might be aptly translated for our own day: "These are the most modern times. Nothing could be worse. Look out!" The Dean also spoke of his annual participation in "High Mass" at Pusey House, and with a flash of the old wit indicated his relish of a Catholic friend's comment:

"When I preach at 'High Mass' at Pusey House, as I do every year, I always remember the comment of a Roman Catholic who was persuaded to attend one of their services: 'It was very well done, but I prefer the simplicity of our own ritual.'

"All believers in the *philosophia perennis* are philosophically my friends. Oxford and Cambridge seem to be whoring after the strangest gods—Wittgenstein and Gilbert Ryle, Professors of Philosophy; Ayer held in honour. Plato, Aristotle, Saint Thomas, Kant and Hegel, it seems, talked nonsense; they were not 'meaningful'! I fear we are in for a dark age.

"George Tyrell once said, 'The time may come when there will be nothing left of Christianity except mysticism and charity.' I hope not 'nothing else,' but these, I think, are the indestructible bed-rock. The poor C. of E. is in a bad way, for the class which mainly supported it is being systematically exterminated by taxation."

In the same letter he writes:

"I shall be 91 on June 6th, and rather hope it will be my last birthday. For *tempora pessima sunt* and I am very lonely without my dear wife; I am glad that you knew her."

XXXIX

Drama Through the Ages

THE PLEASURES that may accrue to an author in seeing his work well performed on the stage have now and then been mine, sometimes in quite unexpected ways and on special occasions. My one-act play *Rada* (*A Belgian Christmas Eve*) was produced in New York during the first world war. My longer play *Sherwood,* of which a special acting edition was published in America for the use of schools and colleges, was performed in many open-air theatres over a long period of years. Some of these were brilliantly produced and beautifully acted. Lena Ashwell's production in London in 1926 was at a small theatre, but it was well done, and gave me at least a taste of what a more successful playwright must feel on a larger scale.

One of my most delightful surprises took place at New Orleans. I had just arrived in that city to give a lecture when I discovered that the annual Mardi Gras was taking place, and that the subject chosen for the pageant which was to pass in procession through the streets was my *Sherwood!* A special supplement in the leading newspaper gave four pages of charming coloured drawings of the various floats in the procession, each of them representing passages in the play, with the verse quotations under each picture.

I quote the description it gave of the twentieth of these floats:

"Once again the gates of dreamland open—through the devotion and sacrifice of the poor fool, Shadow-of-a-Leaf. Robin and Marian, their pathway strewn with ferns, are led to a new life beyond the shadows.

Green ferns in the dawn-red dew-fall,
This gift by my death I give—
They shall wander immortal through Sherwood!
In my great green house they shall live!
They shall pass through the Gates, they shall live!
For the Forest, the Forest has conquered!
This gift by my death I give!

Thus, fading into the mists of memory, passes another stately and glorious pageant, and leaves us but the recollection of a passing dream."

No young poet travelling in a distant country could have received a more heartening welcome. I could hardly have expected to find my own thoughts of English woodlands moving through the streets of that picturesque city in Louisiana, with its memories of old France.

In England some of my poems had the great good fortune to be delivered by one of the truest artists of the nineteenth-century theatre, Irene Vanbrugh. Her recital of "The Barrel Organ" at a charity performance was so successful that she continued, on many occasions thereafter, to invite audiences to "come down to Kew in lilac-time."

Her jubilee was celebrated in His Majesty's Theatre on June 20, 1938, and the Queen occupied the Royal box. The prologue I had been invited to write for the occasion was spoken by Noel Coward. I tried to give expression in it to the very sincere feeling of all who shared in that celebration, by making it not so much a retrospect as a little lyrical drama moving forward from Irene Vaubrugh's first performance as Phoebe in *As You Like It,* to the moment in which the curtain was to go up on her appearance "here and now":

Fifty years back—or was it yesterday
In *As You Like It,* London saw her play
A shepherdess, named Phoebe. . . .
The play nears
Its end before that shepherdess appears.
The player is too young for fame; and yet
At her first words, her listeners forget
The make-believe, the trappings and the stage.
Green boughs are round them, and the golden age.

Fifty years back in Arden—though her name
Was printed small, through that proud wood she came;
And, all at once, old London was aware
That Shakespeare's very shepherdess was there,
The bird-like eyes, the living truth and grace,
The spirit of youth and wonder in her face—
Speaking, as April might or April's birds,
The Master's echo of Kit Marlowe's words:
"Dead shepherd, now I find thy saw of might.
Who ever loved that loved not at first sight?"
Fifty years back—she made the woodland shine
Like youth and morning with that echoed line,
Gave all the poet's life to her small part,
And wrote her name on London's mighty heart.

Irene Vanbrugh—at that name there rise,
In all our hearts to-day, what memories,
What legends of a London, long ago,
When London, Sirs, *was* London, as ye know!
Great days when Alexander reigned in power,
And Ernest was important—for an hour!
But she—our living best—through all those years
Has moved old London's heart to smiles and tears,
And still—with timeless art that grows not old,
Brings back *our* youth, *our* London's age of gold,
When she was Rose Trelawney, or Letty Shell,
Rosamund in *The Liars,* or Mis' Nell
Of New Orleans; or when she swept the stage
As Lady Teazle, or as Mistress Page;
Swayed us with Barrie's magic; or, once more,
Moved to her darker throne at Elsinore.

Whether she played the subtlest of her sex,
Or breathed soft nothings to *The Gay Lord Quex,*
She made them live, whatever part she took—
Clara in *Money,* Kate in *The Twelve Pound Look,*
Belinda, Viceroy Sarah, or Amy Grey,
Flashing from gay to grave, and grave to gay,
And carrying London with her all the way.

Fifty Years back? In Arden? No, that glade
Is of the timeless world where nought can fade—

The world of beauty. Spirits that live there
May play at age, and still be young and fair.
From age to youth, the parts again shall change.
Where'er it will, the quickening soul may range.

So—when that curtain rises—you shall see
Not only scenes that shine in memory,
Forty years back—but, still beneath her sway,
Twenty years back, and *ten,* and *yesterday!* . . .
Yesterday? Here and now, this very night,
London shall still increase its old delight,
With great new memories, ere that curtain fall,
And find the living present best of all!

The prologue was printed in *The Times* on the following day. It pleased me greatly that some of those who admired the exquisite art of Irene Vanbrugh and perhaps were filled with a certain nostalgia for a traditional London which seemed to be passing away, should have felt that her own personality was faithfully depicted in the lines.

In February, 1932, a pageant representing Drama Through the Ages was enacted at Grosvenor House, with Mr. Frank Lascelles as the producer. It was opened by Lady Linlithgow, on the eve of her departure for India. She took the part of the Spirit of the Drama, and delivered a prologue in verse which I had been asked to write. The production was an elaborate one, with scenes from Indian, Chinese, Japanese, Greek and British Drama, a Marie Antoinette episode in which the Queen was represented by Lady Anne Wellesley; and a group of Shakespearean characters, including Juliet represented by Miss Rose Bingham, Ophelia by Miss Vivian St. George, and Desdemona by Miss Peggy Gordon-Moore. Indian drama was represented by the *Rising of the Moon,* an ancient allegory, with Mr. Choudhouri as Reason; Chinese drama by a scene from *The Circle of Chalk;* and Japanese drama by *The Heavenly Cave,* adapted for the stage by Mr. Gonnoske Komai. Professor Gilbert Murray took a great interest in the Greek scene, which showed a procession at the festival of Bacchus, with Lady Dalrymple-Champneys as Helen of Troy, Lady Anne Hope as Antigone, and Lady Elizabeth Hare as

Ismene. A short passage from *Iphigenia in Aulis* was included in the Greek scene, and the beginnings of English Drama were represented by a short scene from the early Nativity play *Bethlehem.*

My prologue was what might be called a slightly dramatized ballade about the first nights of famous plays, opening with an imaginary picture of the first night of *Hamlet,* and the quite possible belief of the audience that this was merely one more "new play." Towards the end of the ballade Touchstone interrupts, asking questions about Barrie and Bernard Shaw, to which answers are given in the *Envoi.* We had a little rehearsal at Hanover Terrace beforehand, with Miss Olga Nethersole directing, and giving unearthly effect to the phrase with which the ghost of Sulla opens Ben Jonson's *Catiline.*

The prologue, which was printed in *The Times* on the following day, has not been included in any of my books:

Ballade of First Nights

When, for the first strange time on any stage,
The sentry cried, "Who's there?" at Elsinore,
The apple-munching crowd of that great age
Stared at a scene that Time shall not restore.
They did not know whose Ghost was at the door
When first they heard the Prince of Denmark speak.
They clapped; and went on munching as before;
And said, "There'll be another play next week!"

They heard the first wild Ariel assuage
Old ocean, and subdue The Tempest's roar;
Thought Caliban more amusing than the Mage
Who buried in the deep his magic lore.
They heard a voice dissolving earth's wide shore,
And all her granite mountains, peak by peak,
Into thin air; then—threw away the core;
And said, "There'll be another play next week!"

The kings go by in glittering equipage,
Sheer night engulfs the robes and crowns they wore.
Dost thou not feel me, Rome? In deathless rage
The ghost of Sulla rends the grave once more.
Our ravening world devours the brood it bore;

And in six months our moderns grow antique.
But Egypt smiles, Time is not conqueror;
And Jonson's Romans may return, next week.

TOUCHSTONE, *interrupting:*

Prince, in a dozen decades or a score
Sir James may still be playing hide and seek;
But will the waves be whispering to the ssh—
Or
Shall we join the ladies for bezique?

THE SPIRIT OF THE DRAMA, *waving him aside:*

Prince, in three thousand years, or even four,
Our barbarous best may still out-shine the Greek!
On with the pageant! Tell the centuries o'er;
And teach old Time the truth about next week!

XL

The Shape of H. G. Wells

IN THE summer of 1929 we made a short visit to the Isle of Wight, during which we explored a garden that had been described as the loveliest in the Island. My wife and Agnes were enchanted with it, and very shortly Lisle Combe became our own.

This was another instance of the way in which the events of one's life fall into an unforeseen pattern, for after we had acquired it we discovered that many generations ago this part of the Island had belonged to the de Lisles, my wife's forbears.

My book *Orchard's Bay* tells how "memory, use and love" made it the place that I call home.

For a year or two after we went to the Isle of Wight we retained our house in Hanover Terrace, but the Island held us more and more, and eventually we decided to give up the London house.

Almost immediately a letter reached me from H. G. Wells, saying he had been informed by an estate agent that the lease was for sale, and he would like to have it. He said he had been looking for a house to die in, and thought mine would suit him perfectly. I was naturally anxious to help him.

Accordingly, after a brief correspondence, he flew down to the Isle of Wight to stay the night with us and discuss a few minor details. I met his plane at the Shanklin airfield. The author of the *War of the Worlds* alighted from the plane with a vivacity which suddenly vanished when he discovered that his luggage had been left behind—but he had no sooner made this discovery than a great thought entered his mind. "This is very serious," he ejaculated in his shrill little voice, which had a queer resemblance to the cry of a bat at twilight. "This is very serious. The whole of my manuscript, *The Shape of Things to Come,* was in my bag. I have no other copy. If I lose it I shall have lost a year's work." He appeared to be really agitated, and in my innocence I took him seriously.

He could get no information at the airfield, and we hurried on to Lisle Combe, where I thought he could sit more comfortably at the telephone and make all the necessary inquiries. To my surprise, however, instead of using the telephone he asked for writing materials and began to outline a kind of publicity campaign, the initial move being a nation-wide search for a manuscript lost at an airport. In fact, it would be hard to think of a theme more inspiring to the composer of headlines: "Priceless Wells MSS Lost in the Air" would surely make the front page of any self-respecting journal.

Incredible as it now seems, the first moves in that prospective campaign, as written down in his own hand on a sheet of foolscap which is now in my possession, ran thus:

(1) Associated Press
(2) Lord Beaverbrook
(3) Scotland Yard.

However, as Henry Adams might have said, my education was incomplete at the time and I really thought that the seriousness of his loss had upset his nervous system. I therefore consulted a neighbour of ours, one of the directors of the Isle of Wight air service. I told him that Wells had what appeared to be the beginning of a nervous breakdown, adding that I was not surprised, for to lose *The Shape of Things to Come* was a serious matter. My friend rose nobly to the call. "We certainly ought to be able to discover what has become of his bag," he said and, going to the telephone, with a few crisp inquiries he elicited the unromantic fact that an old lady named Wells had flown from Heston to Newcastle that day and taken with her everything labelled with that magic name, including, of course, *The Shape of Things to Come*. My friend assured me, however, that they would send for it at once and bring it back by what, in those early days, he called a "racing plane."

I returned to Wells with the good news, and if looks could have killed I would have been a dead man. Apparently I had ruined everything. And worse was to follow: Later in the evening I had a call from my friend in the air service, telling me they had found Mr. Wells' bag at Newcastle; it was too big to be put into the "racing plane," but, knowing how anxious he was, they had taken the liberty of unpacking it and were bringing back all the contents at once. The bag would follow the next day. Then came the devastating climax! "I think Mr. Wells ought to be told immediately that we found his pajamas but there was no sign of any manuscript whatever."

It was not an easy message to convey to the already infuriated novelist, softened though it might be by the obvious implication that here indeed was a case for Scotland Yard. But he dropped the subject completely.

For that night, however, I provided him with pajamas, which he complained were too long in the leg, and a safety razor, which he complained was behind the times. The Island's sunlight, the next morning, he complained was an escape from reality. He said that if he had only been able to meet Kipling, he thought Kipling would have declared him a "pukka sahib."

At lunch that day we had a few guests to meet him, and he appeared to be mollified a little, though he made up for it by airing some of his pet hates. The other guests, fortunately, were old friends of mine, and though they were typical of the conservative and patriotic English of the countryside, they did not gratify Wells by appearing to be shocked when he deliberately dropped a verbal bomb-shell in referring to the Royal Family as "those rabbits and swine in Buckingham Palace." Herbert Ward, son of the biographer of Newman, in outward appearance as typical a country squire as John Bull himself, but a man of immeasurably wider reading and intellectual grasp than Wells, looked at him steadily for a moment and asked with quiet courtesy: "Why do you feel so strongly about them, Mr. Wells?" The novelist gave a curious explanation. He muttered something about his mother having adored them. Ward immediately got under his guard with the one swift retort of which Wells would feel the sting: "Hardly a scientific reason, Mr. Wells."

Wells then proceeded to take it out of Catholicism, and made an enchanting remark about Chesterton and Belloc, who had been having great fun with his *Outline of History.* I don't know who was responsible for calling it "An Outline of Everything," but the title had a keen critical point; Wells felt the smart of their expert skinning, and attributed its popular success to their Catholic conviviality. "Chesterton and Belloc," he said, "have surrounded Catholicism with a kind of boozy halo." At this point someone suggested that we should take our coffee in the sunlight on the verandah, and immediately Wells exclaimed petulantly: "Oh yes, let us get away from reality."

Later in the afternoon the Priestleys came over, but Wells' inner man was still sighing after Lord Beaverbrook and Scotland Yard. Priestley sat beside him in a garden chair and began talking to him cheerfully, as one craftsman to another, unaware of Wells' emotional disturbance. After a few minutes Wells closed his eyes and deliberately began to snore. Mrs. Priestley, seated on the other side of Wells, gave a little start at the sound, looked with some amazement at the face of the sleeping beauty, then turned to her husband and said gently: "Surely, Jack, this is very rude of Wells?" Altogether I had a most enjoyable afternoon.

Wells made no explanation of his mistake about *The Shape of Things to Come,* but he never forgave me for the failure of the Great Idea. People who did not know that we had left 13 Hanover Terrace would occasionally try to reach us there on the telephone, with explosive results at that end. Letters, some containing cheques, would occasionally be delivered there by mistake, and were marked with a furious

"Not Known" in blue pencil, and returned to the postman without any of the aids which I had so freely given to the restoration of Mr. Wells' bag.

But the Fates, to a certain extent, had avenged me by anticipation. When the keys of the house were handed over to Wells, he went there one afternoon alone to explore and decide what he was going to do with it. He went up to a room which had been our nursery, and, as our dear old Nannie once said, sitting before the fire with one of her charges on her lap:

"Nobody knows but me and the Mouse
How cozy it is at the top of the house."

Outside the nursery there was one of those old-fashioned folding fire-escapes, an iron contraption which could be let down from the ceiling in case of need and offered a way out to the roof, from which you could walk to the far end of that long row of Georgian houses. This fire-escape was very heavy, and when folded was held in place by a massive chain. Wells wanted, of course, to see how it worked, and though he was ingenious enough to unfasten the chain, he was also, symbolically, not alive to the fact that the folded ladder would probably unfold. It unfolded, with considerable force, and hit the unexpectant novelist on the bridge of his nose, causing what the old prize fighters called "a-tapping of his claret."

The extraordinary thing about this accident was that although Wells was alone in the house, an account of the accident appeared in the London evening papers hardly more than an hour later. He must have staggered to the telephone with the blood streaming from his nose, and asked for either the Associated Press or Lord Beaverbrook.

In those days a press-cutting agency used to send me all newspaper cuttings relating to my work. I do not think the accident to H. G. Wells could fairly have been called my work, but twenty-four hours later I received a bundle of press cuttings big enough to choke an elephant. "This," I said to myself, "is fame," for I was still young enough in heart to cherish that illusion. But there they were, scores of them, with such headings as "H. G. Wells Gets Blow on Nose in Poet's House." Many were even illustrated with photographs of the injured novelist's rueful countenance peering out under bandages. Some of the stories were not explicit enough to please me. They all mentioned "the Poet's house" but did not make it clear that Wells got the blow on his nose from a machine and not from the poet.

However, there was what might be called a symbolical adjustment of this when, later on, Wells distinguished himself by telling one of his audiences that nothing of any value had ever come out of Palestine, and fortifying this remarkable assertion by saying that "Solomon's Temple was no larger than the average British barn." The opening was really irresistible. In a brief letter to *The Times* I ventured to point out that Mr. Wells' head, out of which so many brilliant ideas had come, was certainly no larger than the average British pumpkin. This contribution to anthropology brought me an amusing letter from Chelsea, saying that the undersigned (there were many signatures) wished to thank me very cordially for my straight left to Mr. Wells' pumpkin!

As an imaginative writer, in his *Country of the Blind,* or as a humorist in *Tono Bungay* and *Kipps,* Wells had great gifts, but his reasoning was often as superficial and even silly as that of the crude "fundamentalist" interpretation of the Scriptures, although of course his approach was from the opposite direction. For instance, he once remarked pontifically, of an innocent little hymn for children, that modern astronomy had put an end to all that nonsense about "a friend beyond the bright blue sky." But as an artist Wells should at least have understood that for little children unseen realities can be represented symbolically or pictorially, and that neither the telescope nor the microscope has anything to do with it.

But in some of these alleged "conflicts between science and religion" neither side understands what the other is driving at. I am reminded of a dispute described to me by the Astronomer Royal nearly fifty years ago. He had been manipulating his big telescope at Greenwich, when quite by accident a church steeple swam into his field of vision. His powerful lenses disclosed that it had a very dangerous crack, of which the parish was probably quite unaware. After some difficulty he succeeded in getting the Vicar on the telephone, and the conflict between science and religion proceeded something like this:

SCIENCE: This is the Astronomer Royal speaking.

VICAR (*with great respect*): Ah, yes. Yes. Dear me!

SCIENCE: I am sorry to tell you that your steeple is cracked.

VICAR (*after a pause, coldly*): If this is a practical joke, I completely disapprove.

SCIENCE: But I assure you my telescope—

VICAR: Don't talk nonsense.

SCIENCE (*incisively*): I am trying to avert a catastrophe. I am speaking from the Greenwich Observatory, and I assure you that your steeple is very seriously cracked.

VICAR: This is really an outrage—

SCIENCE: I will tell you what I will do. I will ring off, and I suggest that you ring up the Greenwich Observatory, and ask for the Astronomer Royal to confirm my statement.

VICAR (*still sceptical, but a little shaken*): A pretty fool I should look, ringing up the Astronomer Royal to ask if my steeple is cracked!

SCIENCE: Then get one of your churchwardens to do it.

VICAR: We-l-l, I think I may have one who is a big enough fool.

And so religion and science were reconciled, with at least the temporary salvation of the Vicar's flock, for the Astronomer's diagnosis proved to be exactly true; the vibration of the organ might have brought the steeple crashing down on the heads of the congregation.

XLI

In the Isle of Wight

VERY SHORTLY after we had taken up our abode in the Isle of Wight there came a telephone call from the other side of the Island, and a pleasant voice said, "This is Alfred Tennyson speaking." A little startling, though I soon realized I was talking not to a ghost but to the grandson of the poet. It was indeed a delightful welcome to the Isle of Wight.

Alfred Tennyson, the younger, might have been a poet in his own right, but, as he told me at Farringford, it was an obvious disadvantage for a young writer to be named Alfred Tennyson. It was like being named Euripides or William Shakespeare, and editors would certainly look askance at a modern poem submitted under the name of John Milton.

After our first meeting there was sent to me from Farringford a small yew tree, a child of the famous yew which had inspired several passages in Tennyson's poems ("O, brother, I have seen this yew-tree smoke, spring after spring, for half a hundred years"). It was accompanied by an off-spring of the Italian laurel which was sent to Tennyson by the Florentines when he wrote his poem on the sixth centenary of Dante:

King, that hast reigned six hundred years, and grown
In power, and ever growest, since thine own
Fair Florence, honouring thy nativity,
Thy Florence, now the crown of Italy,
Hath sought the tribute of a verse from me,
I, wearing but the garland of a day,
Cast at thy feet one flower that fades away.

There also came to us a young cedar of Lebanon, a child of the great cedar in the garden at Swainston which inspired some of the poet's most beautiful lines:

Art thou sighing for Lebanon
In the long breeze that streams to thy delicious East,
Sighing for Lebanon,
Dark cedar, tho' thy limbs have here increased,
Upon a pastoral slope as fair,
And looking to the South, and fed
With honey'd rain and delicate air,
And haunted by the starry head
Of her whose gentle will has changed my fate
And made my life a perfumed altar-flame;
And over whom thy darkness must have spread
With such delight as theirs of old, thy great

Forefathers of the thornless garden, there
Shadowing the snow-limb'd Eve from whom she came.

In some ways those lines are surely the most beautiful ever written about a tree.

Subsequently we saw a good deal more of Charles Tennyson, another grandson of the poet. His devotion to his grandfather's memory has added something of great value to future estimates of the English Virgil. What may be called the official biography by Hallam Tennyson is an extremely valuable book, and contains appreciations of Tennyson by contemporaries as various as Huxley, Benjamin Jowett, Tyndall, Palgrave and Watts-Dunton. It has been seriously underestimated as a biography through the fatuous notion of recent decades that the filial piety of a son, in saying nothing derogatory about his father, deprives his record of authenticity. There is infinitely more to be said for the opposite view that affection and long intimacy are far more likely to enable a biographer to understand his subject than any attempt to replace these things by cheap and easy methods of "debunking." These often obtain their apparent realism by a flagrant disregard of truth. Nor, as I have said, did Hallam Tennyson rely upon himself alone. In the age of Tennyson scholarship was not undervalued as it is to-day, and the opinions of his great contemporaries in many fields have weight.

But Sir Charles Tennyson has the double advantage of remembering his grandfather with affection and of carrying on the tradition of scholarship to a much later generation (he must have been one of the very few men in the City who carried a pocket Homer about with them). His biography of his grandfather contains much new material that gives additional strength to the characterization of the poet, and it is good to think that Tennyson's fame may thus be carried on by a scholar of his own line.

Tennyson's house at that time looked very much as it did when he lived there; his library was exactly as he had left it, with his pipe and tobacco on a large writing table, and a curious little stair winding down from the library to the garden, a kind of escape exit that somehow suggested a miniature turret stair in one of the Arthurian idylls. At the foot of the stair there were still the two wooden bears, very realistically carved, which he had brought from Switzerland in his younger days. Kipling once suggested that a thing so slight as the drowning of a kitten by a little girl might have put the idea of Lady Macbeth into the mind of Shakespeare; and I have often wondered if the two great beasts between which the searcher had to pass in the Holy Grail: "Go forward, or the beasts will tear thee piecemeal" may have originated in Tennyson's mind when, after a moonlit walk in his garden, he passed between those two bears to regain his library. Many great things in literature have sprung from smaller seeds.

During this decade a new form of happiness came to me in the births of our three children, Hugh, Veronica and Margaret. In 1936 my step-daughter, Agnes, was married to Paul Grey, then Third Secretary of the British Embassy in Italy.

Paul was so amazingly like his relative, Lord Grey of Falloden (as a young man), that photographs of them at the age of twenty-seven might have been interchangeable. Robert Wilberforce told me that when he first met Paul, Robert and his colleagues at the British Information Services in New York felt there had been a kind of reincarnation, and they could not take their eyes off the avatar. They hoped that he hadn't thought he was under any darker suspicion.

In those years Princess Beatrice was Governor of the Island. One evening when we were dining at Carisbrooke she turned to me and asked, with just a touch of that German accent which makes a question formidable: "Do you not think Lord Tennyson was a great bear?" She then proceeded to tell me why she thought so.

"When I was a very young girl I was taken to see Tennyson at Farringford. Mrs. Tennyson was an invalid and I thought she had been standing too long, so I said to her 'Won't you please sit down, Mrs. Tennyson,' whereupon Tennyson said in his big voice, 'Please don't think we are standing up for you.' Was not that r-r-rude?"

It certainly would have been, had the poet's intention been what Princess Beatrice thought, but he was obviously trying to make her feel that her presence was a source of complete pleasure.

"He did worse than that," she went on. "When I was married he dedicated a poem to me in which he called my wedding a white funeral. Was not that *awful?*" Again it would have been, if Tennyson had meant what Princess Beatrice thought he meant. Reference to the context shows, however, that while the first part of the poem gives expression to the joyous side of the occasion, the passage in which the misunderstood phrase occurs refers to and deprecates the conventional tears of motherhood, which were sometimes shed over the "white funeral of the maiden life." The phrase "white funeral" exactly expresses the feeling conveyed by the tears and snifflings so often seen in those days; and Tennyson was poetically suggesting that they would be out of place—at least that was his intention. His mistake, perhaps, was in too vividly describing what he deprecated.

At another dinner in Carisbrooke, Princess Beatrice, *à propos* of nothing in particular, suddenly remarked: "You know that my mother, when she was a child, had to have all her food tasted before she ate anything, because they were afraid the wicked Duke of Cumberland would poison her!" I did not know quite what one should reply to so startling a comment on the behaviour of a lady's family, and could only murmur: "Who had the pleasure of tasting it, Ma'am?" to which she replied, nodding her head as if it were a matter of no importance: "Oh, one of her ladies-in-waiting." At this moment I caught the eye of one of Princess Beatrice's own ladies-in-waiting, and had difficulties.

One day in 1933, during the yachting season at Cowes, a telephone call came to us from the *Victoria and Albert,* which was anchored off Cowes: Queen Mary was coming ashore the next day to motor through the island, and would like to come to tea with us. Accordingly, all the preparations were made. Our two elder children, who usually spent the entire summer in bathing suits, had to learn a new ritual from their governess. It was very stormy the next day, with high seas running all along the coast, and quite early in the morning a second telephone message reached us from the Royal yacht, saying that the bad weather would prevent the Queen from going ashore that afternoon, but she hoped to visit us a little later. The children accordingly had a little longer to practice their bow and curtsey, and were almost perfect in both when word arrived that the Queen would be coming to see us on the following afternoon. Her Majesty arrived on the exact second of the time appointed, accompanied by Gerald Chichester, Sir Derek Keppel, and Lady Malmesbury.

When the children were brought in after tea it looked as if the work of the governess had been wasted. Hugh, aged five, made one quite successful bow, but unfortunately continued bowing with a determined air, until he was drawn away.

However, in spite of this collapse of protocol, we had an exceedingly pleasant visit, and another one from Queen Mary the following year.

Her Majesty had a remarkable memory: I showed her a very beautiful edition of Voltaire, printed in 1784, in Baskerville type, which contained in every volume the book-plate of Princess Sophia. She identified it at once and knew exactly when it had been sold from one of the Royal libraries. She also reminded me of the fact, actually used in my book on Voltaire, that the type of that edition had been melted down to make ammunition for the French Revolution.

XLII

The Unknown God, and Voltaire

IN 1928 I published a book entitled *The Unknown God*. This was in a sense an autobiographical work, recording the adventures of my own mind among the agnostics, and its progress towards the perennial philosophy.

In my early reading of the nineteenth-century agnostics (Herbert Spencer, Darwin, Huxley, Leslie Stephen, and a host of others) I had been constantly struck by the fact that each of them admitted the truth of some part of the perennial philosophy, and when all these admissions were put together they made up a body of belief considerably more substantial than that, for instance, of Bishop Barnes.

Herbert Spencer, the leading philosophical agnostic of his age, established the basis of Theism in his *First Principles,* where he distinguishes between the knowable and the unknowable. Behind the "knowable" world with which science can deal, the world of natural causes and effects, he affirmed a Reality that was not merely unknown, but eternally unknowable, utterly beyond the grasp of science, and transcending all the processes of reason because it was the origin and end of all things. In simple language, it "had always been there," needing no anterior cause to produce it. Of this fact (to human reason an impossibility), he said we were more certain than of any other fact whatsoever.

There were times when the simultaneous recognition of this impossibility, and its actual reality, overwhelmed my own mind with an almost crushing sense of the miraculous. Logically there should have been nothing. That, at least, would require no explanation and no permanent uncaused Being.

"Who made God?" said poor little Katherine Mansfield, in a pathetic letter. In this very question she was postulating what she thought she was denying. For if we refuse it the name of God we are still face to face with the uncaused Cause of all things. Spencer was led by his own reasoning process to affirm some of the attributes which this uncaused Source of all things must possess. It was supra-rational, infinitely perfect (because absolutely self-subsistent), and therefore "supernatural," and he arrives at these attributes by a reasoning process which, though expressed in modern terms, is essentially identical with that of St. Thomas Aquinas.

Swinburne, in one of his violent and unnecessary reactions against the cruder forms of theology, had asked the same question as Katherine Mansfield:

Before the growth was the grower, and the seed ere the plant was sown,
But what was seed of the sower? And the grain of Him, whence was it grown?
Foot after foot ye go back. . . .

The best answer to that is to repeat the question. We do not escape that absolute impossibility which confronts us as an ultimate fact, merely by asking how it got there. Incidentally it is the materialist and not the theologian who insists on going back, foot by foot, along the diminishing road that runs out into nothingness; and it is the philosopher and the religious thinker, on the other hand, who affirm an ultimate Reality.

It has been well said that we expect to find in the mind of every honest man certain truths or fragments of truth, even though errors may be mixed with them, and that there is immense value in discovering these truths to his readers instead of concentrating on the faults. I had felt particularly interested in certain admissions of Voltaire. In spite of his satirical tone, so characteristic of the French society of his period (a tone which was used not only towards religious questions but towards every aspect of human life, political and social), he showed real humanity in many secular matters, and he had, beneath the polished surface of his Gallic wit, an *anima naturaliter Christiana.* This was often manifested in profoundly moving ways. The praise bestowed on him by Benedict XIV (intellectually perhaps the greatest of all the Popes) was a recognition of this forgotten element in Voltaire. It seemed to me there was an excellent opportunity to "spoil the Egyptians" and confront the "rationalists" with answers drawn from their supposed leader. With this in view I read his seventy-two volumes from end to end, and as I read I felt that I began to know the man in his inmost self. Here and there, especially when he was angered by some cruelty or injustice, he said things that would have been inexcusable if taken by themselves, torn out of the main body of his work, or extracted from some hasty journalistic pamphlet which he afterwards explicitly regretted. His great arguments for the existence of God and the immortality of the human soul had been forgotten by both his admirers and his enemies, as completely as his final confession of faith and the praise and honours bestowed on him by Benedict XIV.

The purpose of my book on Voltaire, which followed *The Unknown God,* was to show that the atheists and sceptics, who regarded him as their leader, were quite unaware of the support which Voltaire himself, consciously or unconsciously, had given to the central principles and the central beliefs of that faith. To begin with, he asserted his belief in God, and anticipated the famous argument which Paley used in his *Evidences* that a watch implies a watchmaker. The fact that

I want to destroy the rats in my house, Voltaire said on another occasion, does not affect my belief that it had an architect. He argued, moreover, that it was better not to believe in a God at all, than to believe in one who had no love or compassion for his creatures. The God in whom he believed must, therefore, be one who cared for the souls he had created; and by this statement Voltaire separated himself completely from the deists of his own generation. He was reaffirming to that extent one of the main foundations of the Christian religion. To demonstrate this fact, so disconcerting to the enemies of Christianity, was the object of my book.

It carried the argument of *The Unknown God* a stage further. In one of his most serious passages Voltaire spoke of the Founder of the Christian religion as "my only Master," but he was unorthodox in his failure to accept the whole doctrine of the divinity of Christ. I analyzed this departure from the Faith at some length in my book, and attributed it to a failure on the part of Voltaire himself. He had not worked out his philosophy of values. He fell on his knees once before the spectacle of an Alpine sunrise, but this was what any pantheist might do. He knew perfectly well, however, that a child, on the most insignificant of planets, not only embodies a higher value than anything material, but is actually *nearer* to the Centre of all spiritual values, which is God. If the Divine were to be apprehended at all; or if any revelation of the Divine were to be made, it was infinitely more probable, therefore, that this should be apprehended or made through a conscious personality, capable of love and sacrifice, than through a revolving mass of gas and fire. The whole doctrine of the Incarnation turns upon this; and when it is rightly considered it becomes clear that the whole case for a materialistic attack, based on physical dimensions, is completely reversed. The absurdity rests with the materialist, not with the believer in spiritual values who can say with Crashaw, and in despite of all the suns and systems:

Welcome, all wonders in one sight!
  Eternity shut in a span,
Summer in winter, day in night,
  Heaven in earth, and God in man.

In a work of reference on twentieth-century writers, which is to be found in libraries all over the United States, it is said that my book on Voltaire was condemned by the Holy See; that I was asked to make corrections in it and refused; and that afterwards I submitted. These statements are quite erroneous.

The second edition of *Voltaire* (which had received a very cordial welcome from both the Catholic and the Anglican Press as indicating a new line of apologetic) was about to be published when an anonymous letter-writer denounced the book to Rome, taking the absurd line that as I had written a book on Voltaire I must necessarily be supporting the destructive ideas which are commonly associated with that writer; whereas of course I was doing exactly the opposite. Douglas Woodruff, who saw this letter at Westminster House, told me that it looked very much like those of a crazy woman who sometimes sent anonymous letters to *The Tablet;* these were always consigned to the wastepaper basket.

A good deal of trouble and controversy ensued. A letter from the Supreme Congregation of the Holy See involved the temporary suspension of the book; and Cardinal Hinsley wrote to Rome strongly emphasizing the fact that unless we were told what the objections were, we were "simply floundering." By the intervention of Cardinal Pacelli the matter was later referred for settlement to Cardinal Hinsley; who in April, 1939, issued a letter from Archbishop's House (which appeared on the front page of *The Times,* in the *Dublin Review,* and in the whole of the Catholic newspaper Press) stating that the competent authorities desired no alterations whatsoever in the text of the book.

I wrote, by agreement, a brief preface, merely enumerating the many pages of the book itself which should obviate any misconceptions based upon passages torn out of their context.

Later I was told that Pope Pius XII, who had previously intervened as Cardinal Pacelli, had declared the charges against the book to be nonsensical.

XLIII

New Friends and Old

THE YEARS between 1929 and 1939 were spent for the most part at home in the Isle of Wight, with a few visits to Switzerland, France and Italy, and one to the United States. I spoke fairly frequently for various clubs and societies in England. At one of these gatherings I gave a reading from my own poems, with Dame Madge Kendal in the chair.

Dame Madge Kendal was a spell-binding name in those days. She represented the finest traditions of the English theatre. I knew her only slightly, but I was very proud of the fact that in the previous year (1931) she had given an Empire-wide broadcast of my poem "The Exiles." The arrangement had been made by the *Daily Express* for the broadcast to be given on Empire Day at a gathering, according to the Press, of at least fifty thousand people in Hyde Park.

Because the poem was to be delivered by her in a last appearance before the public, it was treated by the Press as the event of the day.

It was not entirely due to the rain that there was no beating of the big drums of pseudo-patriotism during this celebration. After the light-hearted community singing with which it opened, and in which the bad weather, with all the other little troubles, including Mademoiselle from Armentières, were packed up together in the old kit bag, the theme of the pageant that followed was simply the love of every man for his home land, culminating in his love of that other country,

> Most great to those that love her,
> Most dear to those that know.

James Douglas wrote, in the *Sunday Express:*

"The Empire Day Festival vindicated its popularity by triumphantly routing and defeating the rain. The green amphitheatre was quickly filled with enthusiastic men and women, boys and girls, who laughed at the showers. They cheered the massed bands of the Guards. They lustily joined in the community singing. . . . They cheered the pipers of the Scots Guards. . . . The rain seemed to be ashamed of itself as the Pageant of Empire moved out of the trees, and the queens of the festival, Miss Canada, Miss Australia, Miss Africa and Miss India were carried in on litters by stalwart members of the Legion of Frontiersmen. . . . The sun came out for the Procession of the Churches, and the massed choir singing . . . and the Union Jack was unfurled.

"Then Sir Edward Elgar, his white hair uncovered, conducted the massed bands, the choir and the people in 'Land of Hope and Glory.' The Master of the King's Musick sent the great chorus crashing through the rain, and he was loudly cheered as he took cover at the end.

"The thrill of the festival was provided by Dame Madge Kendal. The rain prevented her from mounting the rostrum, but she delivered the verses of Mr. Alfred Noyes from her motor-car in a voice which was amplified so magnificently that every word was heard by the fifty thousand listening people.

"This old lady of eighty-three astonished us by the dramatic fire of her diction, by the modulations of her tones, and by the faultless rhythm of her delivery.

'Meadows of England whispering in thine ear'—her voice whispered in the silence.
'Rivers of England, murmuring as they run,
Doves on the thatched roofs, rustling in the sun,
Blackbirds in hawthorn, drenched with starry dew,
Did'st thou not guess then why so dear they grew?
Month of Our Lady, tell us of thy grace
While we behold all beauty in thy face,
How to our hearts this English earth was given,
Radiant with May, to shadow forth our heaven.'

"The hawthorn was in bloom. The May blossoms shone bright through the showers. The scene was English, as the rain buried its fairy spears in the green trees and the green grass. There was a fair interlude while the Bishop of Willesden read the prayer for the Empire:

"'Almighty God Who rulest in the kingdom of men and hast given to our Sovereign Lord, King George, a great dominion in all parts of the earth, draw together, we pray Thee, in true fellowship the men of divers races, languages and customs who dwell therein, that, bearing one another's burdens, and working together in concord, they may fulfill the purpose of Thy Providence.'

"It was a solemn close to a splendid Festival of Empire."

Dame Madge Kendal wrote to me: "When you wrote those verses you did not imagine they would be said in a car with a man holding a microphone and the wires in an ambulance—while the rain came down in torrents! In spite of all I could not resist the joy of speaking them. Ever since you wrote those verses on Charles Dickens

> A poor boy reading in a garret,
> A great king, seated on a throne,

I have longed to say some words written by you. Now, under the extraordinary conditions of my trying to do so, you may have to forgive much. I sign myself

"Your grateful

MADGE KENDAL"

I had met Dame Madge Kendal first at lunch with Sir Johnston Forbes-Robertson, at his house in Bedford Square. He was one of the very few actors in my memory who understood the speaking of Shakespeare's verse. Most of them try desperately to make it sound like prose, which is obviously not what the poet intended. There is a very real sense in which it may be said that the music of the verse, especially in the great monologues, represents, not something actually spoken, but those quiet undertones and overtones of thought which, as Hamlet said, are often torn to tatters on the stage.

If Hamlet is made to yell those tremendous first questions at the ghost of his father, we lose not only the poetry, but also the dramatic power of thoughts that could be conveyed only by an awe-struck undertone, pulsating in those rhythms in which all deep emotion tends to express itself.

Forbes-Robertson understood this better than any actor of his time and, despite the fact that the American public is sometimes supposed to favour the over-theatrical, the quiet power of Forbes-Robertson's Hamlet won its fullest recognition in the United States.

It was there I first met him, and later we interchanged visits in London. My wife and I shared a box with him at a theatre where, in aid of a charity, he was to recite Shelley's "Cloud." He delivered the poem with magnificent effect right up to the last two lines, and then, by one of those unpredicable tricks of verbal memory, he transposed two words, with what must have been the only disaster of its kind in his life.

> "Like a child from the *tomb,* like a ghost from the *womb,*
> I arise and unbuild it again."

He knew what he had done as soon as he had said it, for a shudder passed over him; but curiously enough, no doubt owing to the magnificence of his delivery, apparently nobody in the audience noticed it. At any rate, the rather appalling announcement was received with tremendous applause. A moment or two later he stole back into the box, "like a ghost from the tomb," and whispered into my ear, "Wasn't it *ghastly!*"

On two occasions I spoke at the Royal Literary Fund annual dinner; also on Poetry and Reality at the Royal Institution with Sir James Creighton-Browne as Chairman; and once as the guest at a "Foyle Literary Luncheon," with Mr. George Lansbury in the chair.

I had met George Lansbury several times; it was Francis Meynell who first introduced me to him. He struck me as a kind of angel disguised as a labour leader. He radiated goodness, and I am quite sure that if politicians and statesmen in all countries had anything like the good-will and honest Christianity of George Lansbury the terrible dilemmas that confront us at the present day would vanish like a nightmare, and his vision of world peace would be fulfilled. But the "if" remains, to confirm the fact that nations are dealing not with a political but a moral problem.

Many friends stayed with us at Lisle Combe during these years: Sir George Thompson who, like his father, had won the Nobel Prize for scientific research, brought his beautiful young wife, whose happy conversation and radiant spirit will always remain with us in memory; Ernest Schelling, the American composer, and his wife came on their way to their chalet in Switzerland. One of Schelling's works, an elaborate composition based on my poem "The Victory Ball," had been performed with great success on the Continent and at the Metropolitan Opera House in New York. He asked us several times to stay with them at their chalet when our fellow-guest would have been Paderewski, but we were unable to go as we had other visitors coming to Lisle Combe.

Among these was Lord Askwith, who had just returned from settling some difficulty between Church and State in Malta. Herbert Ward and his wife came to meet Lord Askwith at lunch one day, and Herbert, who in his association with the Vatican and his general knowledge of ecclesiastical affairs had all the facts about the Malta dispute at his finger-tips, greatly surprised Askwith, who took me aside after lunch asking for further information on that astonishing young man who really knew more about ecclesiastical matters in Malta than anyone he had met during his official visit there.

There were also the Charles Tennysons; Guy Pollock (then Managing Editor of the *Morning Post*) and his wife (sometimes an exceedingly charming Managing Editor of Guy Pollock); L. S. Amery (one of the few Secretaries of State who had his Homer and Horace by heart. Literature and philosophy lost a great deal when Amery gave his brilliant intellect to political life); Sir George Rendel (at that time head of the Eastern Department of the Foreign Office; on his arrival at Sofia he narrowly escaped being blown to pieces when an agent of some "friendly" power placed a bomb in his suitcase); Lady Burghclere, half-way through her very fine biography of Strafford; the Inges, to whom I have given another chapter; E. H. Blakeney, who, among other things, was just then publishing his delightful edition and translation of the *Mosella of Ausonius*—the best in English.

Then there was that extraordinary character Stephen Gaselee, Librarian of the Foreign Office and Fellow of Trinity College, Cambridge, who came attired in a brown tail-coat, with a brown top-hat, carrying a baggy umbrella in one hand and a despatch case in the other, with just that touch of eccentricity which convinced porters and taxi-drivers that he must be a great chief to be treated with profound respect. He was an Anglo-Catholic who revelled in Pepys and wrote little fables about the primitive saints in a style of facetious aestheticism. He had that curious modern tolerance for things that ought not to be tolerated. When I last saw him he spoke of a high honour that had recently been bestowed on a man who was a notorious moral pervert. I said quite frankly that I thought it disgusting, but he merely replied, with a deprecating smile, "Oh, but of course we all know ——'s little weaknesses."

Several times Princess Beatrice came to luncheon with us, on one occasion accompanied by Princess Marie Louise. There were many pleasant tennis parties with our neighbours the Jellicoes, the Mottistones, the Seeleys and the Moulton-Barretts. At one of these, about the time that *The Barretts of Wimpole Street* was giving London one more dose of amateur psychiatry, Colonel Moulton-Barrett led me grimly into his drawing-room and pointed to a very beautiful portrait of Elizabeth Barrett as a young girl. "That," he said, "is the woman who brought the curse upon my family."

A deputation of the Barrett family, I was told, had protested to the Lord Chamberlain about certain episodes in *The Barretts of Wimpole Street,* which, in one rather nauseating scene, suggested that Elizabeth's father objected to her marriage with Browning owing to his own incestuous passion for her. If it had been true, of course the truth might have had to be faced by biographers, but even then the popular stage was hardly the place for its display. Modern corruption sees no difference between the tragedy of Oedipus, who had been led, without knowing it, into a trap from which only death could extricate him, and the direct courting of the very situation which to Oedipus and Jocasta was worse than any death. But amateur psychiatrics masquerading as realism and applied on the public stage to persons whose relatives are still living, can hardly be condoned as "truth." The very simple remark of one of the family, "Grandpapa was not in the least like that" may have been naïve, but it was convincing. I believe the idea was not biographical but was first suggested by the cheerful imagination of "apple-cheeked" Hugh Walpole.

Wilfrid Meynell, who knew Browning personally, gave me an explanation I believe he had at first hand: Whenever a daughter married, Grandpapa had to give up £500 a year.

Sometimes J. B. Priestley and his wife would bring a party over to Lisle Combe from Billingham for lunch or tennis. On one of these visits I thought he seemed a little dejected, and his wife told me it was because the advance sales of his new book were only about one hundred thousand. I told her that if the advance sales of one of my books had reached a tenth of that number I should feel very cheerful indeed. "Ah, yes," she replied gently, "but it's all relative, isn't it."

A little later Priestley told me that I ought to get what he called "the big guns" behind my own work, but I had not the slightest notion how the "big guns" were to be brought into action. However, I was once privileged to see what I suppose might be called an air reconnaissance before the barrage began.

Priestley, who is a keen tennis player, had come over with Hugh Walpole and a small house-party to Lisle Combe. He told me that one of their publishers (Hamish Hamilton) was flying down to the Island that day to see him on important business. The two authors had told the publisher where they were to be found. Accordingly, about three-thirty in the afternoon, Hamish Hamilton's plane (he flew it himself) appeared in the sky, circling above our tennis court where the players were in the middle of a set. The publisher looped the loop several times to draw the authors' attention, and then, as there was no possible landing place in our neighbourhood, darted away in the direction of Billingham. Never before or since has a publisher looped the loop over *my* head, but then, as Mrs. Priestley had remarked, "It's all relative, isn't it."

Oddly enough, about the same time I had a similar experience with the Dean of Canterbury, Dr. Hewlett Johnson. I had been asked to give an address during "Canterbury Week," and chose the subject of Charles Dickens. My wife and I were put up for the night at the Deanery. Our host had not yet become notorious, and I knew of him simply as the Dean of Canterbury. When we arrived we were given tea by a very young lady (afterwards his wife), who acted as hostess, and said that the Dean was out at the moment but was returning in an hour or so. Just as we were finishing tea he made a dramatic entry. He had a wild gleam in his eye and his tousled hair seemed to be standing on end.

"I am sorry I was not here to receive you," he remarked, "but I have been looping the loop over the Cathedral."

Apparently a friendly pilot had taken him up for a joy-ride.

I am always reminded of this symbolical moment when I read of his later exploits.

In the summer of 1932, while we were in the Isle of Wight, my wife and I received an unusual invitation to come to New York for a week-end in November in order that I might speak at the Centenary Celebration of New York University. It was organized on a large scale, with representatives of fifty-one foreign and over two hundred American Universities, and the attendance was more than one thousand.

Dr. Sproul, President of the University of California, was one of the delegates, and it was at this conference that he invited me to give a series of lectures at Berkeley, an invitation which eventually gave me several more years in the *tierra adorada* of the West.

In the meantime, however, there were long summer days among my books, and many games of chess with Admiral Jellicoe on our sunlit terrace.

> Chess on the lawn beneath the rustling trees,
> Where many roses scent the summer air.

These two lines, which I read years ago in some old chess magazine, always come back to me when I think of those afternoons.

The Jellicoe daughters and Agnes were great friends, and there were many young people coming and going in both houses. Agnes in those days was a little shy of giving invitations as from herself over the telephone, and would give them as from her mother or me. About half past nine one fine summer night when the moon was shining, two of the Jellicoe daughters arrived at our house in bath-robes and bathing costumes, with what might be called an expression of mixed curiosity and caution. They explained, very charmingly, that their butler had given them a telephone message saying that Mr. Noyes wanted to know if Lady Prudence would swim with him by moonlight.

Part of the curious pattern that I constantly find myself tracing through incidents and coincidences is the fact that shortly before Admiral Jellicoe's return from his Governorship of New Zealand, almost his last official act there was to unveil a statue to Sir Frederick Weld in commemoration of the work he had done as Premier (this is also commemorated by the Weld Club, which was named after him). When we first met in the Isle of Wight Admiral Jellicoe greeted my wife with the remark, "I have just been unveiling a statue of your grandfather."

Lady Jellicoe told me of another unveiling incident in New Zealand. She had been asked to unveil many War Memorials in that country, and she had always used a form of words which ran something like this: "I unveil this memorial to the glory of God and in memory of those who made the supreme sacrifice in the great war." On the day in question it was a memorial window that was to be unveiled in a church, and the introductory remarks of the clergyman who opened the proceedings were not too clear. When the moment came for the unveiling, Lady Jellicoe said as usual: "I unveil this window to the glory of God and in memory of those who made the supreme sacrifice in the great war," and pulled the string. It revealed on the emblazoned panes only the simple inscription: "In memory of Maria Williams." Lady Jellicoe, being a sailor's wife, unaccustomed to mince matters, and oblivious of the fact that she was speaking into a microphone, remarked in a voice that tingled through the entire congregation:

"Who in hell is Maria Williams?"

When it was all over, Lady Jellicoe, whose kindness and good nature won friendship wherever she went, was able to see the humour of it; but, as she remarked, "wherever I went in New Zealand after that, I found Maria Williams had got there first."

Lord Jellicoe himself came of seagoing forebears and he had seagoing generations in his blood. He had the simplicity and sincerity of greatness. His kindness and gentleness of manner hardly suggested the man who held the fate of the world in his hand at Jutland. Yet once, and curiously enough on the tennis-court, I had a glimpse of something else in that slight figure. It was a very hot afternoon, and he had tied something that looked like a piratical bandanna round his forehead, with a knot behind one ear—and in a flash I saw the companion of Drake and Hawkins.

I saw him frequently during the long period of controversy with the Beatty faction about the Battle of Jutland. One thing I admired about him intensely: Though the other side was extremely vocal and bitter, and (as I learned afterwards) Lord Jellicoe could have given the most complete and crushing answer, I never heard an ungenerous word from him about the others. He was not only a great Admiral of the Fleet but a great Christian gentleman.

I went to his funeral in St. Paul's Cathedral, with Admiral Hopwood, who had served with Jellicoe in the *Iron Duke*. The affection of the Navy for one of the finest and best of those who have commanded it since Collingwood was demonstrated there beyond all question. There has probably never been so great a representation of all branches of the service on any occasion of this kind. Admiral Hopwood, looking at that great assemblage, murmured the words that had been applied to the builder of St. Paul's: *Si monumentum requiris, circumspice.*

At the end of the service, echoing and re-echoing through the great Cathedral like voices from beyond the world, there sounded, not the Last Post, but the Reveille.

My tribute to his memory, a pen portrait of the man as I knew him, was published in the *Morning Post:*

The Admiral of the Fleet

(In Memory of Admiral Jellicoe)

By Scapa Flow
The morning light enkindles the wide sea;
And here, far south, by his deserted home,
His Isle of Wight remembers. The young leaves
In Pelham Woods already begin to stir.
His garden under the crags is full of sun.
It sees theAtlantic shining. But no sail
Can bring him home again.
The alert slight form;
The weather-wise face that showed no ageing sign
But only grew in kindness, year by year;
The shrewd brown twinkling eyes; the gentle heart;
The resolute truth in judgment and in act;
And those clenched lips no enemy could unlock
To answer what the grave could answer best,
These can return no more. No more returns
The quiet strength
That, when the fate of England and the world
Hung on his lonely choice,
Dared to forego the plaudits of the crowd.
His was the signal, deeper than they knew,
Which followed, in the face of calumny,
The predetermined, world-considering plan;
The deep-laid plan, forgotten at their ease
By half the all-knowing crowd; but not by him,
For all the darkness and the leagues of sea,
And all those wide horizons, not by him,
Our little Admiral, in the mist and fire.

Silent, through all those long and clamorous years,
And silent now for ever, where he rests
With Nelson and his captains, side by side.

. . . . . .

Northward, far north, of England's brooding soul
In ice-locked seas, more bleak than Scapa Flow,
There rides a mightier fleet, not made with hands.
It guards and armours with invisible steel
The unspoken thought, the uncheapened memories,
All that our island's inarticulate breed

Buries and hides, from enemy and from friend,
In that dim region, till God calls the hour.
Then, all her history, all her memories speak.
Northward, far north, a signal-gun is heard,
Our Admiral's flag is hoisted yet once more.
Ship after ship, line after line, they come!
Out of the mortal mist—Love, Honour, Truth.
The shining and immortal squadrons bring
For all time now, his mightier victory home.

XLIV

Youth and Memory

IN 1937, perhaps with some instinctive sense of the terrible challenge that was to be made in the near future to the British Commonwealth, a gathering of the youth of the Empire took place in England. Thousands of young men and women from all parts of the Commonwealth attended it. The unformulated idealism in their hearts and minds clearly originated in a very strong feeling that the world was approaching a crisis in its history. Most apparent was a passionate longing in many of the younger generation for a world set free from wars.

There were services in Westminster Abbey and elsewhere, attended by these young people, for whom the land of their fathers was opening up the treasures of its historical past. Its memories lived in their blood, even though they had been born thousands of miles away. Many of their own forebears could have echoed the words of the Scottish exiles:

"From the lone shieling of the misty island
 Mountains divide us and the waste of seas—
Yet still the blood is strong, the heart is Highland,
 And we in dreams behold the Hebrides."

The National Council of Education of Canada made many of the arrangements and asked me to write several things for them, including a new version of the National Anthem, which was sung in Westminster Abbey and has been used on other occasions in Canada since that day.

On May 18th there was a rally of some eight thousand of these young people, most of them in their early twenties. It was held at the Albert Hall in London, and I was asked to speak for about ten minutes and conclude with a poem specially written for the occasion. It was not easy to choose a subject, as I was to follow a formidable list of speakers—Mr. L. S. Amery; Mr. Lyons, the Prime Minister of Australia; the High Commissioner for India; Lord De La Warr, Under-Secretary of State for the Colonies; the Duke of Gloucester; and Mr. Stanley Baldwin, who was to make his farewell speech as Prime Minister.

Many letters have reached me from time to time, some of them from far afield (the speeches were broadcast over-seas), asking for the text of what I said that evening. As only the poem has been reprinted I give the text of the rest here:

"During the last few days this old country of ours has witnessed what may be called a great Act of Remembrance. Many of you who come from overseas must have felt, in a very deep way, that the history in which all our lives are rooted had awakened a thousand memories in your hearts and minds.

"Remembrance is as vital to nations as to men. It not only prevents us losing the real values of the past, but it infinitely increases the worth of our own lives here and now. It enriches them with unnumbered associations. The commonest flower in the English hedgerows is touched with a special glory when we remember how Chaucer and Shakespeare loved it. 'Under our feet in the grasses, their clinging magic runs.'

"The great literature of the past, the great poetry of the past, breathe the very spirit of remembrance among all who speak our tongue; remembrance of the great English ghosts on land and sea; remembrance of the long struggle for that ordered freedom which is still the hope of the world.

"It is no small thing that far beyond this little island, far beyond the widest horizons of our Commonwealth of Nations, men are still able to say, 'Shakespeare was of us; Milton was for us; Burns, Shelley were with us; they watch from their graves.' For Memory is not born of materialism. It recalls to our minds the things that are not seen. Perhaps this is why, in a still deeper sense, the ancients thought of Memory as the daughter of God.

"I am not here to say merely comfortable things to you. You are confronted to-day by a world that has lost something; a world that in the rush and roar of its daily life has no time for recollection; and has almost ceased to believe in real values, or is engaged in falsifying them and confusing the lines of right and wrong. . . .

"Great nations are born in real belief and enthusiasm. They die in unbelief and cynicism. Over a large part of the world to-day the inner life of mankind is suffering from this loss. Whole sections of art and literature, instead of being fountains of hope and inspiration, are fountains of bitter disillusionment, defeatism, and sometimes an all-embracing hatred. The war had something to do with it; but it goes deeper than that. It is largely due—not to a reasoned judgment—but to a tragic loss of memory. There is a vague idea abroad that modern science has revealed a universe in which all the old values of the individual human soul are somehow discredited, and reduced to insignificance; that religion and poetry belong to an out-worn past; and that nothing we can do or suffer is of the slightest importance in the long run. It is a mood, and a mood largely ignorant of the real achievements of the human mind. It is a mood that can and must be changed if our civilization is to survive. Our political conceptions are involved as well as our religion, for the whole of our ordered freedom has been built up on the value, the absolute value, of the individual human soul. Those values are not diminished by the size of the physical universe, which, even in the days of Genesis, was considerably taller than the tallest man. They do not depend on the centrality of the earth.

"They depend on the centrality of their Creator. Rocks and stones may crush us to pieces physically; but, however large, they are not so valuable in the eternal memory, or so near to God, as the smallest human heart that ever sacrificed itself for what it believed to be right, or caught one glimpse of the divine. There is a great saying of Galileo, which is not well enough known, and goes far deeper than may appear at first sight. He was asked if the vastness of his new universe did not make the idea of the universal care of God for His creatures incredible. He replied: 'The sun, which has all those planets revolving around it, is able to ripen the smallest bunch of grapes as though it had nothing else to do in the universe.' We need not doubt the power of that infinitely greater Light.

"Your generation, if it chooses, can restore what has been lost, and capture new heights of vision for the generations to come. The spirit of youth—in every generation—revolts from the easy task; but it responds at once to the really great adventure. As I told you, I am not here to say merely comfortable things. If you are prepared to accept a really great challenge, your generation has the noblest opportunity that has ever been offered to the young in the history of the world.

"You will not be misled into thinking that youth in itself is the one thing needful. Youth is enviable, not because it necessarily sees further than its elders, but because it has time to learn from the past, and even from the mistakes of the past. Mankind is in desperate need of that vital knowledge, the knowledge of the things that belong to its real peace. These things are clearly written in every unspoiled memory. Follow them in simple truth; trust to the hand that wrote them there, and it may be that yours will be the generation chosen to redeem a war-shattered world."

XLV

Footnote to History

NOT LONG before the outbreak of the second world war Lord and Lady Howard of Penrith stayed with us for a week-end in the Isle of Wight, and an episode took place which I think should be recorded here. At the time he was greatly concerned about events in Germany, and very emphatic about the measures which ought to be taken. He said: "I know the character of those men and there will be a catastrophe."

Lord Howard was a Catholic and a man of very wide experience. He had represented his country in Berlin and Washington, and his transparent sincerity was not at all in accord with the conventional idea of the diplomat. At one of our luncheon parties in London he had raised the interesting question whether any one book could be regarded as so completely typical of its nation as *Don Quixote* was of Spain. The works of Shakespeare were rejected on the ground that they were not a single book and that no one play really represented England. Some were about ancient Rome, others about Venice, Verona, Elsinore, Athens, Bohemia, Scotland, and so on, while Henry IV and Henry V, despite their English atmosphere, were limited by their strict historical frame. André Maurois, who was one of the guests, suggested Molière for France, but this was turned down for a similar reason, though if his works were regarded as a single book they might stand. *The Divine Comedy* might represent one aspect of the Italian mind, but nobody seemed able to find a single book which completely embodied the English character. Lord Howard surprised us eventually by voting for *Tristram Shandy,* not because he thought it the greatest English book, but because he thought it embodied just that vein of humour touched with sentiment, and sometimes a little eccentric in its individuality, which is the special quality of the insular Englishman. Uncle Toby had helped to win most of the English battles; he had done most of the English farming; and in various disguises he had carried on most of the business of the City of London.

Uncle Toby would certainly have agreed with Lord Howard in wanting "sanctions" to be imposed at once on Mussolini, who had just taken an army through the Suez Canal. I knew no more than the newspapers had told me about this adventure of the Duce, and Lord Howard's comment illuminated the difficulties of Sir Samuel Hoare, who had just been driven from office: "Of course Mussolini had a secret agreement with Laval!" It is easy to see this now, but at the time there was much indignation in England at our own inaction, caused by this unseen political thrombosis.

Looking back on all that he said then, it seems to me that Lord Howard was clearer-sighted than any of the political leaders in England. He was one of the very few men who were wise before the event.

During his visit he addressed a meeting of the English-Speaking Union at Newport, on the necessity of imposing "sanctions" on Italy. He was convinced that this might avert war and save hundreds of thousands of lives.

It was a very quiet country audience. He had retired from diplomacy a year or two earlier, or perhaps he could not have spoken as directly and simply as he did. He was an old man, and at the end of his address he did something which, if all the political leaders had been able to do it with equal sincerity, would have saved the world:

"In all these things, you know," he said, "we are quiet helpless unless we have that other help. I would like to ask you to say the Lord's Prayer with me."

Everyone in the room stood up and repeated it with him.

I have sometimes wished the world could have seen what, according to convention, must have been an unusual proceeding in an ambassadorial career, but if the world had seen it the world would have assumed that it was a "gesture," and I have never seen a speaker more sincere, or an audience more deeply moved.

In 1938 my wife and I went to Italy. We spent some time in Florence and Venice and had a very pleasant month in Rome, where we stayed at the old Hotel Russie. We motored up to Assisi, and (though we spent only three days there) that little city on the hill has ever since been for me one of the strong fortresses of the mind. The impression it made upon me is recorded in my novel *No Other Man* and in a poem which was afterwards printed in *Orchard's Bay.*

One thing that had a strange effect upon me was the fact that as we drew near Assisi, the city seen from below looked cold and grey, but a little later, as we wandered through its narrow streets, the sunset light seemed to transfigure it, tingeing its stones with exquisite luminous colours. It happened that the streets were completely deserted at that hour, and here and there:

. . . a little lighted window shone, like an altar lit for prayer.

We motored about the country a good deal with Paul and Agnes Grey; we had delightful days among the Alban Hills, made pilgrimages to places associated with Horace, revelled in all the colours of the coast around Sorrento, Capri and Amalfi, and drank Falernian (perhaps we christened it ourselves) among the ruins of Paestum.

Paul Grey was then Second Secretary at the Embassy, where Lord Perth was Ambassador. (Lady Perth was a cousin of my wife.)

One night, after dinner at the Embassy I had a conversation with the German Ambassador, who was one of the guests, and I began to understand the strange and dangerous mood that was taking possession of the German Government. We got on to the subject of the Christian Churches in Germany, and I suddenly realized that some violent hatred was seething under the immaculate shirt-front of the Nazi Ambassador. His face became crimson. "Germany will never tolerate a state within the state," he snapped.

None were for religion,
But all were for the State,

as the old verse might be revamped.

My friend Professor Carlo Formichi had translated some of my work into Italian. He was Vice-President of the Royal Academy of Italy, but really Acting President. He had held office under the nominal presidencies of D'Annunzio and Marconi. He was in close touch with Mussolini, and told me that the Duce had said of D'Annunzio, "He is a rotten tooth. He must be filled with gold or extracted." Apparently, from the sumptuosity of the subsidized National Edition of that writer, the golden remedy was the one adopted.

Professor Formichi invited us to a reception at the Academy and afterwards to dinner at his house, where his sister, who acted as hostess, played Beethoven for us. Formichi suggested that I should write a poem on the long literary friendship between England and Italy, to which so many poets had borne witness, from Chaucer to Keats, Shelley and the Brownings. Formichi said if I would do this he would translate it into Italian and publish it in one of the leading Italian reviews, where he thought it might promote good feeling.

The cause of world peace was first in my thoughts at that time. Accordingly I wrote a poem entitled "England to Italy," and touched not only on the literary bond, but on the crossing of St. Augustine from Italy to England, and the way in which, for many of us, Protestant as well as Catholic, St. Francis of Assisi had made Italy a "second Holy Land":

> We know whose feet,
> Whose piercéd feet, between the cypresses,
> Walked by Assisi on the Umbrian Hills
> And left that glow of beauty on thy walls,
> Like the last light of our lost Paradise,
> The dying sunset of the soul of man.

The poem ended by asking what word or bond could hold or bind in a world which had been grinding its altars into dust. It expressed the hope that distant ages would answer "England's word," and that the old bond between us might help to re-establish the reign of law and save the world from the disaster which threatened it.

> *Qui, in un mondo fuori d'ogni legge, nel quale gli uomini*
> *Hanno ridotto in polvere gli altari; quale parola, quale vincolo,*
> *Quale giuramento può essere valido o legare?*
> *Rispondano; i' distanti evi futuri—la parola dell'Inghilterra.*

La parola dell'Inghilterra—the tribute to the value of England's pledged word, was as clear in the Italian as in the English, and so was the implication that the pledges of Italy's partner in the Axis were valueless.

Without telling me, Formichi took the poem to Mussolini, who at once said that it must appear, not in the literary monthly for which it was intended and where it would have a limited circulation, "but in the *Giornale d'Italia,* where it will be read by thousands of Italians while they are eating their frugal evening polenta."

In that newspaper, therefore, shortly afterwards it appeared and received great prominence on the front page. It was very well received; and there were cordial messages about it to Formichi from the King of Italy and from various Italians of eminence.

Shortly afterwards I spoke to a little group of English and Italian poetry lovers at a meeting in the house where Keats died. A committee had been formed by Lord Rennell of Rodd, former Ambassador to Italy, who wanted to make some suggestion about this beautiful little house of memory. They were going to present an address to Mussolini about it, and asked my wife and me to accompany them. I never quite discovered what they wanted, and I am afraid we accepted the invitation chiefly out of curiosity about Mussolini.

On the morning appointed we were ushered into a long room in the Palazzo Venezia. Mussolini sat at a table at the far end of the room. It seemed to be an essential part of the ceremony that while the visitors were escorted by what Edgar Allan Poe would have called his "dark Plutonian Fascists" down the long shining floor of this immense room, Mussolini should rise and walk—not towards his visitors—but pompously to and fro at the far end of the room, his chin up and his chest well inflated. We were halted a few feet away from him, and after introductions had been made Lord Rennell, who acted as our spokesman, began to read his brief address from a typescript which I understood had been submitted to Mussolini beforehand. Here and there, when a formal compliment was introduced, Mussolini would elevate his chin and inflate his nostrils as if he were snuffing up incense. At the end of the address Lord Rennell made the mistake of extemporizing a few remarks not included in the typescript, and it was clear that Mussolini did not quite understand what was being said. The speaker ended by gazing rapturously into the face of the Dictator and quoting Keats: "Beauty is truth, truth beauty." Mussolini apparently took this also for a personal tribute, elevated his chin, snuffed up the incense, and bowing graciously, exclaimed: "Thank you *vairy* much."

Those were the days when a great effort was being made, by all men of good-will, to save the peace of the world, the days when Mr. Chamberlain, with his umbrella and top-hat, was planning a visit to Rome. I had gone to the Palazzo Venezia fully prepared to find something admirable in the man who had at least drained the marshes, established punctual train service, and made it possible to send your unlocked luggage from Rome to Venice without losing your shirts on the way. But that brief interview shattered my hope. The pompous little man in the morning coat was not a normal human being; every glance, every gesture was theatrical. The vanity of an actor-manager possessed him to the point of insanity. Undoubtedly in public and surrounded by his Fascists, he was always playing a part, but the Perths told us that in private social intercourse he behaved very differently. Once even in public the pomp was broken down by the humour of an American, who brought him a personal message from President Roosevelt. Mussolini received this transatlantic visitor with arm outstretched in the Fascist salute, and the American replied by putting up both hands. At this unexpected gesture of capitulation Mussolini collapsed in a roar of laughter.

At our interview he strutted and tossed his head about in a manner that would have been ludicrous if it had not been for the glare of his eyes, which continually showed their white rings. They were the eyes not of a man but of a wild creature, and human communication seemed no more possible with them than with those of a tiger. However, when I thought about it later, I was not sure whether their strange glare expressed ferocity or a secret and intense fear of the terrible forces that held him in their grip. One could almost think now that those white-ringed eyes had some uncanny prescience of his own ghastly end.

Oddly enough, at this very time Rome began to make immense preparations for the visit of Hitler. German secret police were imported and began to investigate window boxes along the route which Hitler was to take through the city. Armies of workmen began to dig holes in the streets, in which scores of supports were to be set for the flambeaux planned to illuminate his progress at night. Many of the Italians in Rome were cynical about this, and said that the digging was an attempt to find the Axis. Rome was no longer Rome, and we betook ourselves to Florence and then to Venice, where all my dreams of that city were more than fulfilled.

At Venice

Home from their fishing, over the quiet water,
  The coloured sails returned.
Before them all the domes and towers of Venice
  In the deep sunset burned.

The still lagoon was full of coloured shadows.
Your face was like a flower.
The wingéd Lion darkened on the splendour,
And it was Titian's hour.

Over the shining flood the sails came softly,
Saffron and rose and white.
Brown throats among the tawny nets uplifted
A love-song to the night.

The sunset moved before them like a banner
That into darkness flows.
The sunset and the sails moved on together,
Saffron and white and rose.

This visit to Italy was to me something like a renaissance of the mind, quickening and enriching it from the treasure-houses of art and poetry. I picked up editions not only of Ariosto and Dante, but of the fifteenth-century humanists, and I almost felt as if I were a contemporary of Poliziano, Landino and Pontanus.

In March of the following year, 1939, I was again in Rome, and my friend Formichi surprised me with the gift of a beautifully produced edition of my poem "England to Italy," which had been issued by the Italian Academy and was being circulated by them in this form. It was exquisitely printed on hand-made paper, with the watermark of the Roman wolf. It contained a facsimile of my manuscript with all the corrections, as well as of the translator's manuscript, with the versions in Italian and French and a preface. Most remarkable of all, in view of the date, the frontispiece was a portrait of Mussolini himself, under whose aegis and authority alone the Italian Academy had issued this edition in support of an Anglo-Italian entente. I was quite unaware of what had been done. The book was being circulated only in Italy. But it illustrated the complete uncertainty of Mussolini's plans. In 1939 at that particular date he was playing for the friendship of England, and repudiating by implication the methods of his Axis partner.

Formichi gave me a telegram he had received from Mussolini:

"*11 Gen. 39.*

S. E. CARLO FORMICHI—VICE PRESIDENTE ACCADEMIA ITALIA, ROMA.

Duce ringrazia molto vivamente gradito omaggio autografi carme Alfredo Noyes et versioni.

SECRETARIO PARTICOLARE SEBASTIANI"

This at first gave me something of a shock until Formichi explained to me that *omaggio* was the word usually applied to a presentation copy.

Formichi also told me of some remarks made to him by the Duçe, among them this: "It is a tragedy that France has thrown Italy into the arms of Germany. England is our natural friend and France our natural ally."

Following all this, Formichi asked me to send a personal copy of the special edition to Mr. Chamberlain. I did so, and in his reply, dated April 9, 1939, Mr. Chamberlain said, "All my information goes to show that the feeling in Italy for this country and what she stands for is as strong as ever."

In the meantime various incidents had taken place which had made me extremely uneasy. Among these incidents was the sending of Italian troops into Albania, and a report of the mobilization of certain classes of the Italian Army. This report had appeared in the London newspapers, and a question had been asked about it in the House of Commons.

I happened to be in the office of the International News Service in Rome when a telephone call came from the British Embassy, asking for information about the source of these "rumours." It was pleasant to hear the Manager of the I.N.S. explaining in good American that several of these Italian Army posters calling up certain classes had been plastered upon the outer walls of the British Embassy. I could just hear the slightly bored very English voice at the other end of the wire: "Oh, thank you *so* much. I'll just go and have a look."

Formichi himself had told me that Mussolini had no fixed plans; that he was living from day to day, not exactly as an opportunist

(Formichi, being loyal to the Duce, put it more flatteringly than that), but as one who would seize the good of Italy where he thought he found it. Unhappily there were signs that he feared Germany more than he valued the friendship of England.

Before Mr. Chamberlain's letter reached me I was led by these uncertainties to write fourteen lines which the International News Service cabled to America. The New York I.N.S. cabled a reply saying that these lines would be syndicated in a chain of newspapers throughout the United States as the poem was "a political document of prime importance." Of course it was nothing of the kind, but that hard-headed American newspapermen should think so at this moment was an indication of something in the air.

Pope Pius XI had just died, and was lying in state at St. Peter's, his hand raised and frozen by death in the very act of blessing his people, tragically symbolical, perhaps, of the fact that he had been one of the restraining influences on Mussolini. The lines were entitled "The Dead Pope Speaks":

Cæsar, quo vadis? To the Augustan world?
Yet—yet—remember, Cæsar, in that day
The sword was sheathed, the battle-flags were furled,
The trumpet hushed, the war-tents packed away.

The nations doffed their harness. The torn hill
Rippled with ripening waves of golden corn;
And all men listened, as they listen still,
But in that listening stillness Christ was born.

Cæsar, the *Pax Romana* seals my breath.
Cæsar, the *Pax Romana* folds my hands.
Cold, in this *Pax Romana* which is death,
I cannot speak to all those listening lands.

Cæsar, quo vadis? Cæsar must decide!
Peace? Peace on earth? Or Christ re-crucified?

XLVI

Exit Hugh Walpole

I MUST now go back a little to the immediate causes of my visit to Rome in 1939.

In the middle of a children's birthday party at Lisle Combe, the news reached me of the death of Pope Pius XI. Almost simultaneously came a cable from the International News Service asking if I would go to Rome and write a series of articles for a chain of newspapers in the United States on the historical events of the next few weeks, including the election and coronation of a new Pope. I was told that Hilaire Belloc and Hugh Walpole had accepted similar invitations, and we were promised all kinds of tempting facilities.

It was Saturday afternoon when the cable reached me, and on Sunday morning, just as my wife and I were setting out, the London manager of the I.N.S. telephoned, urging me to go by air. He gave one of those grim reasons which move the newspaper world to a callousness of expression perhaps inevitable, if its readers are to be fed. "We have had private information," the message ran, "that the embalming has not been successful, and the funeral ceremonies may have to take place earlier than expected. If you go by train you may arrive too late. Hugh Walpole is flying."

I replied that all arrangements had been made, and that I should be in Rome long before Hugh Walpole, who had to wait hours for a plane and had to go by way of Germany.

I did, in fact, arrive some twelve hours before him. He reached Rome quite late the next night, with a horrible account of trouble in the Alps and a forced landing after one of the wings of his plane had caught fire. By this time my first article had been cabled to New York. Twelve hours later the first of Walpole's articles crossed the Atlantic. He was probably still suffering from the effects of his flight when he wrote it, for there came in reply a fierce cable from New York quite complimentary to my own article but very angry with Walpole, saying it was not paying to hear about his breakfast and shirt-studs. Apparently he had written one of those delightfully chatty articles all about himself, explaining how much he disliked putting on evening dress in the daytime, how he had lost his collar-stud, and how the waiter who brought his breakfast had dropped the tray on entering his bedroom. (After reading his biography I am not surprised.)

Later on he published a vivacious little book entitled *Roman Fountain*. It was described on the jacket as a record of the author's spiritual quest in the Eternal City. Walpole could tell a story (in more than one sense), but here in Rome and at these Catholic ceremonies he had the most naïve notions about the things he had come to describe. Standing at my side in St. Peter's during the solemn funeral ceremony, he asked several times, "When does the incense begin?" and I could see that his mind was filled with the romantic hope of enjoying lots of lighted tapers, operatic organ music in the distance, and above all clouds upon clouds of good rich orgiastic incense smoke.

I could not resist telling him later of the dear old lady I once knew in Boston. For the greater part of her life she had been very Low Church, but in advanced old age she began to attend very High Church services. She explained to a surprised friend, "You see, my dear, I don't hear very well and I don't see very well, so I thought I would like a church where I could use my nose."

On the evening when Belloc arrived, still later than Walpole, he had dinner with the newspaper men, and insisted that they should all take port with him afterwards. The next morning I found the manager of the International News Service in his office, looking very bilious. He glowered at me with a bloodshot eye, and said he had a bad headache. "I'm single-handed here s'morning," he said. "They call this Hilaire Belloc a great writer. Seems to me he's an old soak." Shortly afterwards I met Belloc at lunch. He was quite cheerful, fresh as a daisy, and apparently completely unconscious that he had laid out the entire staff of the I.N.S. But port, it should be said, is not a customary tipple among American newspaper men.

Belloc asked me to go for a long walk with him in the Alban Hills, and I have always regretted that I was prevented by an engagement which I could not break.

Shortly before the election of the new Pope I received some delightful illumination upon the methods of the great news services. The I.N.S. had rented a cell in a little Monastery overlooking the Square of St. Peter's. Immediately opposite was the Vatican and the balcony from which the new Pope would speak to the city and to the world. In the window of this cell the I.N.S. had installed a telescope commanding a window in the Vatican. They informed me that they had made arrangements with a Vatican official to signal from this window the result of the election, and hoped thus to be able to flash the news to New York before it was announced to Rome. A monk's narrow pallet had been arranged for seating accommodation, and under his crucifix a very special telephone had been installed. This was independent of the ordinary exchanges and would enable the I.N.S. to send a message direct to London and from there immediately to New York.

Early on the morning of the election I arrived at this den of impiety, and found the manager of the I.N.S. almost beside himself with rage. "I've been double-crossed," he cried, "and double-crossed by a monk!" His language became sulphurous as he explained that the Monastery had calmly rented an adjoining cell to a rival news service. The gentle little monks, innocently jubilant over their unearned increment, had not the slightest idea that they might be ruining a "scoop."

However, all was not lost. There was only the one telephone line, and though the rival news service had its own extension, it could not use it if the I.N.S. kept the line busy.

"I've had a man reading the Bible over that line since seven o'clock this morning," said the Manager, "and he hasn't got half-way through Exodus yet."

Fortunately perhaps for the Hearst finances, the election was decided before the reader had finished Leviticus. Signals came from the window commanded by the telescope.

"Flash!" yelled the Manager into the telephone mouthpiece; and the result of the election was displayed on the streets in New York nearly half an hour before it was known in St. Peter's Square.

Before I returned to England, Hugh Walpole asked me to go with him to look at the grave of Keats. I did not realize that he had already written the chapter of *Roman Fountain* in which he described that visit, and that he merely wanted to make it more "factual." I went with him because I wanted to see the place again, but our conversation, naturally enough, was not in the least like his anticipatory description of it.

There was a little contretemps at the outset, when Walpole hailed a *carrozza* and got into a tantrum because the driver could not understand a direction which sounded incredibly like "Keatsiano gravy." "These blithering Italian idiots!" he fumed. The driver became equally excited. They both talked at once, and the spectacle of their agitation, apparently over the exact meaning of gravy, held me rocking helplessly in the *carrozza.* Finally Walpole turned to me.

"Alfred, what the hell is the Italian for Keats' grave?" I had no notion; my only Italian had been acquired with a dictionary for my favourite passages in Dante and Ariosto, but I just managed to gasp, "*Cimiterio Inglese.*"

"A-h-h-h-h!" said the driver, with a broad smile, as if he had drunk a bottle of wine at a draught, and off we rattled in the right direction. Walpole looked at me with awe. "My God, Alfred! I didn't know you spoke Italian like that!" It was exactly like that, but I didn't disillusion him.

Not a word of the conversation which Walpole reports in his *Roman Fountain* ever took place. He says that he tried to explain sprung verse to me by the grave of Keats, and when there was a question what was great poetry, "Alfred, who can quote anything, repeated . . . " about a dozen lines of "Hyperion." This happens to be one of the poems which, greatly though I admire it, I cannot quote from memory. What we actually discussed was the epitaph:

Here lies one whose name was writ in water,

and the fact, which Walpole had not realized until he saw it, that the bitter wish of Keats had been carried out, and that the headstone bears no name at all. The name of Keats appears on the adjoining grave as a friend of Severn; and in one of the latest biographies of Keats even Severn did not escape base and ungrateful ridicule for the loyalty that so gently consoled the last hours of the poet.

Walpole may or may not have been telling the truth when he says, in the course of his "spiritual quest," that on an earlier visit he had been introduced to what he most valued in Rome by a vendor of indecent post-cards, and that he had a great longing to meet that personage again. In the biography by Rupert Hart-Davis, Walpole is quoted as saying that he made this statement about himself because he was a professional novelist—a queer conception of the novelist's function. I can speak with certainty only of the passages in which Walpole introduces me personally; but there was something wrong with his mind.

There is one passage in *Roman Fountain* which seems to me quite pathological—his description of the "evil" he encountered in the crowd at a church ceremony. In any case the passage reflects only his own mind, as he himself says:

"Holy? I didn't wish them to be holy, and that was why I saw them as I did, for it is in ourselves that truth or falsehood lies." (A form of solipsism which means that other people are good or bad according to the state of Hugh Walpole's liver.)

I should not give the following facts if it had not been said by Walpole's biographer (as quoted in *The Manchester Guardian,* Feb. 14, 1952) that Walpole "had been virtually thrown out of Alfred Noyes' house-party for daring to admire *Ulysses.*"

Some months before *Roman Fountain* was published Walpole asked if he might come for a day or two to Lisle Combe on his way to the Priestleys at Billingham. We had staying with us at the time a former editor of the *Spectator,* J. B. Atkins, and his wife Lady Gormanston (daughter of Lady Butler and niece of Alice Meynell). Everything was done to make Walpole's visit a pleasant one, and up to that time I had had nothing but friendly thoughts of him. I knew very little about him, as we had met him for the first time in Rome only a few weeks earlier. He had seemed to me quite good-natured, and the tantrums he had occasionally displayed in Rome I had regarded as something like the temperamental explosions of Suzanne Lenglen. Unfortunately I had not realized at the time of his visit that, as his own publishers say upon the jacket of his biography, he was "a perfect subject for a psychologist's case-book," but I must take their word for it. As a guest on this occasion he was quite impossible. His behaviour may have been due to the insulin he had to take, but he was obviously laying himself out to appear the untrammelled genius.

Some of these manifestations were funny. He was childishly annoyed, for instance, that nobody commented on the crimson corduroy trousers in which he appeared one morning at breakfast. He explained that he had bought them in Hollywood, and seemed to think that if there had been a spark of artistic feeling in any of our breasts we should have grouped ourselves around him to admire. There was certainly no intention to slight the crimson trousers. It simply did not occur to anyone to express rapture in words.

After the Catholics in our party had returned from early morning service at Bonchurch, he was good enough to tell me, with a snigger, that during one of the most solemn moments of the funeral at St. Peter's he had seen a priest behaving obscenely. When I asked him to be explicit he pretended to find it unmentionable. I had not noticed this delicacy in him before.

At lunch on the same day Sir George and Lady Rendel and Lord Mottistone were with us. Half-way through lunch Walpole made a remark so personal and so disgusting, about a young girl who was one of the guests, that Lord Mottistone (who was not a prig and could be extremely plain-spoken in the right way) pulled him up short. Lady Rendel, who certainly knew the world, said quietly to me, "I think that was the most atrocious remark I have ever heard." Later in the day there were other incidents of the same kind, and in the evening I found him recommending James Joyce's *Ulysses* to one of my children. He looked up with a grin as I entered the room, and asked me what I thought of the book. He knew perfectly well what I thought of it (as is shown in Chapter XXXIV, though in his biography it is stated that he was unaware of my strong opinions). However, as he had enquired, I said, "I think it is one of the most loathsome books ever written."

He then explained the narrowness of my mind to my guests, and persisted in recommending to an innocent girl a book which he himself describes in his own diary as "filthy." Accordingly I told him I thought it was time that his bag should be packed. He became very white, and ejaculated that I couldn't mean it; but, finding that I did, he hurriedly went to his room and left the house early the next morning.

Later he wrote expressing some kind of regret, and in view of this I made one more effort to convince him that there was nothing personal in the opinion for which he had asked, but that it was based upon a real conviction about the function of literature. He replied, however, that I had "frightened" him.

Afterwards, in *Roman Fountain,* he referred to the incident saying that at the mere mention of *Ulysses* the face of a friend "hitherto sympathetic," had suddenly become "evil" and that this evil was due to his religion.

XLVII

America Revisited

FOR THE first year of the second world war we remained at home in the Isle of Wight. Although our bit of the coast was no longer "a haunt of ancient peace," we still had visitors (the Inges, Yeats-Brown of *Bengal Lancer* and *European Jungle* fame, G. P. Gooch and others).

Gooch had been one of "Acton's Young Men." He had edited the official documents of the first world war, and as a historian probably knew more about modern Europe than any contemporary. He had a magnificent library, and when I was writing *The Torch-Bearers* and *Voltaire* he occasionally sent me books from it which were extremely useful. He was a fascinating conversationalist, and his talk was a brilliant fountain of information about all that was going on in the political world. He was a liberal of the left centre, and already, at the beginning of the war, foresaw exactly how it would end, and was able to sketch in his mind the admission of Germany into the European Federation.

The Isle of Wight lay under the direct route of the air attacks on Southampton and Portsmouth, and if the attackers had anything left on their return journey they frequently dumped it on the Island. There was a radar station at Bonchurch on a hill-top immediately behind the Stacpooles' house. This drew the attention of the bombers, but it was Bonchurch and Ventnor that received the bombs. Our Catholic Church in Ventnor stood at the foot of the hill almost immediately below the radar station. Half-way through Mass one morning the warning siren sounded. Father MacDonald, who was about to begin his sermon, paused and remarked:

"Those of you who wish to stay in the Church may remain. I shall be back in half an hour."

He then disappeared through the vestry. The congregation tittered, but Father MacDonald had neither the time nor the need to explain that he had the task of shepherding a number of school-children into a shelter. When he had done this he returned and went on with the service.

His courage and helpfulness in those many difficult months, with his Presbytery immediately under the direct object of attack, were known to everyone. Several blocks of houses within a few hundred yards were completely destroyed.

Sir John Simeon's house at Swainston, where Tennyson wrote one of his most beautiful poems, went up in flames, and a friend wrote, "Poor John is left with nothing but the clothes he stood up in." Once or twice our own house was badly shaken, and later windows were shattered by concussion, but otherwise it was unhurt. Gradually restrictions were tightened, and it became more and more difficult for any but residents on the Island to come and go.

Returning to the Island one fine evening after a day in London, I saw on the shining stillness of the Solent a strange assemblage of oddly assorted craft (including a paddle-steamer named *Gracie Fields*) obviously drawn up for some definite purpose. It was one of the contingents whose achievements at Dunkirk on the following day were to save England.

Living on an island only a few miles from the mainland, but still in a sense between the opposing forces (for the Isle of Wight received not only enemy bombs but also an occasional sprinkling of our own shrapnel from Portsmouth and Southampton), one obtained a peculiar perspective. One very peaceful afternoon, for instance, we could see in the distance a convoy of ships, diminutive in the great seascape, moving slowly, almost lazily. Suddenly, what looked like a swarm of tiny mosquitoes appeared above them. There were sounds of gunfire, and little splashes in the water round the ships. Then some of our own airplanes roared out over our roof, and the attacking mosquitoes took to flight. The convoy went lazily on its way, and again the only sounds were those of peace—a bee buzzing among the flowers, the murmur of pigeons in Pelham Woods.

In the autumn of 1940 I was asked by the National Council of Education of Canada to undertake a coast-to-coast lecture tour; and at the same time I received invitations to give lectures on English literature in the United States. Sir Frederick White, who at that time was the head of the American Department of the Ministry of Information, urged me very strongly to accept the invitations, saying that the maintenance of these friendly literary relationships was of value.

The proceeds of my lectures arranged by the National Council of Education went directly to their fund for bringing English children over to Canadian schools. I received no fees, but was provided with free transportation on the railway for my wife and myself, and in the Canadian Pacific hotels I had merely to sign chits for our expenses.

On arrival with our children in Montreal we were taken by car to Maplebank, Cartierville, the house of Colonel and Mrs. Ogilvie, the grounds of which slope down to the Richelieu River. Immediately opposite the house is a long island, named by the old French settlers the *Isle de Jesus*. In a house near the Ogilvies there were English children, with whom our own speedily made friends.

The kindness of their Canadian hosts to the youngsters from overseas is something of which I find it difficult to speak adequately, but I tried to commemorate it in some lines on "English Children in Canada":

From an old Canadian garden, among the budding maples
  And slender silver birches that gleamed to the April sky,
The bright-haired English children stared at the mighty river,
  And watched the ice of winter slowly drifting by,

Rending and crunching along the rocky shores of the garden,
  Splintering, cracking and jamming in cove and creek and bay;
While, round the wooded coasts of the quiet *Isle de Jesus,*
  The wind came whispering softly that Spring was on her way.

It touched their golden heads with light unseen caresses.
  They stood there like Spring flowers, while the squirrels drew quietly near,
And the youngest child called out "Look, Mummy," and then remembered;
  And the light failed, and recovered, for one that could not be there.

A moment, only a moment; then radiant bird-like laughter
  Pealed thro' the tall dark pines, and the rocks re-echoed the din,
As they rode on the cracking floes, in the dancing sun-lit shallows,
  Till sunset reddened the West, and a kind voice called them in.

Then the stars and the stillness came; but, out of the night around them,
  What shadowy hands were stretched, in blessing and thanks and prayer;
While a little one called in dreams, on the shores of the *Isle de Jesus,*
  "Look, O Mummy, do look!" And her Mummy at last was there.

After we had installed our two little girls at the Sacred Heart Convent in Montreal, and Hugh at Ashbury College in Ottawa where there were sixty other English boys, my lecture tour began.

At Ottawa we stayed a night or two with the poet Duncan Campbell Scott, then continued our westward journey, stopping for my lectures at many towns on the way. In Vancouver I gave an address on October 12, 1940, at the University of British Columbia, and at the Vancouver Institute. So that I should tread on no toes, the Canadian Authors' Association very kindly gave me a leaflet with "brief notes as to some of those you will meet." There was a nice touch of humour in one of these notes:

"Mr. —— To be taken very seriously. Author of several books on poetry. Considers Shakespeare a much over-rated writer."

Christmas itself, a real Canadian Christmas, we spent with our children at Maplebank with the Ogilvies. As there was an interval before I could resume my lectures for the National Council of Education, my wife and I crossed the border into the United States and went on into California. I had been invited to speak at the Institute of Technology in Pasadena, and also before the World Affairs Assembly under the chairmanship of Dr. von Kleinschmidt, President of the University of Southern California. On this visit we had our first glimpse of the huge mirror for the 200-inch telescope then being perfected at "Cal-Tech."

From then on, I was lecturing almost continuously, sometimes on one side of the border, sometimes on the other, moving to and fro across the continent. The underlying thesis of all my lectures was the dependence of aesthetical and ethical values on those eternal values which are grounded in the nature of ultimate reality, and are envisaged in *The Torch-Bearers* and in *The Unknown God*. My lectures on poetry were in accord with this thesis, and I sometimes reversed the statement of Matthew Arnold that the strongest part of our religion was its unconscious poetry, by trying to show that the strongest part of all poetry was its unconscious religion, the setting up of that right relationship between the transient and the abiding which once held Christendom together. In the absence of that relationship, that religion, the world was heading for "red ruin."

I was occasionally criticized for saying in 1940 what has become only too obvious in 1952. In December, 1940, an American newspaper said, under the heading "Over-Fearful":

> When Alfred Noyes says that the spread of Communism is one of the chief dangers of the aftermath of war, one may answer that that is only one man's opinion, brilliant as that may be, but we do not have to see eye to eye with him. We may look forward to another protracted lucid interval of peace and quiet.

The three Josiah Wood Lectures which I gave in early February at Mount Allison University were published in book form by the University in Canada, and appeared in the American periodical *Fortune* under the title of "The Edge of the Abyss." In the mind of every speaker and writer there must sometimes be an almost desperate feeling that nothing he can do or say really has any effect. It was an immense encouragement to me, therefore, to receive a letter from the publishers of *Fortune,* saying that many people had written asking for additional copies of the article; for a while the publishers had torn it out of extra copies of that issue of *Fortune,* but it finally became necessary to reprint well over twelve thousand copies, of which about five thousand had been sent to college students.

This essay was autobiographical in the sense that it embodied the conclusions I had reached over a long period of time, and had tried to express in one way or another through my writings. *The Edge of the Abyss* was subsequently reprinted in book form by Dutton in New York and John Murray in England.

On February 11, 1941, we arrived in Boston. I had something of the feeling of a revenant; for we were met at the station by the same chauffeur who had taken me to the Aldriches' house at 59 Mount Vernon Street a third of a century earlier. He was a little plumper but otherwise hardly changed; and when we reached No. 59, with its graceful porch of so many memories, my heart thumped, for there seemed no change at all. The door was opened by the same butler, Hannan, very little changed though with greyer hair, and we were led into a book-lined room of which I knew every inch. The senior Aldriches had died years ago, but I could see little alteration in Talbot and Eleanor; and, when they took us into the dining-room, I found in a corner near the door a framed manuscript of my poem in memory of Thomas Bailey Aldrich, exactly where it was first hung in 1913.

In Aldrich's study on the top floor, where I had spent so many good hours, not an article of furniture was changed. The engraving of Apollo and the Muses, the editions of Balzac and the *Arabian Nights,* and his favourite poets, were all in their accustomed places. I could almost believe that the old rocking chair near the hearth had only just been vacated by the poet, and I think his pipe and toabcco pouch were still upon the desk. Moreover, as when I first arrived at that house, my next engagement was to lecture at Wellesley, where none can go without meeting the very spirit of youth.

In March, 1941, we continued westward, with many lecture engagements.

At Salt Lake City I spoke to an audience curiously different from anything I had encountered before. The University at Provo, Utah, was named after Brigham Young, and the atmosphere of his strange sect broods over the whole district. Outwardly Salt Lake City, with its broad clean streets, appears to be one of the most prosperous in the United States, but there is something creepy and secretive about it. A fact, almost startling in its contrast with the rest of America, was that one seldom saw a smiling face. I had an uneasy feeling that, despite its material prosperity, the whole city was afflicted with a queer abnormality for which I could find no name. One symptom was the almost complete lack of humour.

This was curiously illustrated by their attitude towards what they call "the Lion House," the former residence of Brigham Young, which is now maintained as a memorial to him and shown with great pride to the visitor. In a room on the ground floor there is an immense sofa upon which, you are told, Brigham Young used to sit in the evenings, with a large selection of his twenty-five wives, possibly twelve on each side and one to bring in the coffee. I was not shown the nursery accommodation for his forty children.

In his study a cupboard door discloses a little private stairway by which Young could ascend to an upper floor and a long corridor with a great many bedroom doors, each bearing the Christian name of a different wife.

While these things are being shown, you must be very careful not to smile or make the slightest joke. My wife rashly enquired whether these numerous ladies were always at peace with one another. The custodian's eyes flashed:

"It was the most harmonious family the world has ever seen," she exclaimed, "and they had the most wonderful system of household management ever known. All the household work was done by the wives who had no children."

At the magnificent auditorium of the Mormon Tabernacle, from which organ recitals are broadcast over the whole country, our cicerone seated us near the entrance and told us he was going to demonstrate the remarkable acoustics of the great hall. He then walked to the other end of it, and in a husky whisper told us that he was now going to drop the traditional pin. I could not see what he actually dropped, but to my expectant ears it sounded like a dumb-bell. He returned to us triumphantly, and I asked him how these remarkable acoustics had been obtained. An uncanny gleam came into his eyes, and he delivered another husky whisper, this time directly into my ear. "Inspiration," he said.

I was really very glad to get away from Salt Lake City. I have visited many unusual communities and enjoyed the experience, but I am quite unable to explain that sense of something sinister by which I was haunted in this unsmiling and splendid city. I was extremely glad to escape from it. I had never before taken Conan Doyle's "A Study in Scarlet" seriously, but I did now. It is a grim reflection that a large proportion of the Mormon leaders were of English descent.

After some lectures in San Francisco, a city which I have always loved and mentally coupled with Edinburgh (probably because of its steep streets, which remind one of the Canongate, and partly perhaps because of its gracefully romantic memorial to Robert Louis Stevenson), we travelled south, by Santa Barbara, to what Robert Bridges, in his *Testament of Beauty,* calls "rose-hung Pasadena." There I gave another course of lectures at the California Institute of Technology.

Pasadena was a place that had and always will have many memories for me, and its sunlight was now tinged with a certain sadness. Crimson bougainvillea still hung over the "poet's bungalow," as it was called partly because Henry van Dyke had at one time occupied it, and partly because it was my own first abode in Southern California; but George Ellery Hale, my astronomer friend, had gone, and those of his younger associates who were still at the Mount Wilson Observatory were now "grave seniors." Dr. Millikan (recently a

Nobel Prize winner), Hubble, Adams and Seares were still active. The hummingbirds were still thrusting their needle-like beaks into the overhanging blossoms, just as they did nearly thirty years earlier.

My lectures were inaugurated by a dinner at the Athenaeum, a Club which looked like a Greek temple, in its sun-flooded setting among palms, roses and pepper trees, with the San Gabriel Mountains in the background. The long list of guests included Frank Capra and Ronald Colman, whom we were to meet later in Los Angeles and in Santa Barbara.

In the series of about twenty lectures which I gave at "Cal-Tech" I found that (although the Institute is primarily scientific) the students had a sound appreciation of the basic principles of literature. This I think was largely due to the influence of Professor Judy, whose bachelor quarters housed a fine library, and partly to the fact that the scientific student is trained to think with precision, and is not easily misled by the merely eccentric.

I had no intimation at this time that the strenuous series of lectures, involving scores of long journeys and much night travel, was a danger to my eyesight. (During my various journeys through America I had spoken in over five hundred towns and cities, often making three or four return visits.) In the interest and excitement of the experience I did not realize the "tension" which I was undergoing in lecturing to audiences, usually of some hundreds, occasionally of several thousands, and sometimes speaking twice a day. I was told later that this "hyper-tension" induced the glaucoma which in a year or two deprived me of the power to read.

I gave many incidental lectures at other places in California, a dozen or more of them in Los Angeles on which occasions we stayed with our old friends Alice and Belle Cooper. Their house on South Flower Street had seen the city growing up around it, but still retained its country garden with its avocado trees, and roses growing over the gate.

On one of our visits there I had a telephone call from Frank Capra, telling me that he had just acquired the rights of my novel *No Other Man*. He gave a little dinner for us that week to meet Mr. and Mrs. Ronald Colman and Mr. and Mrs. Charles Boyer. I gained quite a new impression of Hollywood. Frank Capra had a fascinating library, with first editions of *Paradise Lost* and Ben Jonson. After dinner, to my great surprise, he showed me the framed manuscript of one of my own poems which, although I didn't remember it, I had given to him when he was a young student working his way through "Cal-Tech" twenty-five years earlier.

No Other Man still has "top priority" he tells me, "when conditions improve." He was planning a great production in Technicolour, with special attention to the scenes at the Vatican and on the Italian coast.

In June, 1941, my wife and I set off once more on the three thousand-mile journey across the United States, breaking it for a day at the Grand Canyon, where again I was a revenant. I met my own *Book of Earth,* with its account of my former visit, in the possession of one of the Forest Rangers.

In Kansas City Henry Haskell, editor of the *Kansas City Star,* was the most hospitable of hosts. On a later visit to him I saw one day an immense funeral procession passing along the main street. A bystander told me that it was the funeral of Pendergast, the Boss of the Pendergast gang. He had recently been released from the penitentiary, where he had served a sentence, after a lurid political career. Midway in the solemn procession there passed a car guarded by armed police on motor-cycles, evidently conveying a mourner of considerable importance. I was told that it was Mr. Truman, then Vice-President, who had flown from Washington to attend the obsequies of his old friend and political creator.

Mr. H. J. Haskell, whose paper had with great courage fought the politician's influence for many years, told me that Pendergast had relieved the State of many million dollars. (All the best and most American influences in the State recognized and respected the fight that Haskell and his newspaper carried on for good government.) However, on the Sunday after the funeral, sermons drew floods of tears from crowded congregations, by inviting those without sin to cast the first stone at the defunct millionaire, and, with a fine confusion of ideas, stirred many young hearts with the unconscious suggestion, "Go thou and do likewise."

alfred Noyes
2 fold task
Interpret an
task more ne
ever been

During the summer there were few lectures, and our children came south for the holidays to join us. We met them in Boston and took them to Haven, a little fishing village on the coast of Maine, where we rented a glorified log cabin from the Harvard poet Donald Parson. It was backed by pine-woods, and stood on a little rock-bound meadow ledge full of wild flowers, overlooking a broad reach of deep blue sea. In the distance it saw three small pine-tufted islands, where only sea-gulls and other wild creatures lived. Beyond these was the Atlantic. The cottage was built of sturdy pine, with a rough stone chimney. In the patch of long grass and ferns around it bees hovered over the wild Michaelmas daisies; and among the rocks there were all sorts of deliciously scented little shrubs where the rambling foot-wide path went down to the beach. In front of the cottage the sun flooded the wide verandah.

There was a large central room, with a wide stone fireplace and an ingle-nook. The room had a gallery running the whole way round it, with a trellised balustrade of silver-birch logs. The prettiest of stairs, with another trellised balustrade of silver birch led up to the gallery from which bedrooms and bathrooms opened. The dining-room and kitchen opened out of the central room.

The village life and scenery formed the background of *The Secret of Pooduck Island,* a story I wrote there. But the place is depicted briefly in some verses which, with the children in mind, and perhaps with some of my own nostalgia as a revenant, I called "The Happy Hunting Grounds":

> I know a cottage on the coast of Maine. . . .
> You walk thro' a wood, by a winding lane,
> Till you come to a clearing where the waves say "woosh"
> And the sea-swallow nests in a wild-rose bush.
> There you will find it, as the honey bees know,
> With the rocks and the tide twelve yards below;
> And, in among the rocks, with the dragon-fly and bee,
> A foot-wide path takes the swimmer to the sea.
>
> And the little wild strawberries redden under foot,
> And the woodchuck nibbles at the rosemarie root,

And the green snake basks on the path as it goes
Down thro' the rocks with the wild red rose.

Then, a shining cloud-winged spirit of the sky,
A lone three-masted ship sails by;
And, out and away, on the deep-sea blue,
The dark pines cluster on an island or two;
Salt, hard, flower-bright islands of the blest,
Where the blueberries grow and the herring-gulls nest,
And the fish-hawk over his pine-tree wheels,
And the cormorant cries to the barking seals,
While you thrust through the firs with their dew on your face,
And the long grass misty with the Queen Anne's lace;
Till the Red Man's ghost in a birch-canoe
Dips his paddle in the creeks *he* knew,
And glides thro' the old old sights and sounds
By the shores of the shadowy hunting grounds.

I know a cottage on the coast of Maine. . . .
Let a salt wave whisper, and I'm living there again.
By the tang of the rosin from a blue spruce bough,
Or the red of a maple, I am living there now,
Looking through a window at my heart's delight,
As the sea falls quiet and the West turns bright,—
Barefoot children, in the sunset-glow
Running up the rocks from the little beach below,
Climbing up the crags from the shell strewn shore
With a bucket-full of clams to the open door;
Through the scent of the briars where the sea-swallow stirs
And the squirrel chirrups in the sun-warmed firs.

I know a haven on the coast of Maine. . . .
Let a pine-wood rustle and I'm living there again,
Writing or reading by a pine-log fire,
Or looking through a window at my heart's desire,—
Skies of vision, and a sea at rest,
And the face of my belovèd as she turns to the West,
On a rock above the water with a creel in her hand,
And her bright eyes gazing at the sunset-land. . . .

Skies of vision, and a world of light,
And a white sail homing at the fall of night.

Haven was about ten miles south of Blue Hill, where A. J. Cronin and his family were staying for the summer. We lunched together occasionally and every Sunday motored to the same church, about fifteen miles away at Ellsworth. Mount Desert, which was described by President Eliot of Harvard as the most beautiful island in the world, was a little further north, and there again we found some old friends in Senator George Wharton Pepper and his family, and Mr. and Mrs. Charlton Yarnall.

In the middle of September we took the children back to their schools in Canada, and as there was still a week or so before the lecture season could begin again, my wife and I returned for a few days to Haven. Most of the little colony of summer visitors had departed and the autumn had already begun to colour the hillsides. There was a long and strenuous programme before us, for I was to lecture my way across the continent again and then deliver a course of thirty lectures at the University of California in Berkeley. These few days on that lonely coast were paradisal. In the evenings there was no sound but the lapping of the water on the crags below. The little pine-tufted islands in the bay, where we had spent long days with our youngsters, were now left to the herring-gulls and the barking seals.

On the first evening after our return to Haven I had what seemed to me a very strange experience in that remote solitude: I turned on the radio, and instantly, to my amazement, heard a man's voice in England, a very fine one, singing one of my own songs.

XLVIII

Failing Eyesight

AFTER THAT week, and until Christmas, I had numerous lecture engagements around New York, Philadelphia and Chicago, and was still unaware of the risk to my eyes from the resultant "hyper-tension." Some of the audiences numbered over three thousand. (For a reading of my poems at the University of California there had been an audience of over seven thousand students.)

At Rochester, New York, we stayed with Judge and Mrs. Van Voorhis at their place on the shore of Lake Ontario. The grounds slope down to the lake very much as our own in the Isle of Wight slope down to the Channel, and among their many fine trees there is a firm beach exactly like our own and in a similar position. John Van Voorhis, a distinguished Judge and a man of wide reading, is also a fine yachtsman and a good chess-player. This meeting was the beginning of an enduring friendship.

Mrs. Van Voorhis, who contributed two charming lyrics to the *Golden Book of Catholic Poetry,* was also the author of a poem addressed to one of her own very young children, in terms which must strike a familiar if unacknowledged note for many women. It began, "You, whom I long to strangle and caress."

We spent that Christmas with our children at the house of Mr. and Mrs. Craven near New York. Mr. Craven was a partner in a legal firm with Wendell Willkie, whom we met with Mrs. Willkie at dinner. Some of Wendell Willkie's ideas about his "One World" seemed to me extremely visionary, but he insisted that the whole of Europe would have to speak a single language, which, one gathered, was to be his own. I put in a plea for those national differences and characteristics of which the various languages and literatures in Europe are the vital expression, but he swept this away quite genially, with the remark that I was a poet.

After Christmas there was another transcontinental lecture tour, followed by lectures in Florida. Once or twice, when I was trying to read on railroad trains, the page became a blank, but I attributed this to the glare of the snow and the jolting of the train, and as I was able to resume reading in a minute or two, the warning escaped me. By April, 1942, we were back in New York. The lectures went on, but without the fatigues of travel. In May, I remember, Ian Hay lunched with us, and told us of the play he was writing on Harriet Beecher Stowe. He was especially interesting about the central scene in England, where Harriet Beecher Stowe is told by Lord Palmerston that, largely owing to *Uncle Tom's Cabin,* there would be a civil war, and she had better go back to America and look for a certain giant. He is not quite sure of the giant's name, but thinks it is that of an English Cathedral city.

In June Syracuse University, where I had lectured on several former occasions, offered me an honorary degree. My wife and I stayed with our friends the Dean of the Law School, Paul Andrews, and his wife, at Wolf Hollow, a delightful house which, despite its name, stood on a height overlooking miles of open country. In many ways, with its fine library and huge open fireplace, it was very like an old English manor-house. Lord Halifax, then British Ambassador in Washington, was to receive an honorary degree on the same occasion, and he and Lady Halifax were our fellow-guests.

There was a huge gathering in the amphitheatre for the ceremony. From the platform where the recipients of degrees were seated I could hear a mysterious voice broadcasting details of the proceedings from some invisible hiding place. I noticed that Lord Halifax was listening with puzzled curiosity to the unseen narrator, whose voice, apparently coming from underground, like that of the ghost in *Hamlet,* was embroidering the ambassadorial achievements with strangely irrelevant remarks about Francis Drake and some probably disreputable ale-house called the Mermaid Tavern.

The friendship formed at Wolf Hollow with Paul and Nan Andrews remains a treasured possession. Paul Andrews, a man of law, became interested in the idealistic movement for world federation—which, if it be a dream, is yet better than the nightmare in which the world is living and moving to-day. He made frequent visits to Europe in connection with it, and occasionally came to Lisle Combe. His idealism was always kept in proportion by his legal training, judicial mind and keen sense of humour. His fund of stories was inexhaustible. He told of a meeting in Scotland, at which speakers from various parts of the Dominions had all dwelt too lengthily on their personal ties with Scotland. The audience was growing a little tired of this when, to their relief, a full-blooded Maori was called upon to speak. Here at least there would be no blether about that grandfather from Inverness. To their amazement, however, the

Maori at once began to claim closer relationship to Scotland than any of the former speakers. "Indeed," he said, "mine might be described as a corporate bond. My grandfather ate a Scotsman!"

A World Federalist who can talk in that vein has great allies.

Paul Andrews told a story about Lord Macmillan, who at another meeting paid an unexpected compliment to a particularly excellent Chairman. "There is a legend," he said, "that every newborn child is visited in his cradle by a fairy godmother who bestows a particular talent on him. If he is to be a great orator she kisses him on the lips. If he is to be a great artist or musician she kisses him on the hand. I don't know where she kissed Mr. Blank, but I have never known a better occupant of a Chair."

In some of his letters Paul Andrews gives glimpses of that America which (as I knew and loved it on the coast of Maine and in Canada) sets the mind of at least one Englishman longing to breathe its unspoiled air again.

Living in more than one country has its pains as well as its pleasures; the distant place is always tugging at the heart. One evening, during our visit to Wolf Hollow, Paul Andrews reminded us that he had taken some coloured pictures of our garden in the Isle of Wight. He put them on the screen for us, and there, once again, were the children running up and down the garden paths, the flowering shrubs around the pools and the willows waving in the wind—all the happy haunts of childhood, now cut off from the sea by barbed wire defences and gun emplacements.

For our 1942 summer holidays we were again joined by our children in the log cabin at Haven, where they had another happy interval swimming, sailing and fishing. Our own happiness was in theirs, but it was inevitably shadowed by the terrible events of the time. The Cronins were again at Blue Hill, and Mr. and Mrs. George Wharton Pepper and the Charlton Yarnalls at Mount Desert. Donald Parson, the Harvard poet, was also at Haven, and we had many pleasant visits with our old friends George and Claire Waterman at Pooduck, their Sabine Farm, as they always called it.

Donald Parson had a motor-launch which he had placed at the

disposal of the American Navy, with himself in charge as skipper and his two brothers as crew. They looked completely nautical in their naval uniforms, but the launch was really better adapted for pleasure than for coastguard work. However, they were under Navy orders and they were glad to combine duty with pleasure. One morning they set out with excellent provision for luncheon on board, and were quietly cruising into the open sea beyond the islands when they came upon the floating body of a Russian General. He was only identifiable by his medals, and was probably the victim of some air accident. They got him onto the bows of the boat and returned to port, but they ate no luncheon. . . .

In those years places that had hitherto seemed remote to me had a strange way of suddenly becoming central to what was going on in the world. San Francisco with the Golden Gate, which to "Old Grey Squirrel" had seemed more distant than Cathay, was soon to become the meeting place of the United Nations. One evening during these holidays, from our log cabin on the coast of Maine we saw the *Potomac* dropping anchor behind Deer Isle. It was bringing the President back from the conference at sea with the British Prime Minister. The lights of the *Potomac* shone there all that night, and there were very few other lights on the Atlantic between that little ship and war-torn Europe. The verses that I wrote about this incident were published in the *New York Times* (after permission had been received from the White House), and I was subsequently asked to broadcast them for the American Navy Day.

There is one very curious thing that I have often noticed in the writing of poetry—that it unconsciously anticipates events. As I have said earlier, I had no conscious hint that the strain of lecturing was having any unusual effect upon my eyesight. Indeed, on a visit to Pooduck Island I had and recorded what will always remain to me the most beautiful visual experience that I remember. The island (only about 250 yards long) was a mile or so from the mainland. It had everything in miniature, a bit of woodland, a meadow full of wild flowers, blueberry bushes, patches of wild strawberries, and a water-spring. I have described it at greater length in *The Secret of*

Pooduck Island. One day, while my wife and the children were lighting a fire on one of the tiny beaches, I saw the picture I have recorded in that book. This I attributed to Solo, one of the characters in the story:

"He rose to his feet and went a little way up a miniature woodland ride of tall bracken through a clump of fragrant red cedars. He did this because he thought he saw a light shining at the end of it. Suddenly he stood quite still and caught his breath in a gasp of sheer wonder.

"A few yards in front of him there was one of those gaps or ragged arches in the wood through which you saw the sea again, just as if you were looking through some wild cathedral window, in which all the coloured glass had been replaced by the shining and living colours of the sea beyond. But this time it was more beautiful than it had ever looked before; for the lower part of that wild window, arched by its dark cedar boughs, was a glowing mass of tall purple loosestrife, with the opaline sea shining *through* the blossom as well as above it; while, away in the distance, he saw a three-masted full-rigged schooner of the old days, growing slowly brighter as she crept along the dark background of the coast to take the first colours of the sunset on her crowded sails.

"He stood there for nearly five minutes, watching her. It was like looking through an eye of his beloved Island, and seeing things more clearly and beautifully than he could see them elsewhere. Then, slowly, the opalescence of the sea changed into a light mist, rising in wisps and wreaths and at last veiling the magical picture completely. It was like the mist that, once or twice, had dimmed the eyes of a wounded herring-gull, he thought. Then he turned and went back to the spring where he intended to camp. It was the same there too. Filmy curtains of mist had hidden both the mainland and the islands, leaving only a narrow ring of sea around Pooduck, which had once more become a world in itself. Yet, most curiously, Pooduck Island and its narrow ring of sea were still bright with the last of the sun."

This is almost an exact description of what happens to the narrowing field of vision in glaucoma. There seems to be a further premonition in the following passage:

"The radiant picture he had seen, and tried to paint later, would still be radiant in other summers; but its radiance, apparently, was dangerous for him. There was no unhappiness in it; but his own thoughts of it were tinged with all the deeper sense of loss. . . . The phrase he used,—*Pooduck Island has an eye*—meant something beautiful to him when he said it, and he had said it as though it were a line in some mysterious poem. . . . Now it came back to him as if the very stillness of the woods outside were solemnly warning him that nobody must speak or think like that. It was a voice of infinite sadness, breathing its music into his troubled brain from a world beyond our world. It was the same voice that had gone through the autumn woods two months ago. . . . But to-night it was a silent voice, in his own heart and mind. . . . It could never be put into words; but, if it could, this is what it seemed to say:

Pooduck Island has an Eye.
   Ne'er look through it!
'Ware that lovelier sea and sky
   Or you'll rue it.

Eye that in a little wood,
   Boughs all round it,
Opens on a world as good
   As youth found it.

Window in a world of pain!
   Up, lad, flee it;
Lest your heaven be born again,
   And you see it.

Birds and men that once had wings
   And have lost them
Know (with those who see such things)
   All it cost them.

I can attach no other meaning to those passages now except that some quite unconscious apprehension or warning was at work within me. I don't want to make too much of this, but I quote the passages for those who are interested in the workings of the subconscious mind.

In November I went to see an oculist in New York about what I believed to be some minor eye trouble. He informed me that I had glaucoma in one of those insidious forms which inflict no pain and can destroy a great part of the field of vision before the danger is recognized. In my own case the damage had come very near to the point of central vision, and I had a choice between trying to hold it in check with pilocarpine or an operation. As the central field was so nearly involved it appeared that an operation might do more harm than good. I was later advised that, as the eye-drops seemed to keep the tension down to normal, my lectures might continue, especially as the projected course at Berkeley involved no travelling.

At Berkeley I gave about thirty lectures. These were open to the public as well as to the students, and there were usually about three or four hundred present. President and Mrs. Sproul were kindness itself, and there were delightful gatherings at their house. Mr. James K. Moffitt too, one of the Trustees of the University, and his wife, showed us great hospitality at their home in Piedmont on the hills across the Bay from San Francisco. Mr. Moffitt had a very fine library, including a notable collection of the early editions of Horace; and there was much good talk at the luncheons he gave in a private room at the University Club in San Francisco, to which there usually came three or four members of the faculty and one or two of the leading lawyers of the State. Towards the end of the San Francisco Conference some of the British delegates were among the guests, including Mr. Peel of the India Office, and it was a shock a few days later to hear that the plane on which they were returning to England had been lost over the Atlantic. The suspicion with which the Russians were viewed in San Francisco may be gauged by the comment, "Oh, yes, they got them," which I heard more than once.

Strange things that might have come out of a story by John Buchan could happen at that time in San Francisco. Mr. Moffitt himself, who was in his eighth decade, tall, spare, white-haired but very active for his years, was one day kidnapped in a main thoroughfare of the city. He was seated in his car, waiting for his wife who was doing some shopping, when another car drew up in front of his own, a man alighted, walked up to Mr. Moffitt's car and, seating himself beside the chauffeur, poked a revolver into his ribs and said: "Drive on! I've killed two men today, and I don't mind if I kill two more!"

As they drove off, Mr. Moffitt, who was in the back seat, without attracting the attention of the gangster quietly threw his hat out of the open window on to the sidewalk, as a possible clue for anyone who might be interested. In fact, only a minute or two later his wife found it, but the car had gone.

The police had been on the lookout for the car which the gangster had abandoned, and he was now leaving the city in the car of one of the leading bank directors of the western world. The kidnapper repeated from time to time his assurances that he had already killed two men and would be quite happy to kill two more if his orders were not obeyed.

When they were out of the city the chauffeur was ordered to stop, and the gangster began to get out of the car. In doing so he accidentally pulled the trigger of his gun. The bullet glanced off some metal-work and struck him in the face. The chauffeur seized the opportunity and at once grappled with him. Even in those circumstances it was no easy task, for though the injury bled profusely it was only slight, and the man was in fact an ex-prizefighter. At last the police arrived and secured him.

"I suppose it was unchivalrous," said Mr. Moffitt to me afterwards at the fireside in his library, with Cyril Bailey's edition of Lucretius open on his knee, "I suppose it was unchivalrous, but as they were taking the man off, I ran after him and gave him the hardest kick I could in the seat of his pants."

From what Mrs. Moffitt said, I suspect that Mr. Moffitt had done more than he told us, to help his chauffeur in the tussle, for the front of his coat was smeared with blood, and even Dr. Watson might conclude that this was not the result of kicking his assailant in the seat of his pants.

The gangster went to the electric chair. His boast that he had killed two men that day was true.

XLIX

Santa Barbara

FROM BERKELEY we went to Santa Barbara, where a branch of the University of California was being developed. There I gave another course of lectures, which were attended by the general public as well as by the students, and though my sight was beginning to give me great difficulty, I was able to depend on my memory for the many passages from the poets on which the lectures were based. At this time I was also writing my *Horace,* and the great kindness of Mrs. Elmer T. Merrill gave me access to many books in her very fine library, some of them from the collection of Professor Merrill (to whose edition of *Catullus* I paid a very inadequate tribute in the preface to my *Horace*). Her friendship, in fact, reopened the world of books for me at a very difficult time, and there are many pages which for me will always be associated with the readings in that sunlit house between the Sierra Madre Mountains and the Pacific Coast.

Santa Barbara has been described as an earthly paradise where elderly people sometimes go to visit their grandparents. Since it has the best climate in the world, this is partly true, and may be explained by the charm of the grandparents, but it omits a great many other aspects of that delightful oasis.

Among those whom we met there Stravinsky stands out vividly. He talked simply and sincerely, and without any of the affectations which advertise the second-rate. With all his conversational lightness of touch, one felt that there was a philosophical depth and richness of thought behind almost everything he said. In fact I liked the man very much more than I like his music. This, for me at any rate, despite its intellectual brilliance lacks the humanity and the spiritual values of which he seemed to be fully conscious in real life. You cannot hear Beethoven without being aware that you are listening to someone who understood the heights and depths of love and compassion, justice and mercy. In Stravinsky's music I can admire the fireworks and the mathematics, but I cannot find the deeper qualities which were manifest in the man himself. He once affirmed that music must not be accused of having a meaning, but in this perhaps he was merely rejecting the view of that other composer who waxed indignant because a critic had failed to gather that the subject of one of his most brilliant passages had red hair.

Two poets, Leonard Bacon and Hermann Hagedorn, and the author of the *Song of Bernadette,* were among our neighbours at Santa Barbara while we were there. Leonard Bacon, whose translation of the *Lusiads* is itself a classic, rivalled Yorrick in his devastating humour, and upset his flagons of Rhenish on many a devoted head. Of a Czecho-Slovakian visitor to a neighbour's house he wickedly reported the following passage between the visitor and his hostess:

CZECHO-SLOVAK (*imperfectly acquainted with English, and conscious that he has stayed too long*): I hope you will excuse me so much for cockroaching on your time.

HOSTESS (*anxious to improve the efficiency of the melting-pot*): You know, in English we usually say *en*croaching.

CZECHO-SLOVAK (*with sudden illumination*): Ah-h-h-h, I see, ze feminine, *hen*croaching. I will remember.

Santa Barbara often had interesting visitors passing through. Young David Astor, representing the *Observer,* and certainly not visiting his grandmother, came to see us. Sir Alexander and Lady Cadogan (on a peaceful vacation from the United Nations) came to tea, and Sir Alexander dwelt upon the impossibility of penetrating the Russian ear-drum either by logic or by demonstrable facts.

While we were in Santa Barbara we had first a house of a Spanish or Mediterranean type, built round three sides of a small patio, with a low balustrade on the fourth overlooking the sky-blue blossom of jacaranda trees and a garden which sloped steeply down to a lake. It was in this Mediterranean setting that I wrote my *Horace.* There were one or two orange and lemon trees in the patio, and overhanging one corner there was a crimson bougainvillea. Hummingbirds flitted to and fro, and sometimes one would bury its head so deeply in a hibiscus or oleander blossom that Hugh, who is something of a naturalist, was able to take both blossom and bird in his careful hands for a moment. Of this little corner of Paradise Margaret Webb gave a delightful suggestion in a book-plate which she did for me there.

Ever since my first visit to California nearly thirty-five years earlier, certain happy valleys, vine-clad slopes and bits of palm-fringed coast had remained in my mind like memories of Elysium. It has been said that those who once visit it never forget that delicate fragrance in the air, the smell of the burning eucalyptus leaves and the long leagues of peach and orange blossom.

But there was now for me another aspect of this beautiful country with a deeper significance which in the new paganism may gradually be overlaid and forgotten, and yet is by far the richest in its history. Place names that to the decivilized may suggest nothing more than a setting for a "Western," are still to the historical sense, from San Diego and Santa Monica to San Francisco, jewels in the rosary of their godfather Junípero Serra. There are still high and lonely places among its mountains from which one sees, below, five miles of Paradise sinking down to the Pacific Ocean. Groves of citrus fruit, peach trees, walnut trees, bordered by tall white-stemmed eucalyptus, and breathing delicious fragrances, remind one of the name that Junípero Serra had given to this beautiful coast—*Tierra Adorada.*

Above, the aromatic sage brush and tumbled rocks mark the beginning of the mountain wilderness. Bushes of wild lilac were mingled with strange forms of cactus that cast fantastic shadows over the hillsides. But even in that rugged landscape the early pioneers had found the symbols of peace, and when all over the slopes of the hills the wild yucca was in blossom, the Franciscans had called those tall waxen spikes of white bloom God's Candles.

Looking to the west over the ocean, one saw the islands of Santa Rosa, San Miguel and Santa Cruz. To multitudes in the modern world these names are merely labels like any other place names—pleasant sounding, because they are in the golden tongue of Spain, but their actual significance for the crowd is no more than that of Pine Ridge or Crow's Nest. Yet each of them, like San Juan Capistrano or San Bernardino, opens a great glowing window upon the vital history of a past loaded with significance for the future, and pregnant with the fate of the universe. There were times when, in the course of my lecturing engagements, motoring along that radiant coastline from one golden name to another, I felt as if I were journeying through the pages of a gloriously illuminated breviary. There were many grotesque signs by the wayside, but neither these nor the shock of arrival at a place called Watsonville could mar the natural beauty or the historical associations of that magnificent landscape.

Very soon after I had corrected the final proofs of my *Horace* I underwent an operation for glaucoma. The operation was unsuccessful, and a consultant was called in who advised a second operation a week or so later. While I was waiting for the first operation I read John Buchan's *Mountain Meadow* from the first page to the last; but from the day of the operation I have never been able to read again.

During my convalescence we took another house in Santa Barbara, also of the Spanish type, in Plaza Rubio. There were grapefruit, orange, lemon and tangerine trees in its walled garden, and round two sides of it there were nine tall olive trees. On the wall facing the old Monastery there were some very lovely roses, and on one side of the patio some glorious red and white camellias. In a bed more sheltered from the sun, under my study window, there were English violets. In the little summer-house which faced the Monastery we found a Della Robbia plaque of the Madonna, with the Child stretching out His arms to a cluster of tall lilies—an exact replica of the plaque on one of our garden walls at home. Near the summer-house we were delighted to find English spring-flowers, primroses, snowdrops and daffodils. I could still see the colours.

Immediately opposite, across a broad green space, arose the beautiful old Franciscan Monastery. When I had first seen it, years earlier, the evening light had flushed its long arched cloister and one of the bell towers with faint tints of rose. Built by the Franciscans themselves with the help of the native Indians, half wrecked by earthquake and nobly restored a few years later, it is still in its simplicity the loveliest piece of silent architectural music on the western coast. At that hour, when it stood out, rose-white and luminous against the dark purple of the many-canyoned mountains behind, it was not of this earth.

Although I was now quite unable to read, and a veil had been drawn over the landscape which had given me so much joy, the beauty of the visible world was not entirely closed to me. The silhouette of the old Monastery against the sunset sky on many and many an evening rose before me like a benediction. We had not come there through any plan of our own, yet I somehow felt that all this was intended. At least it came with a strangely poignant consolation when I most needed it.

L

Seventieth Birthday

IN 1949 we returned to England, where I underwent two further eye operations. They were performed by Mr. Williamson-Noble, to whose skill I owe what little sight I now have (nothing could repair the damage that had been done earlier).

More than the deprivation of books is the inability to receive the "full assurance given by looks," in the faces of those around me, which are now veiled in shadow.

At Lisle Combe, where I know every part of the ground, every slope and every tree, I can still feel that for me *ille terrarum mihi praeter omnes angulus ridet.*

For my seventieth birthday a dinner was organized by my friends. It was held at the Hyde Park Hotel, and Sir Shane Leslie took the chair. There were about a hundred and fifty present. Sir Shane Leslie, Mr. L. S. Amery and Mr. Frank Sheed spoke in terms too generous to quote here.

I venture to quote my reply, because it expresses, not only my gratitude for the friendship shown to me, but some of the beliefs which, though they were implicit in my work from the beginning, have become ever clearer:

"For the great kindness shown to me this evening it is quite impossible for me to express myself adequately. The only ground for that kindness is that, whatever the defects and limitations of my own work may be, I have truly loved the art of poetry and given the best of my life to it. One cannot love a great art in this way and devote one's energies to it through a lifetime without learning something of one's own limitations and something about the nature of that art, perhaps more than even the youngest critic has discovered.

"You may remember what Newman said about the Greek and

Roman poets: 'Passages that to a boy were only commonplaces of rhetoric, come to him after long years and experience of life, and pierce him as if he had never known them before, with their sad earnestness and vivid exactness. He understands then how a few lines, born of some chance morning or evening at an Ionian festival or among the Sabine hills, have lasted generation after generation, for thousands of years, with a power upon the mind and a charm which the literature of his own day is utterly unable to rival.'

"When Virgil touches us with the sense of tears in mortal things, or enables us to see that newly arrived throng on the brink of the dark river, stretching out their hands in longing to those upon the further shore; or that fleeting moment in the land of shadows when Anchises greets his son with those poignant words of welcome, 'Art thou come at last? And hast thou overcome the difficult way?' There are no posturings, no quirks and turns of mannerism, no search for the scarlet word, but the voice of nature, the simple and sincere cry of the human heart, caught up by the universal orchestra, and through its music brought into relationship with eternal things.

"For more than two thousand years the distinguishing characteristic of poetry has been the element of song. From the ocean music of Homer to the lines in Swinburne,

> Where the thundering Bosphorus answers
> The thunder of Pontic seas,

the poets have all described their work as a kind of song. It is a music that, as Mr. Amery remarked in a recent address to the English Association, comes to us naturally out of the very fountainheads of language. The famous passage in which Tennyson almost literally translates Virgil,

> The moan of doves in immemorial elms,
> And murmuring of innumerable bees,

may also be said to translate the voice of nature into that human language which, as Mr. Amery has told us, completes the undertones of sound with overtones of thought.

"But the music has a deeper and richer beauty when it rises from nature into the realm that transcends nature, through the subtler intellectual symbolism of language. It was only a legend, of course, that the eyes of Virgil were the first to see the Star of Bethlehem, but he did catch glimpses of the City of God, and seen from a distance the City of God may look very like a star.

"An eminent scientist of the nineteenth century, W. K. Clifford, once wrote an essay on what he called the cosmic emotion of great poetry, in which he showed that the music of poetry, linking things together in a way that outran the discursive reason, sometimes lifted the poet above his immediate subject, so that 'the glory of the sum of things' flashed along the chords for a moment. This, of course, was in line with the famous essay of Wordsworth on poetry, in which he compared poetry with religion, saying that the function of poetry was to represent much in little. It is the function of all great art, in fact, to establish a right relationship between things temporal and things eternal, so that what may appear chaotic and fragmentary in our daily life, seen in another aspect is part of a perfect whole. The harmonies of great art are symbolical, a little cosmos, enabling us to apprehend a greater cosmos that transcends our faculties. The famous phrase of Keats, 'beauty is truth, truth beauty,' might seem false to the superficial realist, but Keats had been lifted by his music, perhaps unconsciously, to the height from which Plato and Plotinus saw beauty and truth as aspects of the divine perfection. A Jewish writer told us recently that just as in madness an individual loses his sense of the real meaning of things, so when nations lose their sense of the divine meaning of the universe the world is plunged into collective madness. Perhaps in this we have the explanation of the psychopathic brutalities of certain sections of contemporary art. Representations of the madness of the modern world can, of course, be multiplied indefinitely, but they will get us nowhere.

"We have lost a very great thing, which has to be regained. If the words of Virgil can still pierce the heart, there are certain other words that strike infinitely deeper. They are the words upon which Christendom was founded. Once or twice in the English translation, and once, strangely enough, in the Greek also, they fall into the measure of Shakespeare, and allow us, therefore, to discover the infinite difference between the greatest words of Shakespeare and the words of eternal life. Perhaps the most beautiful line in Shakespeare is the cry of Hamlet, 'Absent thee from felicity awhile,' but it fades into insignificance before the words upon which Christendom was founded. These last have one quality which differentiates them from all other human words. Merely human words, even those of the greatest poets, may express the desire of the moth for the star, the desire of the exile for a better country, but the words upon which Christendom was founded come to us from the centre: 'I am the Resurrection and the Life!' "

Index